THE
CAPTIVE
DREAMER

CHRISTIAN DE LA MAZIÈRE

THE
CAPTIVE
DREAMER

TRANSLATED BY FRANCIS STUART

INTRODUCTION BY NICHOLAS WAHL

SATURDAY REVIEW PRESS/E. P. DUTTON & CO., INC.
NEW YORK

For Françoise

Library of Congress Cataloging in Publication Data

La Mazière, Christian de.
The captive dreamer.

Autobiographical.
Translation of Le rêveur casqué.
1. Nationalsozialistische Deutsche Arbeiter-Partei. Waffenschutzstaffel. 33. Grenadier-Division "Charlemagne." 2. World War, 1939–1945—Campaigns—Eastern. 3. World War, 1939–1945—Personal narratives, French. 4. La Mazière, Christian de. I. Title.
D757.85.L3513   940.54'12'44   73-20004

First published in the United States by Saturday Review Press.
Copyright © 1972 by Éditions Robert Laffont, S.A.
Translation copyright © 1974 by Allan Wingate (Publishers) Ltd.
All rights reserved. Printed in the U.S.A.

First published in the United States by Saturday Review Press.

10 9 8 7 6 5 4 3 2 1

Published simultaneously in Canada by Clarke, Irwin & Company Limited, Toronto and Vancouver
ISBN: 0-8415-0319-2
Designed by The Etheredges

CONTENTS

INTRODUCTION BY NICHOLAS WAHL   vii

PROLOGUE   1

PART ONE

I. THE HOUR OF DECISION   9

II. AT WILDFLECKEN, IN THE EDDIES OF THE "CHARLEMAGNE"   26

III. IN WHICH I GET TO KNOW WHAT A GERMAN TRAINING SCHOOL IS LIKE   60

IV. IN THE HELL OF POMERANIA   86

V. THREE WEEKS BEHIND THE RUSSIAN LINES   108

VI. THE SURPRISES OF CAPTIVITY   128

PART TWO

VII. OTHER MORNINGS, OTHER TUNES   159

VIII. FRESNES, PALACE OF MADNESS   176

IX. THE HOUR OF TRUTH   199

X. THE CLOISTERS OF CLAIRVAUX   230

INTRODUCTION

This is the story of a young man who almost carried political commitment to the ultimate sacrifice. It will often seem strange and implausible, yet there is much in it that is really quite familiar. Political fanaticism remains a contemporary reality and everywhere the choice is still being made to "live one's ideals," to be "true to one's self"—in violence, terror, and death. Christian de La Mazière's story seems especially curious because of the peculiar circumstances in which he acted and the unique personal commitment he chose. Simply put—as it was by his contemporaries—La Mazière donned the uniform of France's wartime enemy and fought side by side with German soldiers in the last months of World War II. Yet he was not the usual turncoat who went over to the "other side" and broadcast propaganda to his countrymen, as did the handful of Americans who joined the enemy in World War II and the Korean War. For him remaining in France was treason, and he voluntarily joined the most politically activist and highly trained unit of the German armed forces in order to be at one with himself. Even stranger is the fact that La Mazière's case was hardly isolated: almost ten thousand of his compatriots chose his course between 1941 and 1945.

Why did he do it? To a large extent, this book offers an answer. But another question is almost as intriguing: How did La Mazière survive to tell the tale? Many Frenchmen who chose, as he did, the German uniform ended their lives on the guillotines of the restored French Republic or were broken by long years of imprisonment. He himself was engaged in the last furious weeks of combat, when most of his comrades fell before the victorious Soviet armies. The answer to this question also can be found in the book, but it is less easy to find. Part of the answer is—as always in matters of survivorship—sheer good luck. Another part is La Mazière's social position, his friends, connections, and his presence of mind to lie about what he had done and be believed at the time it was most necessary. But much of the answer is in the quotation the author has placed at the beginning of his story: "One is more faithful to an attitude than to ideas."

The man who wrote those words, Pierre Drieu la Rochelle, the French fascist writer of the thirties, actually remained faithful to ideas above all, right to the end: he committed suicide in his Paris hiding place in early 1945, at the very time the Nazi world he had chosen was coming to an end. La Mazière, however, abandoned the idea of a doomed Nazism, although he remained faithful throughout his ordeal to the attitude that he had grown up with since his childhood. It was an attitude conditioned by his age, his experience, and his unconscious. But it was not a system of ideas into which he had folded a mature personality. As a result, La Mazière's physical suffering, the extreme tensions of battle, and ultimately the threat to his neck were all that were needed to help him reaffirm the primacy of life over death. Part of the attitude that led him to the Waffen SS was an elemental thirst for life, an admiration for vigor, a search for community— all the qualities he felt had been lacking in the France of his adolescence. In the end it was this thirst that saved his life, for unlike the fascist ideologues he learned—in a flash—to shun suffering and death.

But before more can be said about the motives of his extraordinary commitment, the exact nature of the commitment itself must be understood. While the Allied forces pushed toward Paris in the summer of 1944, La Mazière continued to work for a minor collaborationist weekly in Paris, *Le Pays Libre*. Founded by Pierre Clementi, one of the lesser known French fascists of the prewar years, the paper lived on handouts from the Germans and subsidies from businessmen who wished to be on good terms with the Occupation forces. Just before General de Gaulle marched into liberated Paris in late August, La Mazière, according to his own testimony, was faced with a choice: he could turn his back on collaboration and offer his services to the Gaullist police, helping the new regime track down his fascist colleagues; or he could continue his commitment in a more extreme form by joining the Charlemagne division of the Waffen SS.

Ever since mid-1941, after the Nazi attack on the Soviet Union, Frenchmen had been officially encouraged to join what was being called a "European" crusade against communism. At first they were urged to enlist individually in the Germany army, much as Americans had enlisted in the Canadian and British forces before Pearl Harbor. However, by the end of the year the Vichy regime had organized the Legion of French Volunteers against Bolshevism or LVF (*Légion des Volontaires Français contre de Bolchevisme*), conceived as a major contribution toward fuller cooperation with Hitler. By the winter of the next year thousands of these volunteers, from all walks of French life, were fighting in German uniform on the Russian front. Most of them, it must be said, were from the ranks of the fascist and pro-German political movements active in Paris and areas of France beyond Vichy control. Vichy realized, therefore, that it would not be receiving maximum credit for the initiative; and it tried to organize still another volunteer corps, fighting this time in French uniform, wholly dependent on Vichy, and baptized the Tricolor Legion. But the Germans said no to this idea, for by this time they had soured on the idea of a separate French volunteer corps. Even though the activists in the LVF had been highly effective members of the "Storm Brigades" in the German army, often credited with heroism against the Russians, they remained essentially French in their choice of loyalties. Most of the volunteers suffered from low morale, submitted poorly to discipline, and seemed to live only for the occasional visits of their French *Führers*—Doriot, Déat, and Bucard, the leaders of the parties from which most of them had come. The obvious solution for the Germans was to transfer the volunteers directly into German armed units, and for this the Waffen SS seemed ideal.

The Waffen or "fighting" SS was the most recent creation of that state-within-a-state, which Himmler's SS had become by the late war years. Originally the SS had been the bodyguard of the

Nazi party leadership. By the end of the thirties its role had expanded, however, as it grew into a vast internal security force, paralleling the official police, the Gestapo, and the counterespionage services of the Wehrmacht. Then the SS "Death's Head" battalions were formed to take charge of the concentration camps and later the extermination camps. When the going became difficult on the Russian front, Hitler's nagging suspicions about the loyalty of the regular army led him to accept Himmler's prodding and to create an elite corps of SS to be used in the front lines. This Waffen SS soon became a crucial element in German counteroffensives against the Russians and in punitive missions throughout occupied Europe. And since the attack on Russia in June 1941 had been justified by Hitler as a crusade against communism in which all of Europe had an interest, the decision was made to recruit about half of the Waffen SS from among nationals of Germany's allies and the occupied countries. The first of the "foreign legions" in the Waffen SS was the Belgian "Wallonia Brigade," organized by the prewar fascist leader Léon Degrelle. This was to be the model for the French unit, the Charlemagne division, named after the Holy Roman Emperor whom Frenchmen and Germans shared in common.

By the time La Mazière arrived at the Waffen SS training camp in Germany the need for manpower had become acute. Not only were the LVF volunteers shifted en masse into the disciplined ranks of the Waffen SS but also all the pro-German French forces—official and semiofficial, paramilitary and political police forces—were being pressed to show their zeal by swelling the numbers of the Charlemagne. Thus in addition to the early fanatics of the Paris collaborationist movements, the Vichy *Milice* were now sending their shock groups to the Waffen SS. During these last desperate months, this particularly sadistic paramilitary organization and its leader, Joseph Darnand, had become powerful forces in occupied France. Much like the SS, the *Milice* had originally been a security force for Vichy's embryonic government party, the *Légion des Combattants*. (Ironically, organizations like the *Milice* had been intended by Vichy to minimize German interference in French affairs by keeping the repression of communists and Gaullist resisters "within the family," so to speak.) But by 1944 Darnand had become an officer of the Waffen SS and was competing with the original pro-German French party chiefs in showing enthusiasm for the lost Nazi cause. As a result, in the fall of that year the Charlemagne was beset by divided loyalties and was in fact a mass of marginal zealots of uneven quality, posing a real challenge to German training efforts. La Mazière's testimony on this strange Babel of ideologies, social and indeed ethnic and religious backgrounds offers an interesting insight into a minor yet hallucinatory moment in history.

As the snows began to fall in the winter of 1944–45, most of the Frenchmen fighting in German uniform were those who had no choice, given their deeds during the Occupation, or those who chose to remain loyal to an extreme form of anti-communism—one bordering on madness given the odds and the conditions of the war in the east. But La Mazière was not mad and it is worth pondering the circumstances and motives that led him to join the Waffen SS at a time when Paris and much of his country had been liberated, when the Vichy government was in flight, and when the war had clearly been won by the Allies. His reasons seem to be located at the confluence of national, international, and purely personal traumas, a convergence of causes that in many ways was uniquely French.

La Mazière tells us that he joined the Waffen SS in order to be true to himself. If by that "self" he means—as we think he does—the self of his adolescence and early adulthood, between 1934 and 1940, the sources of the attitude that forced his commitment are obvious. He came from a Catholic, traditionalist, provincial and military family for whom the ineffective democracy of prewar France had long been the enemy. The Third Republic was corrupt, incapable of maintaining French influence in the world, and so weak as literally to invite a communist revolution. La Mazière tells us, moreover, that he was brought up reading the demagogic royalist newspaper *L'Action Française*. This was the organ of traditionalist and antidemocratic France for whom, in the words of its ideologue Charles Maurras, there were four "confederated states of anti-France"—the Jews, the Freemasons, the Protestants, and the foreigners living within her borders. After 1934 this outlook was increasingly shared by much of the French middle class, for as the depression wore on and political instability increased, anticommunism became an obsession. When the left, including the communists, won the elections of 1936 the obsession became a panic.

What should be more natural, then, but that a romantic youth who had dreamed of the torchlight parades of the Nazis at Nuremberg, who had joined an extreme right-wing youth movement, who had helped to arm the peasants of his province when a Jewish socialist became Prime Minister in 1936, should seriously consider fighting the Soviets by joining the Finns in their hopeless struggle during the winter of 1939–40? By the time of France's defeat the following summer, the basic political content of La Mazière's attitude was anticommunist, and everything else depended on that. But the musty, conservative anticommunism of Pétain's Vichy, as well as that of his family, appeared to the twenty-year-old as totally out of date and ineffective. More important, it seemed to offer no outlet for his desire for action. La Mazière was a pilot trainee, but he had seen no active combat in the brief encounter of French and German arms. For a moment, he tells us, his hunger for action and for personal renewal in war led him to consider going to England in pursuit of the testing he so wanted. But his father, loyal to Vichy and its aging leader, talked him out of such an extreme "second thought."

Meanwhile, under Pétain France drifted into a backwater of world events, ruled by a coalition of old conservatives, technocratic businessmen, and Catholic bigots who together declared that France was embarking upon a "National Revolution." The motto of the new regime, "Work, Family, Fatherland" must have seemed especially ridiculous to men like La Mazière. What they wanted was action in the name of an ideal, not just the quietism of work; male comradeship on the battlefield, not the confines of family from which they were just liberating themselves. Finally, going beyond their inherited patriotism, they gave their highest loyalty to a Europe united by its strongest nation, not to a fatherland that had failed to offer them pride for so long.

André Malraux has written that he who is at the same time active yet pessimist will surely become fascist unless he maintains a fidelity to something human. La Mazière had no faith in a formal ideology or in religion; he had only a vague attitude, inherited from his family background, nourished by the frustration of having missed combat, and finally given purpose by Nazi propaganda in favor of a European crusade against the barbarity of Soviet communism. Certainly there was little of the human in such a heritage. It was this lack of any systematic faith, as well as a striking political naïveté and ignorance of the world —typical of his milieu—that led him to join the pro-German collaborationists in occupied Paris.

The Frenchmen who gravitated to these movements saw in fascism the wave of the future: it was a modernist "third force" situated between communism and capitalism, combining the best of both while avoiding their flagrant defects. For them fascism rejected the established order, which they had fled, while still conserving certain familiar values that remained important to them, if only unconsciously. Fascism allowed a rebellious young man to reject his past without making the complete break demanded by communism. But above all, the fascism of wartime Paris was an eclectic hodgepodge—ambiguous, vague, well conceived to attract the politically immature and the fuzzy-minded for whom posture and attitude had more meaning than ideas. La Mazière's attitudes was attuned to this amalgam: anti-communism, anti-Semitism, anti-capitalism, a fear of outgrowing adolescence and making compromises with what were thought to be ideals, the romantic's love of action, and finally a terrible thirst for community—a loss of the self in a higher cause transcending the self-interest that marked the world he had left behind.

At first this attitude found embodiment in his articles for the collaborationist press. Clementi, the editor of his paper, had originally come from the political left and in the early thirties had founded the practically unnoticed "French National Communist Party." Long before 1940, Clementi had moved to the right with *Le Pays Libre,* and after the German occupation, all fascist movements, no matter how small, became useful to the occupiers. Soon Clementi became the principal Paris recruiter for the LVF and his paper joined the chorus urging young Frenchmen to rally to the anti-communist crusade in German uniform. Part of a small, close-knit editorial team, La Mazière was finally a member of a real community, and soon he felt obliged to live the ideal he was pressing upon others, and that his comrades were undoubtedly pressing upon him. In the perpetual adolescence of small-time fascism the influence of one's peers in the "gang" must have been compelling, if not decisive. From the dreamer simply hoping for action, he was soon to become the dreamer in jackboots, voluntarily captive of a dream that quickly became a living nightmare.

At first the Waffen SS seemed to realize his hopes for comradeship in arms, for a European community above the parochialisms of class and nationality. All ranks mingled in training and no one was allowed to say "thank you" for it was understood that all received what they needed and nothing more. The Charlemagne seemed imbued with the ideals and faith he had never possessed and it offered the supportive pride in community his delayed adolescence continued to seek. Probably it also seemed to offer a chance for personal renewal and purification. The hatred of bourgeois democratic France had become for many Frenchmen a kind of self-hate that had to be purged. Some ultimately turned to communism and the Resistance, others to fascism and collaboration in their quest for this rebirth.

In the summer of 1944, however, collaboration had become meaningless, with France back in the war alongside the Allies; and for someone who had chosen collaboration as a means for personal renewal, the Waffen SS could well have appeared to be the only "honest" solution. It was too late for La Mazière to become a resister, it was unseemly to become a stool pigeon for the new regime, and he knew he was not important enough to find a place in the pseudo-government in exile formed by the collaborationist leaders in Germany. His political education, indeed, his adulthood were still ahead of him—on the frozen fields of Pomerania, in the Russian prison camps, and in the jails of post-Liberation France.

Perhaps the first doubts about his commitment came in the smallest of ways—for example, in his growing revulsion for the battlefront filth in which he lived his last weeks as an SS man. Within the attitude that drove him to the Waffen SS there were certain bourgeois and human reflexes that his account does not attempt to hide: to be clean, to be warm, to be well fed. A number of times in his description of the days before he allowed himself to be captured by the Russians, La Mazière lingers obsessively over his appearance, especially his dirt-encrusted fingernails. One almost senses that capture had become an escape from a new kind of self-hate when one reads about his relief in finally discovering the means of making his fingers presentable.

From then on everything fell into place for him, and his survival became the great reality. La Mazière set his course of self-preservation above all, and the compass of a bourgeois upbringing did not fail him. To begin with, he denied any connection with the Waffen SS and passed himself off to the Russians as a forced-labor draftee, a member of the S.T.O. (*Service du Travail Obligatoire*). Then he used family connections to get out of Russian hands and into, of all places, a soft job with the Free French general serving as Ambassador to Moscow—whose wife actually helped him to gain early repatriation. Practically home free, he was unexpectedly arrested. But after a relatively pleasant incarceration among the elite of the captured collaborators, luck and good legal counsel succeeded in getting him a light sentence. Again he was assigned to the "luxury" section of his new prison where the warden ended up asking his charge to help with the entertainment and seating arrangements at formal dinner parties. At this point La Mazière was pardoned, after serving only about half his time—among the very first of the collaborators so to benefit. Back in civilian life he continued to unlearn the lesson of living one's ideals, which had almost cost him his life. But his "education" was undoubtedly crowned by the great irony that befell him years later. On the eve of his fiftieth year La Mazière became something of a public personality as the most articulate "witness" in the moving documentary film on France in the war years, Marcel Ophuls' *Sorrow and the Pity*. By rejecting in public the follies of his Waffen SS commitment, he gained a notoriety in bourgeois democratic France that bordered on sympathy. He had come home.

As he claims in this book, La Mazière grew to hate fanaticism and bloodshed; but while this is surely true, I doubt that it came as a result of long reflection and the traditional repentence of the sinner. Since he was never a fascist intellectual, La Mazière did not have to rid himself of deeply held beliefs. His loyalty was to an adolescent attitude and, as it turned out, the will to live, to prosper, to have clean fingernails proved to be more important than his naïve anti-communism and romantic hunger for comradeship. In this sense there was, indeed, a fidelity of some sort behind him and, when so many others like him paid high prices for being true to themselves in situations like the Charlemagne division of the Waffen SS, it was this fidelity that helped him survive.

One is more faithful to an attitude than to ideas.
—DRIEU LA ROCHELLE

PROLOGUE

I thought I had dismissed my past, but one morning it caught up with me. A film was being made about the years of the Occupation, those famous and difficult years that history has oversimplified. Resistance and collaboration, the pure and the damned: this rigid division has gone unquestioned ever since the end of the war, when Naziism was revealed to us in all its horror. But the French, in the grip of events with which the future had not yet come to terms, obliged to make decisions in the midst of confusion, compelled to a hand-to-mouth existence in order to survive—how had these French people actually behaved? Suddenly the truth became complex and painful, to be deciphered only in terms of sorrow and pity, as in the title of the film, *The Sorrow and the Pity*. The truth had a hundred aspects, and I represented one of them.

Who was I to have to testify? A veteran of the Waffen SS[1], survivor of the French Charlemagne division, which, in the

---

[1] The elite fighting troops of the German army, as distinguished from the notorious SS used as extermination squads and as concentration camp guards.

spring of 1945, was sent to be massacred in the snows of Pomerania. Since then more than twenty years have passed and gradually I had taken up again the threads of my life. The post-war period posed new problems, which I hoped to approach in a new spirit. I felt no nostalgia for my past and the one lesson I had learned was to hate fanaticism and the shedding of blood.

Now, however, I had to rake through the ashes that I thought had grown cold. An idea that phantoms are best exorcised by daylight made me agree, and, in the film, I did my best to reply frankly to the questions put to me. But did I say everything? Did I really manage to evoke the person I had been? I was not sure; the process of reassessment had started and I had to participate. I was on the screen as an example, or personification, of an attitude. But I began to want to know why, at a certain moment in my life, I had chosen, and remained faithful to, that attitude. I had finally to speak of, and for, myself; in short, write a book.

It was as though I had a rendezvous with a long-lost brother. To understand him I had to endow him with a voice. I searched my memory to find where he was waiting, and suddenly I was reliving a sunny morning in August, 1944. I was driving toward Nancy, at times threading my way through retreating German convoys. Behind me lay Paris, about to be entered by the Allies. I was heading east to join up with the French volunteers who were being assembled for the last throw of the dice. That was where all this began.

I had taken a decision that, like every total commitment, was strangely stimulating. It suited my political attitude, but it was not a choice forced on me by circumstances. On the contrary, I could easily have disappeared in France, or, better still, been of service to the Resistance as I had been asked. I believe that it was the very ease of taking the course I did, more perhaps than that it accorded with my convictions, that led me to my extreme decision. It is precisely when the house is on fire, as I said to myself, and there is a good excuse to flee, that one should defend it all the more energetically. I suppose I acted less because of an ideology than to be true to myself. Today, I see clearly that such an attitude may well have contained a naïve desire to act in an exemplary fashion; and not to understand this is never to have known what it is to be twenty.

Indeed, at that time I was still activated by an enthusiasm rooted in the depths of my adolescence, having been fascinated by politics since the age of fourteen. My officer father had given me a traditionally intransigent and nationalist education; the cavalry school at Saumur where he taught had become a sort of seismograph on which were sharply recorded the shock waves of French political life: February, 1934 . . . the Popular Front. . . .

As was customary in such a milieu, I was brought up on the royalist newspaper *l'Action Française*, but rather than to the speculations of Charles Maurras, which meant little to me, I responded to the passionate anger of Léon Daudet, the paper's most demagogic editorialist. What I needed was a stimulus to which to vibrate and not an abstract philosophy, and in this I was like my high school friends; and I doubt if those of my classmates who had joined the Young Communist movement knew Marxism better than I did. The causes we defended were primarily a reflection of our family background and social class. Our youth gave them a consecrated fervor, and outside the classroom we often fought over them in a manner no less violent than the struggles taking place today in high schools and universities.

However, I soon began to tire of the punctilious conservatism of the Maurras group. In the first place, I wanted to be a revolutionary, no doubt because of the desire to question that turns us, at a certain age, against our family and the paternal ideology, but, above all, I dreamed less of the past than of an exultant future. To me, the contemporary world seemed enslaved to money and rotten with social injustice.

Not that there was anything that impelled me to rally to the Communist revolution; I was brought up in an atmosphere where it had been always condemned, and instinctively I regarded Bolshevism as a diabolic force. Thus what attracted me was the revelation of National Socialism that I received through the banners and floodlights of Nuremberg. And when I plunged into reading various and contradictory books, its attraction was only increased for me. It struck me that this doctrine formed a balance between the great traditions of the past and a new kind of socialism, offering a logical goal to my revolutionary instincts.

Then came the Spanish Civil War, which I followed in this new and impassioned state of mind, seeing in it a closed arena where Fascism and Communism were meeting face to face. I had become convinced that the capitalist democracies had had their day, and had I been able I would have gone to fight my first battles side by side with the nationalist heroes of Toledo.

Then came the German-Russian alliance against Poland, something that I did not understand and that made me turn, for a time, to a stricter form of nationalism. It was in this mood that I enlisted in 1939, but when Russia was invaded by the Reich I began once more to dream of a new world in which Europe would become the beacon of socialism, and this hope inspired the editorials I wrote for a Parisian newspaper with a minuscule circulation.

With the arrival of 1944 events moved quickly. As I have explained, I found myself at the crucial point where the only kind of commitment was to steel helmet and gun. I took the leap, choosing action and adventure, and it was there, at the end of the great ideological dream, that I found reality—my own reality, first and foremost; like everyone else, I was a contradictory being. I felt the sincerest need to sacrifice myself for an ideal, but equally strong was the desire to live and be happy. Indeed, this desire, which I had suppressed in the depths of my nature, never ceased to speak to me and warn me, even in the moments of my greatest exaltation. I see clearly that it was on this account that I was able to face danger, and that, for the same reason, I cannot act like an unflawed hero of popular fiction. I owe my life to this desire and it would be strange if I were reproached for it.

In a broader way, I discovered those great, simple truths that had escaped me in the kind of magic circle I had shut myself into: that war is hideous, fanatical beliefs murderous, and death the supreme evil. Youth likes to live in a kind of mental theater, concocting roles for itself to fit its impulses, and it was onto this inner stage that I had projected the Spanish Civil War and the National Socialist ceremonies of Nuremberg; it was there also that I experienced the war of 1939–40. In 1944, despite the Occupation and the different choice made by my friends, I knew too little of the concrete reality of Naziism, which continued to seem to me an admissible hope. The disaster of 1945, and, above all, the revelations of the postwar period, were to destroy my illusions.

This happened in a brutal and somewhat cruel manner: I saw the milieu that had nourished me with its ideas turn its back on me. Yet my adventure formed, in a sense, the logical conclusion of that ideology. There remained my friends, old and new, and friendship knows nothing of doctrinaire patriotism, and, for the rest, things were going well enough. I had turned my back on my youth, together with the bountiful imagination that had so excited it, until, one day, there was this film, and this present book, in which I resurrect it, only to relegate it to the past once and for all. Is this a repudiation? I think the question is now meaningless. Anyhow, can one deny the experience of passion and belief, and the attempt to act in accord with one's convictions? I shall never be so embittered as to discourage the faith of those who are twenty years of age. I believe, though, I have earned the right to urge prudence, not as regards the act of commitment itself, but in the choice that leads to it.

PART ONE

I.
THE HOUR OF
DECISION

On that August day of 1944 Paris was stifling under the sun. A few pedestrians meandered along the Champs-Elysées. The streets were as empty as in the peacetime vacation season. But close at hand in Normandy hell had broken out. The front was crumbling everywhere and in a last sidestepping maneuver the German divisions were trying to break loose from the vise that was tightening on them.

Only the day before I had been in Rouen. Like its cathedral, the town had been badly damaged. Processions of haggard-looking refugees and ambulances with blacked-out windows were moving with difficulty through debris-strewn streets. I had gone there with the authorization of the town council and the Ministry of the Interior, and my task was to set up a newssheet for distribution among the local population. It was to publish reassuring reports and offer recommendations for the preservation of public order.

A good idea, no doubt, but coming rather late in the day. Besides, there were no printers left and the whole administration was breaking down, and the Germans had ordered those still faithful to the Vichy government to fall back on Paris. The only thing still functioning with some stability was the security forces, which, between the aerial bombings and machine-gunning, helped those in greatest need, evacuated the wounded, and dealt with looters.

There was nothing for me to do but to return the way I had come. Having filled up the gas tank, I got into my front-wheel-drive car with all the necessary authorizations in my pocket. With me were a couple of companions, Roger Pingeault and François-Charles Bauer. The former, who had once been a seminary student, had been employed, like me, on the newspaper *Le Pays Libre*, the latter, a well-known journalist, had been sent to the front by *Je suis partout*,[1] but the Germans had forbidden him access to the battlefield, which was becoming more fluid with every hour.

We left, late in the evening, with dimmed lights, in a procession of blacked-out trucks, crossing the Seine on a huge ferry. It was a night of confusion and anguish, during which we were constantly harassed by Allied fighter-bombers. At regular intervals searchlights illuminated the countryside and we seemed to be afloat on a sea of flame and scrap iron.

We did not reach Paris until the following morning. I drove as far as the Invalides, stopping on the square, where there seemed an unusual air of tranquillity. We were demoralized by what we had recently discovered. During the journey each of us, in his own way, had taken stock of events.

We got out of the car and François-Charles held out his hand.

"You're leaving us?"

"Yes, it's only a couple of steps to where I live."

"What are you going to do?"

He smiled slightly. "I'll take my own precautions."

And he went off. Pingeault and I made our way to the office of the newspaper we worked for at 34, Champs-Elysées. For the last year and a half five of us had been putting out this weekly, which had no more than a few thousand readers. Its publication had enabled its director, Pierre Clementi, to amass considerable secret funds from certain industrialists. He had lived in a grand

---

[1] A French anti-Semitic periodical of the Occupation.

style while paying his editors and the printers in Lyons miserably.

We entered the offices, which looked as though a hurricane had blown through them. Numerous files had disappeared, the floor was covered with scattered and trampled papers, the telephone wire was cut. The myopic old concierge wandered from room to room moaning to herself.

Pingeault, who had sat down in a corner, snickered. "That's what terrifies respectable folk, but, if I could choose, old fellow, I'd take the revolution that really counts."

I looked at his round head covered by a shock of black hair. Curls covered his left ear, which was completely withered, so that his glasses were continually unhooking themselves and slipping down his nose. He hated all establishments and it did not greatly matter to him by what means they were overthrown. At the seminary he was attracted to Marxism, dreaming of the barricades of the Commune. Then he had rallied to the banner of National Socialism, but for him this was only an intermediary step.

While listening to him I thought of my own path. I was less well informed than he and at twenty-four I was full of passionate impulses and a jumble of mental pictures. I remember how as a student the martyred face of Horst Wessel fascinated me. Each week at the movies, the newsreels showed me the forward march of a people that, overcoming humiliations, wished to regain its dignity and national greatness. And I also recalled the tranquil autumn of 1936 in my native Loire Valley when my thoughts had been far away at Nuremberg in the midst of a sea of banners, emblems, and torches. Under the arches of the cathedral of light that searchlights created against the night, a new religion was born. Its impetus crossed frontiers and its songs were of a kind that inspired our hearts.

Pingeault seemed to be reading my thoughts: "Wake up, old fellow. Hitler is finished. It's time to give him up."

"Have you forgotten the men from all over Europe who are fighting on the eastern front?"

"You can be sure that they'll be quickly forgotten when the war is over."

What answer was there to that? I suddenly thought of a young worker who had passed through this very room on his way to don the uniform of the Waffen SS. "It was reading your articles," he told me, "that made me realize which road led to a better future." Having followed my convictions, he had gone further, and I felt bound by his decision. If I didn't want to live in fear and shame I had to follow his example. I suddenly knew that as far as I was concerned the die was cast. I got up and asked, "Is there anywhere you'd like me to drop you off?"

Pingeault looked at me sadly. "You're going to see Maud? I'll come along."

We took a last look at the devastated room. All that remained of my years of journalism was a worn presscard in my wallet.

Maud lived in the rue du Renard with her mother, a big energetic woman who had begun her career selling oranges from a street stall. She was now head of one of the biggest businesses in the market of Les Halles. She had not been able to avoid working for the Germans and had let the Todt Organization[2] have the use of many of her trucks. But she helped her friends with the money paid her by the Kommandantur.

She led us excitedly onto the balcony from where, around the Hôtel de Ville, there stretched a sea of roofs, house fronts, and small streets.

"Keep this to yourself. For the last few days, I've had an English parachutist hidden in a first-floor room. He's very handsome."

Already in love! Pingeault gave a slight sigh. "Well, that puts you in the clear."

She didn't appear to understand. She never worried and had attached little importance to the threatening letters she received in the mail every day. Now a stroke of good luck had fallen out of the sky, but she wasn't thinking of the use she could make of it.

The speed of events was certainly accelerating! A ring at the door, and it was Maud, accompanied by Alain Ballot, a lawyer, who, like myself, came from Touraine. But he worked for London as a liaison agent and had come for the parachutist. Seeing me, he smiled. "Glad to meet you here; I'm going to need you. You've been acting stupidly long enough, now you've got to listen to me."

How easy it was to wipe out the past, to change sides!

[2] The army of conscripted workers, many foreign, that constructed Hitler's grandiose building projects, including the *autobahnen*, and later the west wall fortifications.

Maud—brown curls, small, golden Spanish face—took my arm and devoured me with her large eyes.

"Listen to him, he's right. . . ."

Pingeault was struggling with his glasses while watching me ironically. As if a new being had been liberated in me, somebody I still didn't really know, I heard myself say, "No . . . I've come to say good-bye."

"You're crazy!"

They all agreed. And I saw that I had best leave right away. There were many things I wanted to tell Maud, however . . . I opened the door. Maud caught up with me on the staircase and held on to me, crying, "Don't go."

She was seventeen and I think she loved me. How could she understand? I took her face, wet with tears, between my hands, as if to fix it in my memory. I would have liked to have kissed and comforted her gently, but there wasn't time.

I returned to my apartment in rue Chevert, which consisted of three rooms in a middle-class building where the other tenants were distant but polite and kept well informed about each other by the concierge, whose husband was a policeman. Outside, children were playing on the sidewalk and a few steps away the esplanade in front of the Invalides bristled with antiaircraft guns. The gunners, stripped to the waist, were sunning themselves.

A few letters under the door, nothing important. I was turning things over in my mind; my decision worried me. I had to get my mind off it. I ran a bath. Evening was falling, I was hungry, I went to the cupboard only to find it empty. I went into each room, examined each knickknack, every piece of furniture, my library. I was about to leave them all. Would I ever see them again? I had a momentary temptation to go back to the Garcias, to see Maud once more. But it was too dangerous, it threatened to reopen everything. All the same, hadn't they been right, wasn't I crazy? I started as the phone rang.

"It's Jean Chatrousse. Listen, you must come to Neuilly tomorrow, rue de l'Eglise at 6 P.M. sharp. Ask for Mme James, it's extremely urgent."

He hung up. Chatrousse was second in command of the French security forces in Normandy, and I hadn't expected to see him again so soon. What did his phone call mean? I turned on the radio. From all the successive communiqués I concluded that the Allies were in control of the situation, and that they might be already here had not the Germans been mounting such a desperate resistance. However, all seemed quiet in Paris, there was not as much as an air-raid warning.

I was truly at the end of my strength. No chance of having dinner, unfortunately. I had a bath and went to bed, first taking the telephone receiver off the hook so as not to have to answer a call from Maud.

It was the telephone, however, that woke me. My room was full of sunlight, as I had forgotten to let down the blinds. I felt good, rested. It was eight o'clock:

"It's Pingeault. I must talk to you; you're quite wrong. And then there's Maud. Can I see you?"

"Yes, come on over."

He must not have been far away because I had hardly started to shave when the doorbell rang. As I let him in I realized that he was more a part of my life than I had imagined, more, perhaps, than I wished. His acute judgments impressed me and, at times, made me uneasy. Beneath his sarcasms I sensed a great vulnerability when faced with life. He dared confront it only through me, and I had always seen him attracted to the women close to me. I was sure he felt a warmth for Maud that he wouldn't admit.

He expounded a whole line of reasoning to make me see where my true interests lay and to persuade me to go back on my decision. He emphasized the pain I would cause to those close to me. But the longer he talked, what had been confusing and in doubt the evening before became clear and obvious.

"No, old pal, it's too late. I've made my decision and I'm going through with it to the end. It'll work out all right."

He said no more. I told him of Chatrousse's request and asked him to go there with me. But this he couldn't do; he had changed course and was going to join the underground. We had a coffee in a bistro in the place de l'Ecole Militaire, and then we had nothing more to say to each other except good-bye. We made our farewells and he disappeared into the metro.

My heart was somewhat heavy. I felt like someone entering a religious order who must now divest himself of his past. I had chosen solitude, but it still frightened me.

There was also the problem of my father and what to tell him. While returning home to rue Chevert I was composing the letter I must write him. But what explanation could I give? For more than a year he had known almost nothing about me, and with the discretion that was one of his principal maxims, he had never questioned me.

I knew, all the same, that he worried about my future. An exemplary officer, he had been shaped in the old traditions of the French cavalry, and recognized only one commandment: loyalty. He had taken his oath to Marshal Pétain and refused to join any Resistance network despite the appeals made to him. But after the Germans had invaded the unoccupied zone in November, 1942, he ceased all cooperation with the Vichy authorities.

This reserve of his shocked me. Sometimes I had tried to explain my own evolution to him. After all, we belonged to a common universe. At the time of the 1940 Armistice, when I was a young student pilot in the air force, I had wanted to go to England. He had dissuaded me and his reasons had convinced me. Like him, I came to the conclusion that the defeat was more a matter of the regime than of the people, and I told him of my hopes for the National Revolution extolled by Marshal Pétain. Since then, all I had done was to follow the successive stages of a journey whose logic seemed evident.

My father had made a pretense of understanding me, although this he would not admit. If I were to write this letter it would have to be long and closely argued. I dreaded a final judgment: for my father the German uniform, and even more that of the Waffen SS, even if it clothed a respectable ideal, was, above all, the uniform of the enemy. Thus, in his eyes, I was going to betray everything he had raised me for.

Yes, I ought to write to him, but I lacked the energy and everything was going too fast. I gave up the idea. I had chosen my bed—now let me lie alone on it.

It was afternoon, near the time of my appointment with Chatrousse. I drove through deserted streets to Neuilly and stopped at a small apartment house. A wheezy elevator took me to the fifth floor, where Chatrousse was waiting for me with a serious expression. He wore an elegantly sober suit of gray flannel. All I knew about his career was that he had been at Saint-Cyr.[3]

"Mme Ellen James."

It sounded like a pseudonym. She was a little older than us, attractive and, judging by where she lived, wealthy. She offered

[3] Saint-Cyr: French military academy, roughly equivalent to West Point.

us whiskey, a drink I had not tasted for four years. I sat down somewhat warily. Glass in hand, Chatrousse turned to me. "Remember the tense situation in Rouen? Well, the general position is deteriorating all the time."

He gave me an outline of events and then touched on the reason for our meeting. He told me that Ellen James belonged to an information network. What he said seemed to me rather confused. Had he doubts about me, or was he himself not very well informed? Mme James played the role of a hostess but kept her eyes on us.

"We're expecting two men. It is on Ellen's advice that they are coming to meet us. All I know about them is that they're from London."

I experienced a sense of uneasiness. Now that I had made a clear choice and was at one with myself, it looked as if destiny was contriving to complicate matters. In any case, it was out of the question to tell Chatrousse that I was about to apply to join the French division of the Waffen SS.

Five rings at the bell sounded, one long, three short, one long—no doubt the signal. I recalled playing at conspirators at the age of ten with my friends: the underground evidently mingled the infantile with the tragic. The two men entered, the first dark, with a crew cut, the other with light chestnut hair and carrying a hat in his hand. The kind of people to be seen on any street corner.

Mme James introduced Chatrousse and me. They did not give their names and regarded us coldly. Then the man with the crew cut started to speak, talking in a neutral tone of voice, slowly and precisely. His was the language of the professional who counted on a mission being resolutely carried out. It mattered little who we were or what we were thinking.

"The Allied armies will soon reach Paris. According to our information, the Germans intend to turn the city into another Stalingrad. This will be easily accomplished if groups from the Resistance engage their troops district by district. The Allied staff is worried, fearing that the Communist-inspired elements in the Resistance will start fighting before receiving any order. Thus a revolutionary committee could seize power and proclaim France a Socialist Soviet republic.

"You are aware that General de Gaulle is now recognized by the Allies. The Americans do not want, in the middle of a battle, to be confronted with a political problem that could endanger the agreements they have reached with the USSR. What we want is to have the French security forces take up positions that we shall indicate if you and we come to an understanding. They would intervene if the Communists act in the way we fear."

We must have looked astonished, because he smiled briefly.

"Our choice no doubt surprises you, but the Paris police are going on strike and won't be able to offer any resistance to the Communists, who are full of a fierce revolutionary spirit as well as being well trained and armed. We have got to oppose them with dedicated anti-Communists. When things settle down, what you have done will not be forgotten."

An absolute hornets' nest! My hands were clenched and damp. His lips pressed together, Chatrousse remarked, "It's possible. We'll have to think it over."

The other man's tone became dry. "It'll have to be done quickly. We've come to find out if you agree or refuse. You have, M. Chatrousse, a certain number of the militia,[4] an important force, under your control. A word from you will be enough."

"I'm not so sure."

He was of two minds, vacillating, but finally ready to be persuaded, less by conviction, I think, than for the sake of Mme James's blue eyes. As for me, I was silent—I did not want to get mixed up in this business. We emptied our glasses and the two callers rose; they had no time to lose. They took Ellen James aside, and after a short discussion I heard the outer door close.

I felt like laughing. It was like waking from a dream. The whole thing was dissolving in my mind. Who were these phantoms that had just vanished?

Our hostess reappeared. "You would have been wrong to refuse. It's clear that Germany is defeated. What's going to become of you? This is your chance."

I started to speak. "This coup de main that we're being asked to undertake won't weigh very much against our past activities. Who's going to believe in this last-minute patriotism, even if it is inspired by anti-Communism? Besides, I'm not at all sure that Chatrousse's men will obey. . . ."

But he had made up his mind. "A pity, because I'm going to try to bring off the coup and I'd like your help, not uncondi-

[4] The French militia, a paramilitary organization created by the Vichy government in January, 1943, under the aegis of Joseph Darnand. It collaborated with the Germans.

tionally, but simply as liaison officer, so you have still a little time to think it over."

Then he explained his plan. "My troops should reach Paris by evening and they'll be quartered at the Saint-Louis high school. It's better that I don't join them. I'll see Maréchal, one of my agents, and give him precise orders. At a predetermined time he'll assemble the francs-gardes[5] in the place de la Concorde in small groups, with arms and packs. They'll be in their trucks from the Mortier barracks. Then I'll take command again and lead them to the meeting place that the gentlemen from London named. You can trust Maréchal. He'll know whom to rely on."

It all struck me like a bad detective story. But the situation was so fluid that success was not impossible. "All right, if that's what you want. But on one condition: once the operation is over, I go my own way."

"Agreed. I understand your reservations. I'll phone you early tomorrow with the final instructions."

We shook hands. A last glance at Mme James and I was in the street. I wanted to shake off the low spirits that weighed me down. What about a visit to Maud? No, that was a mad idea.

Then I remembered a house of prostitution in the rue de la Lune, where I had been some months before when writing a story on prostitution for the paper. The manager, Janine, was a small, attractive, laughing brunette. I had had a brief affair with her, in the course of which I had gathered the needed information. Now I wanted to find her again.

When, a little later, I arrived at the house, Janine seemed very pleased. We went to a bistro in the rue Saint-Denis where they did not ask for ration coupons. We sat, pressed close together, at a small rustic table behind red and white curtains. There was a good smell of wax polish, a fan hummed on a shelf. I felt a breath of lightheartedness for the first time since my return from Rouen.

Janine was understanding and a good listener. Coming from a simple southern family, she had had dreams of taking Paris by storm, but soon found herself on the street. Shrewd and willing, she had known how to get herself noticed by an iron merchant who had entrusted her with the running of his establishment, whose principal function, under Kommandantur patronage, was

[5] The shock troops of the militia.

to make members of the Wehrmacht forget the hardships of the eastern front.

She put her hand on my wrist and gently pressed it. I gave her a sketchy account of my existence since I had last seen her while, keeping her dark eyes focused on me, she filled up my glass. I told her of my love affairs and of the fears I had about the future.

"My iron merchant, who always plans ahead, is making me learn English," she told me, laughing. "He said it would make my work easier."

She suggested my coming to live with her in a small first-floor apartment she had off the reception hall. "But the main thing is that you do what you want to."

As is the custom in her circle, she insisted on paying the bill, then turned to me. "Come on."

I was back once more in her room. Her caresses were gentle, motherly, just what I needed. We made love with a great tenderness. Then she went out, leaving the bedside light on. I smoked a cigarette, thinking of nothing in particular, and then closed my eyes.

It was five in the morning when I awoke, and dawn was breaking. Janine was asleep, curled up beside me. It was time for me to go home, Chatrousse would soon be telephoning. I dressed silently and gently opened the door. I asked the night watchman for a piece of paper and an envelope. I wanted to say good-bye to Janine and, above all, thank her.

I walked toward the grands boulevards where I had parked my car. It was going to be another beautiful, warm day. Workers were heading for the early subway trains. The only thing that disturbed the early morning calm was some German convoys.

Back in my apartment, I began tidying up while waiting for Chatrousse to call. I burned all my personal correspondence, then I looked through the pile where my newspaper articles had accumulated. No, they were not bad, always sincere, though somewhat exaggerated perhaps. Suddenly I felt incredibly remote from all that. Strange, how I had grown older in a couple of days. . . .

The telephone roused me from my reverie.

"Christian? Well, here it is. At ten o'clock you meet Maréchal at Saint-Louis. You'll tell him what was decided yesterday. I have already given him an outline of the plan. The meeting is at two o'clock this afternoon in the place de la Concorde in front of the admiralty building. See you then."

I went out again and headed for the boulevard Saint-Michel. The high school was in the grip of a great commotion, with trucks arriving to unload arms and ammunition. Stacks of guns and packs filled the corridors. On my way through the dormitories, looking for Maréchal, I passed militiamen from the north, from Brittany and Normandy.

Finally I got hold of him. He was a huge man, debonair and sly. It was obvious that he understood hardly anything about what Chatrousse expected of him. Afraid of being indiscreet, I was evasive, talking only of a special mission. But to be honest, the whole business seemed pretty chancy to me. It was quite impossible for such a concentration of armed men not to arouse curiosity. In principle, these companies could not be moved except by order of the head of the militia, Joseph Darnand.

When I had given him the information, I left Maréchal with "Be punctual."

I took up position in front of the Chamber of Deputies a little before two o'clock. Strolling with an air of unconcern, I crossed the Seine and arrived at the place de la Concorde. The sun beat down and the pavement was burning my feet.

Soon there rose before me the massive edifice of the former Naval Ministry, now the German Admiralty, the Kriegsmarine, with the German flag flying from the roof. Sentries, with measured step, helmets down over their eyes, submachine guns across their chests, big circles of sweat under their arms, surveyed, as they passed each other, the narrow passageway between the barricades. The militiamen waited on the sidewalk with their guns and packs.

Time passed. A truck drew up at the Tuileries gate and the francs-gardes climbed in. I stood still. This, I sensed, could turn out badly. In fact, two vehicles full of German soldiers appeared. An officer got out of the first and went up to the truck. He spoke French, and I heard him ask the militiamen what they were doing there. I kept out of sight, keeping a lookout in order to intercept Chatrousse as soon as he showed up.

The discussion seemed animated. Finally the francs-gardes got down from the truck and the Germans lined them up by twos. Other militiamen arrived on the scene, and as they did they were apprehended and regrouped. Nobody seemed to know what was happening. Suddenly Chatrousse emerged from the metro. I quickly went to meet him. He took in the situation and came to a halt. I asked him what was going on.

"Well, I'm too late. I only just had a phone message. Some militia commanders became suspicious at the hullabaloo at Saint-Louis. After being informed about what was going on, they came to the conclusion that the franc-garde was being led astray by dangerous elements. Knowing of the meeting in the place de la Concorde, they summoned the Germans. Don't worry, the boys will return to the high school and no harm will have been done. As for me, I'll have to think up an explanation that'll satisfy Darnand."

As we talked, we went back toward the Madeleine. One of the last opportunities to swing over to the Resistance had vanished, but Chatrousse was not worrying about the future. For the moment he would be occupied in exculpating his men before his superiors. As for himself, he would probably get off with a severe reprimand.

We walked a short way together and then embraced, wishing each other luck. I watched him as he walked away; he was the last of the witnesses to these lost, feverish Paris years. With him gone, it was a little as if the whole of occupied France vanished before me. From now on adventure lay in the east. Nothing remained but to present myself at the Hotel Majestic, where the German headquarters of Greater Paris was situated, and to pick up my enlistment papers.

My file was ready, but I seemed to have been forgotten. The Germans were feverishly getting ready to depart. Finally I was given the documents making me a future member of the Waffen SS, as well as German marks and ration cards. I felt awkward having to admit that I was not going to travel by train but in my own car. During a rather painful discussion it was not easy to explain that I needed a few days of liberty to take leave of my past.

It was then that one of the officers surprised me by announcing that Darnand, head of the militia, but also national secretary of the French security forces, had come to an arrangement with Himmler by which the francs-gardes, the armed contingents of the militia, were to join up with the Waffen SS. With the survivors of the Storm Brigade (Seventh Sturmbrigade), the first SS unit to be made up of Frenchmen, they would constitute the nucleus of a new division. Consequently, I had a part in this sudden transfer to the auspices of the Ministry of the Interior.

I was dumbfounded. So it was possible from one day to the next to dispose of thousands of men whose oath of allegiance was to Marshal Pétain. The militia was a fiercely nationalistic unit, commanded for the most part by veteran officers. It was hard to imagine these people in German uniforms.

As for me, I did not feel involved. I had come to my decision alone and I would make my departure alone. After a good deal of fuss I obtained gasoline coupons, all sorts of passes, and a road map to Sennheim, a small Alsatian village between Thann and Mulhouse, which before the war was called Sernay. That was the site of the Storm Brigade's training camp.

Curious, however, to get confirmation of what I had heard, I went to the place Beauvau and asked to see Max Knipping, Darnand's private secretary. He was evasive; no, he had not heard anything about it; all he knew was that Darnand was going to regroup his men in Alsace. A strange coincidence, all the same!

"Wait for his orders," he added. These stories didn't give me much enlightenment.

Next day I started to drive to Nancy. The countryside was peaceful. Apart from the German convoys—some were advancing, others falling back—the war seemed far away. I was headed for a new adventure and this filled me with a kind of intoxication. At times, however, I was overcome by a profound anxiety: what if my choice was only a flight into disaster, a challenge lost in advance that nobody would acknowledge? I made a stop at Sézanne and, in a small bistro, ordered red wine and a sandwich in an attempt to recover my spirits. The place was full of people, and when I was given looks of suspicion, I wondered what was in their minds. What would have happened if I had pulled out my papers stamped with the Swastika?

After Nancy, I made a detour by way of Strasbourg because I wanted to see this town, which had been semiofficially annexed to Germany for the last four years. I strolled through the narrow streets around the cathedral; hams and sausages were displayed in the windows of the pork shops. In spite of rationing there seemed a better-balanced distribution of food in these parts. The people seemed cordial and relaxed, but they had lost all but the memory of our language. It was true that its use was strictly forbidden, as was the wearing of the Basque beret, the recognized symbol of French elegance.

Somehow or other I got into conversation with a maid at the

hotel where I was staying. From her remarks I obtained an idea of the trials of these people, profoundly affected by the war, who obviously were awaiting its outcome in order to know their destiny. As she was talking, martial songs rose from the street through the open window. A company of Hitlerjugend were marching, with tense faces, in perfect order. There was no doubt I was in Germany.

Next day I headed for Sennheim. I did not want to delay too long. I had hardly got there when two plain-clothes members of the SD[6] arrived at my hotel to examine my papers. Politely, but unambiguously, they told me that this was no time for touring around.

I had also made a detour by way of Sélestat, recalling that it was in this district, according to Knipping, that the militia were to assemble. I saw no sign of them, and finally I arrived at the Storm Brigade's training camp. I parked my car at the entrance and had a look at the huts across the barbed wire; the place seemed deserted. I went inside, walked around for a bit, and finally ran into some soldiers. These belonged to the camp administration and had stayed behind to close it down. The last contingents of the brigade had been sent to Greifenberg, in Pomerania, but soon they would be sent back to Wildflecken, where all the French in German uniform would be regrouped to form the new division of the Waffen SS. It was to this camp, northeast of Frankfurt-am-Main, that I had to go.

All at once I was aware of a marked lowering in the pressure of events. This new division seemed to be in no hurry to be formed. Fate was certainly casting me back on my own resources. I had wanted a few days of liberty, and now I was getting more than I had bargained for. I filled up with gas and set out again in the direction of the Rhine. I was curious to see what a nation that was being strangled looked like. I had got enough authorizations and gasoline coupons to last several weeks.

In this manner I started on a tour the details of which I no longer recall. What I do remember, though, is the friendliness I encountered everywhere. I hardly came across any except elderly people and I was treated with the greatest hospitality. More than once I was given the room of somebody who was at the front and ate meals without being asked for ration coupons. Because I had

[6] *Sicherheitsdienst:* German security police.

volunteered to fight the Bolsheviks, I aroused some admiration and much astonishment.

I drove where fancy took me. I cut across the Rhineland and stopped at Ulm, where Darnand and the militia were supposed to arrive after reassembling in Alsace, but they had not appeared. From there I turned toward Nuremberg, having long been eager to get to see this birthplace of National Socialist pageantry.

This lack of occupation was something strange and there were times when I came to reproach myself. But, after all, I was going to fight for this country and I had the right to get to know it a little. So, in a peaceful state of mind, I continued my travels in spite of police controls, air-raid alerts, the military convoys I overtook, the strategic points bristling with artillery I passed, and all the bombing that was laying waste German industry and about which I daily heard the somber details.

Finally, one morning, I came to Heidelberg. As a high school student I had dreamed of this university town, where the best professors taught, as the inspired heart of Germany.

In September, 1944, however, there were only a few students about. As well as it being vacation time, total war was raging. The seventeen-year-olds who could carry a weapon had been called up. The young men, and many girls as well, were all gone. Only invalids and the disabled were left.

I took a long walk, admiring the fortifications and the ancient houses, right up to which had spread ultramodern faculty buildings. It was on one of these peregrinations that by chance I met Inge. She was altogether the romantic German type, tall, slender, with some of the flowing suppleness of a swan, the very opposite of the "Gretchens" mocked at by the French ever since the First World War. She had a gentle, modest smile, large blue eyes, and long fair hair that hung straight down over her shoulders.

She spoke a little French and I a little German, out of which we made, with the help of looks and gestures, a private language of our own. She was eighteen and a student. But, having volunteered for war service, she was waiting for her marching orders. In this respect she was no different from the youth of my country. I do not know whether they were really followers of Hitler, but Nuremberg had left its mark on them and they were deeply imbued with National Socialism. They had a serious awareness of their communal ideal and of their European mission. Their development had coincided with an uninterrupted series of victories and it was hard for them to entertain the idea of defeat even when the tide turned. They felt a total engagement.

Inge and I spent two wonderful days, though nothing happened between us that was not perfectly proper. She came to get me at my hotel but did not linger there. Hand in hand we strolled along the medieval streets that went constantly uphill and down, and where light and shade alternated. She told me about herself and I told her what I was going to do. This both aroused her enthusiasm and surprised her. For her the French were hard to grasp, superficial, and as fascinating as sin. Our conversation was punctuated by peals of laughter caused by misunderstandings that I cleared up by consulting a pocket dictionary.

But I could not stay forever in Heidelberg, where I was beginning to be an object of curiosity. My Citroën, with its front-wheel drive, in a country where only Auto-Unions, Mercedes, and Volkswagens were to be seen, stood out. I well knew that the Germans had looted us, as is the recognized right of the victor, and that they had taken our railway stock, for example; but our cars obviously did not interest them. Furthermore, I cut a figure in my French attire among those whose style of dress, devoid of elegance, tended to be uniform. Besides, I was being constantly stopped and checked. Like any besieged country—the Allies in the west were near her frontiers—Germany was at that time experiencing a spy phobia. On every wall was displayed the warning: *"Feind hör mit*—the enemy is listening to you."

The moment for me to leave had come. Paris, which had fallen more than a month before, was far away, and in my memory the face of Maud was becoming blurred. I was with Inge and it was as if the long detour I had made had had no other purpose but to lead me to her.

My resolve was fortified by her calm courage. To be honest, I was not sure if I shared the general optimism. Everywhere there was talk about the V1's and the V2's, the forerunners, it was thought, of far more terrible weapons. The newspapers mentioned von Braun, a man who was making his name. Airplanes were coming that would exceed the speed of sound, which struck me as fabulous.

I asked myself if all this would be ready in time. But this question no longer mattered and I rejected it. It was time to go on. I said good-bye to Inge and, for the last time, took to the road.

II.
AT WILDFLECKEN,
IN THE EDDIES OF THE
"CHARLEMAGNE"

The camp at Wildflecken was situated on the slopes of a wooded hill. I drove up a winding road, tarred and in good repair, and emerged into a kind of park entered through a large arch supported by two pillars. On it could be read in German: "My honor is named fidelity." A beautiful phrase, full of meaning that touched me. This was the motto of the Waffen SS, and not, as too often supposed, that of the SS in general.

At the entrance, soldiers of the French Waffen SS were on sentry duty. They watched me arrive in my civilian clothes and I produced my papers.

"Right; proceed to staff headquarters. It's a good kilometer but it won't take long by car."

I drove through the gateway and the road led through well-kept woods, between copses as carefully trimmed as in a garden. I was impressed by the simple air of nobility about the place. As I reached the top of the hill there suddenly loomed up a dream camp. On each side of the road were small buildings, and well-laid-out driveways led through the greenery. The road ended in a wide space, Adolf Hitler Platz, according to the signposts. Around it were stables, garages, various other buildings, and finally the camp headquarters. I stopped and got out of my car, which I then completely forgot and never saw again.

Up to now I had seen almost no one. The place seemed deserted, dead. In contrast, the staff offices were quite animated. Privates, noncommissioned officers, and officers, in their tight-fitting SS uniforms, some wearing the Iron Cross, were coming and going. These were sections of the Storm Brigade from Greifenberg, a part of the unit that had been decimated in August in the fierce Galician battles. Their fighting spirit had been duly recognized by their commanders.

I also encountered members of the first LVF[1] echelon, and the difference was obvious. The Storm Brigade troops had been thoroughly assimilated. They had acquired a Germanic appearance and exchanged salutes in the German fashion. Their bearing was impeccable and they looked to have been trained in an iron discipline.

I introduced myself and was examined curiously. In my civilian attire, with my well-cut blue suit and necktie, I felt almost naked before these men whose muscular bodies were one with their uniforms. I was both startled and fascinated.

"Just a minute, please."

As in every office there were guys who typed, who exchanged remarks the sense of which I did not grasp, and whose jokes belonged to another world. I had, of course, tried to imagine this universe that I was entering, but I felt with a vague unease that I did not grasp it all the same, and that becoming part of it would not be so easy.

An orderly came over: "Sturmbannführer Zimmermann expects you."

I entered an office very sparsely furnished, as is usual with the Germans. There were maps and charts on the walls (they were called "graphs") and troop lists. I stood to attention and bowed slightly.

"Good day."

I did not know how to address the Sturmbannführer; what was his actual rank? Major, captain? I settled for captain and later learned that it was major.

I faced a German whose glance was sharp and precise. I was

---

[1] Légion de Volontaires Français, a Pétainist militia.

impressed by his row of decorations, the buttonhole ribbon of the Iron Cross, second class, the Iron Cross, first class, clipped to his close-fitting jacket. I had learned about all these "bonbons" from reading *Signal,* the French language magazine published by the German army in France—the close-combat and assault medals, the decorations belonging to the Polish, Russian, Cretan, and French campaigns.

He was strapped into his uniform. At the right side of his collar were what are called "icicles," that is, the silver SS insignia in the ancient runic characters on a black ground; on the left, the black studs that indicated his rank. His silver-gray braided epaulettes matched the color of his uniform. I handed him my papers and he began to question me. "What made you come here?"

His French was correct but he had a pronounced guttural accent, as with Germans who have learned it from the theater or movies. His delivery was slow as he searched for words. "Were you ever a soldier?"

I told him that as an adolescent I had belonged to a flying club and that I had enlisted in 1939. I had been a student pilot attached to Base Twenty-seven at Terrefort near Saumur, but the infantry was a new world for me. He nodded his head reflectively.

"It's leaders like you that we need. I'll go over your case with Brigadeführer Krukenberg. Meanwhile you'll wear the stripes of Oberscharführer."

This rank, that had no equivalent in the French army, was bestowed on those about to enter an officers' training school. Once admitted there, they became Oberführer—that's to say, officer candidate. An Oberscharführer had in practice the prerogatives of an adjutant (Hauptscharführer), but not his duties. In fact, in the Waffen SS there were very few adjutants and they were mostly given administrative jobs. In general, the hierarchical grading had not the same institutional rigidity as in France. Among the Germans rank served, above all, as an open door to the top. It was the ability to lead that counted, and the actual training was always greater than that implied by the number of stripes worn. In order to become second lieutenant (Untersturmführer), for instance, one admittedly worked at company level but everything that had to do with tactics took place at battalion or regimental levels. Thus there were no promotion problems. Platoon commanders, normally noncommissioned officers, could prove themselves capable, at a moment's notice, of taking charge of a company. And one often saw company commanders becoming regimental commanders.

Major Zimmermann rummaged among a lot of old documents. Then he looked up. "Wait a minute. I'll see if General Krukenberg can see you."

I was rather surprised; this did not coincide with what I had expected. I had counted on seeing the French and meeting General Puaud. Indeed, it was to him, as former leader of the LVF, that the command of this new division, which had not yet definitely been named, was to have been given. It was expected that it would be called "Charlemagne"—Charles the Great—as I heard while I was waiting to be interviewed, but here at HQ there was constant discussion about it. (This name was in fact adopted.) This name pleased the French, who looked on Charlemagne as their own as much as did the Germans, who considered him a great Germanic emperor. And for both, Charlemagne meant the Rhine, a connecting link full of significance.

I was taken in to Krukenberg, who had just arrived and was seated at his desk, without having taken off his outdoor clothes. He wore a general's leather overcoat with braided epaulettes and white lapels (*Wehrmacht* generals had red ones). He had deposited his helmet with the skull and crossbones on the table. He was a lean, cold individual with an obstinate-looking jaw, who made a striking impression and looked like a man of resolution. Behind him lay a successful career as political activist and soldier. Having come through the First World War with honor, he had become one of the early members of the National Socialist party and had taken charge of the German radio. Although only a brigadier general, he had considerable influence; he was listened to in the highest political circles and personally received by Hitler.

As he spoke French tolerably well, he had been placed at the head of our future division and it was now a matter of forging a soul for it—no easy task. It was already necessary to resolve the insidious antagonism between members of the Storm Brigade and the LVF. The latter looked on themselves as Frenchmen who were temporarily in German uniform. They had distinguished themselves on the eastern front alongside the Axis forces, notably at Tcherkassy and in rearguard actions against the partisans. However, they had their own way of conducting the war as French soldiers of fortune, imbued with a spirit of mockery.

Their lack of discipline had given rise to some unfavorable comment at headquarters.

It was quite another story, as I have mentioned, in regard to the Storm Brigade. It had really acquired the German mentality, using only German commands, ranks, and designations. Its members had a certain contempt for the manner in which the LVF guys stood to attention and used the formula *"Mes respects, mon capitaine,"* and the LVF sneered at the "Heil Schutzstaffel"[2] by which the officers of the brigade saluted their men and at the "Heil Hitler" with which the men replied.

As for me, I fitted into neither category and this puzzled Krukenberg.

"You've been a journalist, I see. So you want to join the *Propaganda-Kommando?*"

"No. I would like active duty and, if possible, in an elite unit."

"Good, we'll see." He got up. The interview had only lasted a couple of minutes. "Heil Hitler!"

I raised my arm: "Heil Hitler."

It was my first Nazi salute.

This raised arm—I was both proud of and embarrassed by it. I felt I had crossed a threshold and, in so doing, had, in an obscure fashion, taken leave of something from which I had sprung: my native soil, my past, and the traditions of my country. But these men fascinated me and I wanted to be assimilated into their ranks. I saw them as a race apart. They struck me as strong, courageous, and ruthless beings, without weakness, who would never become corrupt.

I had no more than a sketchy understanding of the ideology in which they were reared. But its major outlines awakened familiar echoes in me, recalling a little, in a different manner, the climate in which I was steeped. First of all, anti-Communism, with its crusading spirit; part of my youth had been spent at Saumur, in the shadow of the cavalry school, where my father had been an active-duty officer. In the twenties he had fought with the Poles against the Russians. In my environment anti-Communism had been a clear and sacred cause that the formation of the Popular Front had made still more urgent.

[2] Defense squad. Originally the SS, which stands for Schutzstaffel, served as bodyguard to the Nazi leaders.

There was also anti-Semitism, a tricky problem. I did not feel then, and have never felt, any racial hatred. To me the Jews were a symbol; to oppose them was to fight against international capitalism. In the closed world in which I moved they represented the forces of evil. In recent years we have seen in Asia, Africa, everywhere, ideological conflicts creating myths that incarnate everything against which the fight is waged. And who can deny that in Russia itself anti-Semitism under Stalin and even in the post-Stalin era does not contain some of this element?

Much later, at the end of the war, I learned of the phenomena of the concentration camps. But in 1944 and during my whole period in German uniform I knew that camps existed—what country has not had its camps?—but not of the extermination plan that they served. The Waffen SS were fighting troops and had nothing to do with the SS Totenkopf Verbande put in charge of the camps; each was confined in its own watertight compartment. The discovery therefore gave me much food for thought. For by then I had been subjected to many ordeals, seen plenty of horrors, so I knew that death is not an abstraction and that even the most honest commitment cannot lightly resort to it, that it has a concrete, hideous face. I know, too, that this aspect is universal. Millions perished in the camps beyond the Rhine. The Germans had been defeated and these corpses could be thrown in their face. There were likewise millions of dead in the camps in Siberia that were scarcely mentioned because the Russians had been victorious.

At Wildflecken, however, all this was still far from my mind. The ideology of the Waffen SS was, all things considered, less important than the rules of conduct that were part of it. I was conscious of the demands made on me, of the inner transformation that the cult of an ideal, whatever it may be, implies. I was proud of the Hitler salute because it struck me as signifying a new start, and through it I was entering an order of things where nothing was easy but where all was more pure and honest.

Now I can smile at this fervor. But I do not repudiate it. It is, above all it *was*, a part of my truth. Through it I rediscovered that emotion which had gripped me when as a child I read the story of the Spartan boy who hid the fox he had stolen under his clothes and, rather than give himself away, let the animal devour his entrails. Pain was in the order of things and restored the much-scoffed-at-discipline. And it was just such a discipline that I expected from the Waffen SS, founded not on caste or compulsion but, to the contrary, on a kind of internal justice, accepted by each member as a matter of course because it was based on a communal ideal in which all were equal, even the higher ranks in the hierarchy.

One detail quickly made me conscious of this inner sense of justice that governed our relationships. In the Waffen SS nobody ever said thank you. A soldier never thanked an officer; nor did an officer thank a soldier who, for instance, handed him something he had asked for. The principle was that what you were given was what you needed. *"Danke schön," "vielen Dank"* were words that, if uttered, drew down an immediate punishment. Even today—it is one of the few habits I have retained from my time at Wildflecken—I find it hard to say thanks and feel that I belittle the person to whom I give something by expecting gratitude. What I give him is what he wants and needs.

So everyone received what he had a right to and nothing more. There were no privileges such as those in the French military tradition of which I had had inside experience, first through my father and then on my own account. In the Waffen SS, for instance, everyone ate together and the food was the same for all. There were no separate messes for officers, or noncommissioned officers, or privates. If there was any schnapps, it was first distributed to the ordinary soldiers. The officers got what was left and, generally speaking, received less than the troops. One of the fundamental precepts was the higher the rank, the more numerous the duties and the fewer the advantages.

This egalitarianism was also shown in the weekly meetings called *"Kamaradschaft."* They were cheerful command dinners, where a soldier of the lowest rank had the right to pull his superior's leg and poke fun at him. And it was forbidden for those of higher rank to take revenge, under threat of punishment. There you had socialism of a sort, where the rank and file exercised some critical control over its leaders. It was primarily the leaders who were the representatives of the lower ranks, which gave them an additional responsibility.

They were therefore always the first to have a rough time of it, a fact I quickly realized during training. When, for example, in a French army exercise a river had to be crossed, the officers sat on the bank watching their men exert themselves—"Look out where you put your feet, pay attention to your packs!" After that they got into boats and waited for the soldiers on the opposite bank. In the Waffen SS, on the contrary, and, indeed, in the whole German army, the higher-ranking officers and noncommissioned officers always went ahead. The men, generally speaking, did not go where their leaders had not been before them; such was the rule. This explains why Germany had the largest number of high-ranking officers killed in the war of any of the Western powers.

This desire to create a superior type of human being, to produce a model race, led the Waffen SS into a certain moral puritanism. Homosexuality, for instance, was brutally repressed, while it flourished in the Wehrmacht. One day an adjutant from my company caught a couple of young fellows engaged in these forbidden games. I had to make a report about it. I supposed that they would automatically be sent to a camp where, as we thought at that time, they would be disciplined in the special SS manner. Much later I found out that it was quite simply a concentration camp. The homosexuals were relegated to the mass of subhumans, Untermenschen, and destined for the "final solution."

I certainly had no special prejudice against homosexuals, among whom I had some fine friends, and I had no wish whatsoever to report these two. But I was obliged to act immediately. I announced that I was going to punish them personally, and for part of the night I put them through the "stand-up, lie-down" or "auf-hinlegen" drill until their legs could no longer support them. Then I gave them a telling off while letting them know what was in store for them if they did not change their habits. They said nothing, but they had had a narrow escape and realized what they owed me.

The discipline was indeed merciless, and I believe I liked it that way, even if, in my inmost self, I remained incapable of accepting its utter harshness. As for the philosophy behind it, however, I was not to have the time either at Wildflecken or later at Yanovitz to get to know it better. We were the last to arrive in the later months of the war and instruction had to give way to military exigencies. The SS mystique was presented to me only in its most general and idealistic manifestations and what, above all, won me over was its emotional atmosphere.

It must be recognized that National Socialism had an astonishing flair for propaganda. Unlike Communism, where the indoctrination, however elementary, is always didactic, it endeavored to touch those emotive depths present in everyone through the theme of a joyful communion with the earth (the cult of nature played an important part in the ideology of the

Third Reich), as well as through the stress laid on individual achievement and the grandeur of the collective destiny, the purity of the race, and its great European future. Various social reforms affecting conditions in industry and commerce and some spectacular shows such as the 1936 Olympics had succeeded in winning over a people whose Marxist indoctrination at the time of Hitler's emergence had been almost as widespread as that of the Russians.

The survivors of the Storm Brigade at Wildflecken were the guardians of this mystique, at the same time absorbing and vague. They had returned covered with glory and weighed down by their death toll. In three weeks they had, I believe, lost 60 percent of their fighting force, and they flung in your face their sacrifices and their heroes: Noël de Tissot, for instance, former teacher of history and geography in Nice, originally from Joseph Darnand's unit. When the latter wished to give the Germans certain pledges, he had more or less ordered a number of his officers to enlist in the Waffen SS. They had gone against their will, but in the camp at Sennheim in Alsace they had been put through the psychological mold.

The men who found themselves at the officers' training school at Tolz, a regular religious establishment that reshaped bodies, minds, and spirits at the same time, were dazzled. Suddenly France, Darnand, and everything to do with them became very remote. They felt they had been reborn into a new European race, neither French nor German (for them the German language was no more than an instrument of thought and command), but new beings critical of the superstructures of the Third Reich, who returned to the earlier National Socialism of the time of Röhm.

This mutation, it is true, depended largely on the fact that over half the Waffen SS came from outside Germany. They were made up of French, Belgians (both Flemish and Walloons), Dutch, Balts, Central Europeans, Italians, and even Hindus. The Scandinavians were well represented, principally by the Swedes in spite of their famous neutrality. There were even some Swiss. I later met a certain number of German-Swiss officers whose country, as was well known, had been infected by propaganda from her German neighbor.

Historians have not finished their studies of this astonishing transformation. The real spirit of National Socialism had been destroyed by Hitler himself when he was forced to come to terms with the Wehrmacht and the big industrialists at the time of the "Night of the Long Knives," when ironically the SS became its own executioner. This compromise compelled him to sacrifice those who were the yeast within the revolution that he had seized power to bring about and, while denouncing international capitalism, to capitulate to national capitalism. The military victories legitimized the triumph of the industrialists, who, in a return to the old pan-Germanic dream, turned their thoughts to dominating Europe. From the start of the Russian campaign up to the first signs of defeat, the revolutionary spirit ceased to exist; it was necessary to reestablish it.

It was then that Himmler, in the face of considerable odds, took the Waffen SS in hand. The moment was well chosen inasmuch as the Wehrmacht, worn out by several years of war, had become slack overall. Its generals had initially hated the SS divisions as a marginal army, but later they were glad to have them to hold the front without respite in the face of the severe pressures multiplying from all directions. And in the end headquarters stopped at nothing to get hold of these incomparable troops made up of activist volunteers.

In the case of a victorious outcome, the Waffen SS would undoubtedly have dominated the situation. They would have reclaimed power; Hitler might have remained, but a large part of his entourage would have vanished forever. It would have meant the emergence of a new Europe without frontiers for which the Waffen SS doctrine had seemed to prepare the way. And this doctrine, it should not be forgotten, had been deeply explored by the Heidelberg professors, among others, who had studied the most ancient European traditions.

A gigantic dream! and today I recognize our illusions and the extent of our naïveté. Yet, with the perspective of time, I see how easily it could seduce and lead a youth hungering for a revolution. And what was extraordinary was that this renaissance took place in the midst of utter disaster, as if disaster itself had revived vital energies. For it must be said, it was thanks to the Waffen SS that Germany's collapse was postponed for at least a year.

Good fortune thus seemed to smile on us, but at the same time we knew that we were the instruments of this last chance. It was in this dichotomy that our morale was forged. While I stood stiffly at the threshold of Krukenberg's office I had had no more than a glimpse of the world that I was entering and that attracted me so powerfully. But I already knew I was as likely to have chosen death as victory. That is how things were; there would be no way of going back.

Zimmermann was waiting for me. "Here are your papers. Go and pick up your equipment. I have just signed your appointment, which will appear tomorrow in the official journal of the division, but you can stitch on your stripes now. Later you'll be given details of your duties; we must wait until everyone has arrived."

Everyone: in other words, apart from the last contingents of the LVF and the Storm Brigade, some of the French, who up until then had served as volunteers in the Kriegsmarine, the Luftwaffe, the Todt Organization, the NSKK[3] and, above all, an important part of the militia, not to mention the individual volunteers from various political groups. In short, it was the great enlistment.

I was immediately given a complete pack: uniform, Norwegian-type cap, helmet, boots, belt, revolver, practically the same attire as an ordinary soldier except for the lapels and epaulettes. I was lucky to be among the first to arrive; later the German administration was faced with some shortages, particularly overcoats. And, as it could be as subject to whims as any other military administration, on occasion Italian caps were distributed, which drove the guys mad.

Next I was assigned a room. I searched patiently for it, my complete kit on my shoulders, along the streets and past buildings meticulously numbered in true Germanic style. Certain buildings served particular purposes: stores, commissary, study and lecture halls. The living quarters were in buildings that could accommodate up to 180 men. The washrooms, complete with showers, were luxurious and sparkling clean. The men slept in dormitories and the noncommissioned officers in rooms for two or three, while the officers had individual bedrooms.

After a long walk I finally found and took possession of mine, which was in impeccable order. I sewed on the epaulettes, stripes, and the tricolored patch on the left sleeve of my uniform. I dressed and suddenly there I was: Oberscharführer! Being hungry, I went out again; in the street the soldiers gave me salutes and I returned them; it was fun.

---

[3] Nationalsozialistiches Kraftfahrerkorps, the motorized section of the party.

I started out in search of the mess hall and had some difficulty finding it. Since the division was far from full strength, only some of the cookhouses were functioning. When I was seated at a table, a young fellow came and sat down beside me. He said, "General Puaud knows you've arrived and is surprised that you haven't yet gone to see him."

"I didn't know he was here. I'm very sorry. I was taken in hand by the Germans right off."

"Yes, but things aren't going too well between Puaud and them. He expected to command the division, and a German general has been put at its head, while he himself was given the rank of Oberführer, a rank somewhere between colonel and general. Besides, the men of the Storm Brigade won't have anything to do with him and he's a little sore. So he'd rather stay with his LVF guys. It would be a good idea if you'd ask him to see you tomorrow."

As we chatted away, this fellow began to give me details about the place. Wildflecken was something of an exception in Germany, where barracks were no pleasanter than anywhere else in the world. It had originally been conceived for the training of the Leibstandarte, the Führer's famous Black Guard, embryo of the Waffen SS, which one saw parading beside Hitler in the prewar photographs, at receptions in Berlin or Berchtsgaden, at Munich airport when Daladier or Chamberlain arrived. It was composed exclusively of blue-eyed blonds between five feet ten and five feet eleven inches tall.

From 1941, however, the men of the Leibstandarte swarmed into the various divisions of the Waffen SS, then in the process of being formed, where in fact they constituted the framework, by the example they gave of an exceptional kind of courage. Thus Wildflecken, having gradually lost its original purpose, had to begin with been used to train the Walloon brigade, which, at that moment, was engaged in hard fighting on the eastern front; its commander, Léon Degrelle, had become a real hero among the Germans, a darling protégé of Hitler. Then it had been decided to use the camp for the formation of the French division.

Next day I asked to be received by Puaud. His office was in the headquarters building but somewhat out of the way. He was the old type of cavalry officer.

"La Mazière . . . Wasn't it your father who was the head of the French horse-show team?"

"That's right."

"Yes, yes . . . Sit down, my boy."

This language belonged to another age. Puaud belonged to the rather outdated tradition of those who fought and killed in white gloves. A tall, vigorous man with an honest look about him, he had fought brilliantly in the First World War, then in the East. In France he would have ended up as a general in command of a division, as was the way in the thirties. His switch to the LVF had not taught him anything; on the contrary, he had fought for the survival of the civilization that had nurtured him. A fine officer, all the same, who commanded respect. I thought that he felt somewhat helpless; he was under the shadow of Krukenberg and asked himself if he would ever become head of the division. Besides, he was obsessively worried about the French political leaders; he did not understand Déat at all, mistrusted Doriot, who, however, had furnished him with a considerable number of men for the LVF, and above all feared Darnand. For him these men were so many enemies, and at the high-level conferences in Berlin he had cleverly managed to make them appear undesirable for the Waffen SS.

He was particularly apprehensive of the militiamen who would soon arrive. They had sworn loyalty to Darnand and were devoted body and soul to him, from the highest officer to the newest recruit. At Uriage, in the camps where the SOL[4] and then the militia were formed, in the southern zone of France, they were united to him by a political mystique. It was therefore with stupefaction that they heard the announcement that Darnand had been loaned to the Waffen SS. He had, in fact, received from Hitler the rank of major (Sturmbannführer), which had further confirmed Puaud in his determination to get rid of him. With his militiamen behind him, Darnand could quickly rise above the rank of colonel and would gradually increase his influence within the division.

One could well imagine, however, that the militiamen, once over their confusion, would do their best to accept the enlistment of their chief into the SS, even though it entailed his absence, and thus reaffirm their allegiance. This thought tormented Puaud, exposed both to the secret disdain of the men of the Storm Brigade and faced by the SS myth into which he could not fit himself. He had an idea that Krukenberg, with diabolical cun-

[4] Service d'ordre légionnaire, Pretorian Guard of the Pétainist legion, out of which grew the militia.

ning, was leaving him the task of eliminating the French factions, which was what headquarters wanted. It would then only have to beat the ideological drum before turning the settlement to its profit.

Our meeting was fairly brief: Puaud had quickly understood that I had made my choice. I returned to my room and started to arrange my things in it. I took out some nice photos of Maud, then, hesitating to pin them up, put them back in my pack. I checked that I still had Inge's address. I rested a short time and then had lunch. Little by little I got my bearings and settled down; I had some coarse tobacco and quite a few packets of Gauloise cigarettes. We talked all day long, because for the moment we had nothing to do except wait for the arrival of people who were being pulled in from all over the place.

It was early October and the weather was still fine. Fall was gently reflected in the trees that were turning golden; from the whole forest emanated an air of tranquillity. One felt more inclined for reading and meditation than for handling arms. Awaiting command, I lived a vegetative existence, as if a visitor to this well-run camp, strolling the streets, watching the men of the brigade going through their maneuvers. They certainly were not wasting their time! They ran, crawled, did the "stand-up, lie-down" drill under the sharp eyes of LVF veterans nonchalantly tagging along after them, as they did what the latter had had to do in barracks behind the Russian front.

It was at this time that I got to know of the death of Marshal Rommel. The German radio had broadcast the news, which we heard more or less by chance; it was only when the others came with sets in their packs that we had radios with which to listen to foreign stations, French ones in particular. All we knew of this event was the official version. Rommel had died from wounds received on the western front, his car having been machine-gunned by either an American or a British plane, it was not known exactly which.

News of this event, however, reached us through the last reverberations of the shock produced by the attempt on Hitler's life. Since then, Goebbels had roused public opinion by a dramatic speech and the conspirators had been hung. But rumors persisted that Rommel had been involved in the plot. The German authorities had had to deny them while eulogizing the man who was one of the Wehrmacht's outstanding heroes, who had reached the highest office and received the highest distinctions, and whose martial figure had widely appeared in the illustrated papers of the Third Reich. They let it be understood that if the battle of Normandy had not been won it was because Rommel had been wounded and unable to assume command.

The marshal was to be buried at Ulm on October 18. Zimmermann sent for me. "I have your travel papers ready. Since you're quite well dressed, you will attend the funeral ceremonies with a delegation of officers."

This was the first time I had left the camp. We arrived in the evening and I strolled once more through this beautiful old town that I had visited the previous month and that was shortly to be destroyed by the Allied air raids. It was entirely in the traditional German Gothic style, with a wonderful city hall decorated with seventeenth- and eighteenth-century paintings.

Next day I became part of the thousand or more assembled delegations. Except for a few insiders, nobody appeared to know that Rommel had been forced to kill himself (though the English radio had suggested the probability that he had been liquidated). All the same, there was some surprise that nobody from Hitler's immediate entourage, except for Rosenberg, was present. The Wehrmacht delegation, however, led by Marshal von Rundstedt, looked imposing.

The colorful scene in front of me was extraordinary. There were contingents from the Waffen SS, although, I believe, several of its officers had taken part in forcing Rommel to commit suicide. Among the flamboyant uniforms, I picked out Degrelle, back from the eastern front to attend the funeral and whom I recognized by newspaper and newsreel photos. He was in the full dress uniform of an Obersturmbannführer (colonel), with the insignia of the Knight's Cross. There was also Darnand, wearing for the first time his Sturmbannführer's uniform, to which he had rather ridiculously attached all his French decorations.

I was deeply impressed by the occasion. I can still see the coffin under the profusion of wreaths and, on a cushion beside it, Rommel's medals and his marshal's baton. All around, black-uniformed troops of an armored division formed a guard of honor. I recall the pageantry, the impressive solemnity that is part of important official ceremonies, and I can hear again the music, slow and spellbinding, which the troops had to march to with a distorted step, heels almost dragging along the ground.

Next day I returned to Wildflecken; and some days later we heard of the arrival of the franc-garde volunteers.

It was decided that the thousands that had come over with Darnand should be made use of in three ways, according to their individual choice, their age, and their physical ability. Some would join the French workers in Germany, others the units fighting the Italian partisans, and finally there were those who would be assimilated into the Waffen SS, following their chief's example. This was the choice, because of their loyalty to him, of most of the young francs-gardes and of their officers, whether on the reserve or active list, say twenty-five hundred all told. A little later, however, they heard that Darnand would probably be taken from them and that he had been summoned to Berlin to arrange this splitting up of his troops.

Thus their arrival on November 5 was marked by contention. They came from Ulm, by train or in trucks, and reassembled on the main road leading to the camp. They started off in columns, singing "Sambre et Meuse" and "La Madelon," and reached Adolf Hitler Platz marching to the cavalry step (Darnand came from the cavalry), with arms and packs, berets pulled down over one eye, decorations displayed on their khaki or dark-blue uniforms.

Their feeling was very anti-German, and they were not afraid to show it. All the same, this was somewhat surprising when one recalled the engagements that they had taken part in in France against the maquis, less effectively, it is true, than had the GMR,[5] which had constituted the Vichy government police after having served the Third Republic in that same capacity, shooting and clubbing on order, just like all those who have no problems in working for successive regimes.

Side by side, Krukenberg and Puaud phlegmatically watched the march past. They were not long, however, in taking the imperative decisions, even though these involved the risk of a fine old row. The Frenchmen stuck up their emblems of allegiance to the walls of dormitory or mess, the ex-militiamen pasted up pictures of Darnand, the ex-legionnaires pictures of Doriot or the badges of the LVF. Toward the end of the long day, feelings were running high, with jeers being exchanged, to say nothing of the rows with the Storm Brigade veterans, who, having pledged their loyalty to Dodolf (as Adolf Hitler was called in French slang), recognized him and no one else.

Krukenberg swiftly gave an order that all photos, posters,

[5] Groupe mobile de réserve—mobile reserve group.

and trinkets be removed. He confirmed the report that Darnand was not coming here, having been invited to join the French provisional government at Sigmaringen; as for Doriot, he was permanently settled at the headquarters of the French Popular Party on Lake Constance. He further gave instructions that all the arms that the francs-gardes had brought with them—Sten guns, English submachine guns taken from parachutists, American Colt revolvers—were to be confiscated. The Brigadeführer then assembled the officers of the militia. It was a matter of picking out the entirely trustworthy veterans among these. Before their departure, Darnand had done away with ranks, and the militia, on its arrival at Wildflecken, had only its recognized leaders. Krukenberg restored the stripes, but only on those about whom he had private information that they were reliable, giving them a rank inferior to that which they had had previously.

All these officers, Victor de Bourmont, Monneuse, Vaugelas, Bassompierre, Boudet-Gheusi, etc., made up a proved core of real worth. They had passed through the legion, the SOL, and then the militia. They had a fanatical admiration for Darnand, despite his not being of their intellectual level, revering him as a military hero and a natural leader. And now they had their backs to the wall. They knew that those who had stayed in France had been arrested and summarily executed, sometimes simply because they had belonged to the militia, and that those who had not been rounded up were at the mercy of the first denunciator in sight. They were outcasts with no alternative but to fight on. This they had the more readily agreed to since Darnand had obtained a formal promise from Himmler that the Waffen SS would never be sent to the western front or employed against the British, Americans, or de Gaulle's Fighting French. Indeed, this had been tacitly understood by those who had already enlisted.

After he had restored their officers' ranks, Krukenberg asked these militiamen to take in hand the training of the men previously under their command. To these he added, in equal parts, men from the Waffen SS and veterans of the LVF, like a chef preparing a smooth sauce. In this way the fusion made easier by the change of uniform was inevitably brought about. The severe training, frugal diet, and Spartan existence, by leveling the basic conditions of our lives, would succeed in transforming us into a homogeneous company.

The unassimilable elements, moreover, proceeded to fall away of their own accord. One of these was Major Bridoux, son of the general who had been war minister under Pétain and had sought refuge with him at Sigmaringen. The son came from the LVF, where he had distinguished himself. At first he had helped Puaud at assimilating the ex-legionnaires into the Waffen SS, but, discouraged by the difficulties of the task, had quarreled violently with him. When his father had one day presented himself at the camp and, although in civilian clothes, had been refused entry, he went to rejoin him and they left together. It was also said that some of the legionnaires had refused to go over to the Waffen SS from the first, had wanted to desert, and, in spite of having fought for two or three years in German uniform, were arrested and shot.

The Storm Brigade had had its own troubles. One of its best-known officers, Captain Cance, had left; and an entire barracks had gone off to join Degrelle, whose prestige was high and whose troops had a different kind of cohesion. Finally, a number of militiamen had, after several days, become defaulters.

In general, however, it could be said that the amalgamation had taken place quite quickly. In this the prime instigator had undoubtedly been "Monseigneur" Mayol de Luppé, one of the most colorful characters in the division. Prelate to His Holiness,[6] as distinguished from bishop, army chaplain in all those campaigns where religion had flourished in the midst of gunfire—1914–18 at the Dardanelles, 1939–40 in the Levant, then attached to the LVF—he was certainly the ecclesiastic who had worn his soutane less often than any other at that period.

From morning to evening one saw him, notwithstanding his seventy years, riding a splendid chestnut thoroughbred that he had come by goodness knows where. Made a Sturmbannführer, he had had a uniform tailored in Berlin from the finest cloth: the getup of a high-ranking SS officer with gold-braided epaulettes. To it were attached three rows of decorations won on the most diverse fronts, the Legion of Honor, plus French, English, Turkish, and Egyptian medals—all nations seemed to have vied in strewing these stars over him. On his chest hung a magnificent oriental cross, in the form of that of Saint Andrew, swaying to the stride of his mount.

He was like a German *Reiter* of the sixteenth century, a monk who fought in the manner of crusaders of past times,

[6] An honorary title given by the Pope that carried with it the title "Monseigneur."

brandishing the crucifix and, when that did not suffice, unsheathing the sword in order, with great sweeps, to send his adversaries' heads spinning. The only difference was that, instead of a sword, he carried a revolver at his hip. He evoked, in short, a Renaissance figure by his energy, his affectations, and his culture. In his case, the crusader's ardor outdid the Monseigneur's unction. Once when I saluted him with the words, "My respects, Monseigneur," he replied, "Leave out the respects, my child, and give me your filial affection." We could not help smiling at this figure, ambiguous and fascinating, who changed masks with the virtuosity of a commedia dell'arte actor, yet whose sincerity was unquestionable. Belonging to one of the oldest French families, he lived at once among his ancestors and among us, in a piquant time lag.

He had done everything to persuade the LVF to join the Waffen SS and Puaud could not have had a better assistant. What is more surprising, he managed to fascinate Himmler and the members of his staff. Hitler had, indeed, arrived at a certain concordat with the different religious sects, with the exception of the Jews, but, after all, the SS doctrine in its original purity constituted a kind of religion that excluded Catholicism, even though it tolerated a rather vague deism. I think that Mayol de Luppé both astonished and impressed the leaders of the SS. Furthermore, they realized that his imaginative virtuosity would be a great help to them in fusing the several counter-currents into the mainstream of the Charlemagne Division.

His opinions, in fact, based on daring syntheses, would, if reported to Rome, have made the Pope's last few hairs stand on end under his skullcap; as it was, the Vatican looked on him with natural suspicion. He linked, without apparent difficulty, Hitler and Christ, on the basis of anti-Communism. With an astounding rhetoric he resurrected the idea of the Christian warrior for whom the cross was replaced by the "Spiegel," as the SS insignia was called in German military slang, on the jackets of our uniforms.

In the riding school he had turned into a chapel he indulged in flights of eloquence: "The democracies are dead and National Socialism is opening the gates of the future to us. It contains the elements of our faith; who dare deny it? God is inscribed on our belts and in the oath we have taken to our German and European Führer. You are aware that in this army you are serving God. Yours must be the strength that allows Him to repulse the powers of evil that rise from those steppes where shivering ghosts vanish forever in the cold and ice. . . ." We had no theater, but Monseigneur Mayol de Luppé, a figure somewhere between Bossuet and Jean Rigaux,[7] more than made up for it.

Krukenberg himself remained admiring but puzzled. He had always been hostile toward the practice of religion and, besides, had been afraid that Monseigneur Mayol de Luppé with his use of Latin might arouse in the men a nostalgia for certain memories of France: the small village church with the café opposite, the clock that counts off the hours. . . . He soon saw, however, that in these potpourris everyone could find whatever he wanted to. The riding-school chapel did good business. Ecumenical ahead of his time, Monseigneur Mayol de Luppé conducted a Protestant service after Mass. Had there been any Moslems he would have doubtless converted the riding school into a mosque, introduced Ramadan, and climbed a balcony to summon the faithful to prayer by the muezzin call. He wanted to be a witness to the spirit among us, and to become such he was ready to assume the most varied priestly offices.

Almost all of us attended his services, myself and some others, I confess, out of amusement; Catholicism seemed incompatible with our new faith. Certain members of the brigade passed the riding school with a feeling of contempt, but others who felt a nostalgia for mass religious ceremonies took part, while thinking of the Nuremberg liturgies. For them the Mass was a sacred symbol in which they immersed themselves in another dream, that of Germanic paganism.

There were also real Catholics, who were militant conservatives. These were principally Darnand's men who, round the campfires, had dreamed of a national rebirth by means of the traditional religion, a return to a social class of craftsmen and the old order of guilds that constituted, for them, man's dignity. They had donned the SS uniform grudgingly in order to fight Communism, whose ideology appeared to them even more noxious than that of National Socialism.

This diversity of beliefs, motivations, and ideas contributed to making the Charlemagne exceptional among the other divisions. Except for a few, the French—and this is what is so marvelous and at the same time so infuriating about them—are never

[7] The former a famous seventeenth-century preacher, the latter a popular post-war nightclub comedian.

happy joining groups. Whatever activities they take part in, they always preserve a certain reserve, a kind of faith in themselves, in their individual superiority, which impels them to contradict and find fault. They often only enlist in a great cause by way of their private paths. How many of my comrades, for instance, would have let themselves be killed at the front without really knowing for what, simply because, through the Waffen SS, they re-created the epic of the Saumur cadets or, even more, the heroic myth of 1914-18?

Krukenberg was aware of all this. That was why, as I have said, this rigid theorist of National Socialism recognized the true worth of the service rendered by Monseigneur Mayol de Luppé in his transformation acts. Besides, he held him in esteem and knew he could rely on him. This did not prevent our Brigade-führer on certain evenings heaving a sigh at the thought of the strange soup he had to stir.

Stranger, perhaps, than he imagined. One day a guy presented himself to my company—attractive-looking, with a nonchalant manner, going slightly bald: "Prince Genghis Khan Eristoff, interpreter at headquarters."

I was rather surprised. He told me he was descended from the last Eristoff in France, a well-known name among aristocratic Russian exiles.

The truth was somewhat different. He was only the illegitimate son of Eristoff and had never borne the name, but when he had expressed a wish to enlist in the Waffen SS his father had signed an affidavit giving him the right to it, and since it was one held in esteem in Russian émigré circles, the Germans had accepted him without further inquiry.

As I learned after the war, the prince had a Jewish mother and his name had been officially registered in France as Abraham Eisler. It was this that, later, enabled him to come out of the affair very well. He was tried in Poitiers, where his mother had fled. The local rabbi testified in his favor and it was argued that he had enlisted to protect his family from being deported.

He was, as I recall, an intelligent and congenial fellow, surprisingly gifted in languages; he had grown up in a very cosmopolitan milieu of Russians, German Jews, and Poles. The Germans held him in high regard: Prince Genghis Khan Eristoff sounded well in an army that had not renounced all hope of conquest. I introduced him to the company; with his perfect knowledge of Russian we thought of how useful he would be for interrogating the prisoners that we expected to capture in large numbers. But, as it turned out, he never went to the front.

There was also a noncommissioned officer who arrived with the militia called Lehmann. I knew that this was a common enough name in Alsace, but this poor fellow looked extraordinarily like one of these caricatures of Jews that one saw in the National Socialist newssheets and, in France, in *Je suis partout*. He had a nose like a soldering iron that met his chin. What is more, although he had plenty of provisions, he jealously guarded everything for himself. Just to make him angry, everyone used to say to him, "Come on, admit that you're a Jew." But the unfortunate fellow defended himself energetically. I do not know what became of him; doubtless he got stupidly killed. He was in fact Semitic, I imagine, and had enlisted to protect his family, using the Alsatian name of Lehmann, which was what led to the confusion. It was a little surprising that he had been recruited without question. But at that period the Germans were not very particular and cared little about the standards of the SS charter; they needed the maximum of men with the minimum of delay. They had to work in double-quick time, as was noticeable during training.

With the effective force finally assembled, the officers were summoned to headquarters and ordered to assimilate the spirit of the Waffen SS. There was no political indoctrination course; time pressed and Krukenberg was a little apprehensive of French irony. Not much more was inculcated than German words of command. Our equipment was scanty; nevertheless, we started training with what was available.

I had been assigned to the PAK,[8] the division's antitank company. It had the privilege of being directly attached to headquarters, along with a company of FLAK[9] and a communications company. Together they made up the heavy arms battalion, commanded by Sturmbannführer Boudet-Gheusi, a former lawyer from Nice. The division was built up around this battalion: two regiments, the fifty-seventh and fifty-eighth, and three field-artillery batteries, the sappers and attack artillery. Finally there was the honor guard, an elite unit, linked to battalion headquarters like the heavy-arms one. Its leader was Obersturmführer Weber and second in command was Oberjunker Jacques Pas-

[8] Panzerabwehrkanone—antitank unit.
[9] Flugabwehrkanone—antiaircraft unit.

quet, a rather remarkable young man who at various times had been the best athlete in Europe and, once, in the world. This unit, mostly made up of troops from the Storm Brigade, had been given its name in order to set the tone in style and discipline. It could be seen drilling in every corner of the camp, a living example to the other troops.

The command of my company had been divided between myself and a young fellow called Vincenot, who, however, having enrolled in an officers' training course, left us after forty-eight hours. He was supposed to go to Bad Tölz, but since the school had been moved, he was finally sent to Neweklau. On his return it would be my turn to go.

Work began in what were pretty appalling circumstances. Since the end of October, snow had been falling over this whole region, which is torrid in summer and freezing in winter. Our equipment was not at all suited to the conditions and we were short of supplies. We had some 75-millimeter cannon, but being short of ammunition for them, our firing practice was strictly limited. Even weapons were in poor supply and had to be used in rotation. We had been promised trucks and all-terrain vehicles but were still waiting for them. Luckily we still had a few reliable old horses, which we harnessed to carts. It was a burlesque.

We got up at six in the morning, with lights-out at eight at night, and, in theory, our day was regulated by a timetable. In reality, it was constantly being turned upside down. In three months the men had to be both broken in and then formed into a military unit, a task that normally needed a year of progressive training. We had to learn a minimum of German for giving orders and for communications in particular, familiarize ourselves with our arms, and in general accustom ourselves to a very special spirit and discipline.

The urgency of the situation forced this tempo on Krukenberg, who had just received secret instructions, but in any case events spoke for themselves. As winter came the Russian offensive was going to get its second wind. And the OKW[10] was not unaware that the Red Army was about to draw on the fantastic supplies that the Americans were delivering, a part of which might benefit the German forces. Little by little the Russians were slowly restoring the heavy industries in the overrun territories that had fallen into their hands.

---

[10] Oberkommando der Wehrmacht—the German High Command.

Furthermore, fresh divisions were pouring in from eastern Russia and Siberia. Since the beginning of the year the race to Berlin was on among the Allies. The Russian offensive would be all the more menacing because, in December, 1944, the Germans would withdraw some troops, armored units for the most part, from the east, and throw them into the Ardennes offensive that had, at one point, so worried the Allies and on which the Third Reich had placed its last hope, one that was quickly dashed.

Our training progressed in a frenetic manner and according to an unforeseeable schedule. There was little keeping to routine, except for getting up in the morning. Even before breakfast the company assembled with full equipment and the second in command, or a noncommissioned officer, presented it to the commanding officer. The latter saluted with a "Heil Schutz-staffel," and the men replied, "Heil Hitler!"

The SS salute was made with the arm slightly bent, and this distinguishing mark annoyed other troops because it indicated that we were an elite unit. In the Wehrmacht, and contrary to what was generally supposed, the salute was effected by a hand raised to the forehead. It was only after the attempt to kill Hitler that an effort was made to have the outstretched arm, the political salute of civilians in uniform and militants in the Nazi party, made compulsory.

After the morning ceremony we had our breakfast. Then followed a frantic succession of activities: drill, quick-marching, long and exhausting sessions of the "up-down" exercise, and, for our company, anti-tank-gun practice. All this was interspersed with courses on strategy, armaments, etc., generally given by those from the LVF or the Storm Brigade who were, in fact, best qualified, and these were most often noncommissioned officers, a fact which was not considered important—in matters of instruction all that counted was competence, and the men could very well teach the officers.

The nights were almost always disturbed by the noise coming from the command post; on an average we had only four hours' sleep. We had hardly fallen asleep when the whistle woke us with a start and we had to rig ourselves out in a hurry with all our equipment. We found ourselves outside the building, legs weak, eyelids swollen, and plunged into the darkness without even a cup of ersatz coffee, stung by a sharp wind that froze the muscles. During the whole time we spent at Wildflecken I do not know if we had as much as a couple of good nights' sleep.

By this means, we became new men. The guys were staggering with fatigue, but it was a healthy fatigue that made them forget the meager but well-balanced diet, the proper sustenance of fighting troops. At that time the study of calories had not become widespread, but the Germans were already calculating them, for both civilian and military requirements. In this way, food intake was reduced to what was essential.

In general the situation beyond the Rhine was very different from what one saw in France during these same war years. Obviously, with us, outside the main agricultural districts—in Paris, the other large cities, and the Mediterranean region—there was severe privation. The more exposed and accessible places were especially denuded. A young fellow in my command who had earlier lived near a railroad switchyard told me one day, "I wasn't brought up on chocolates but on bombs." But one could say that the French population in general had managed tolerably well, thanks to the black market and, above all, the system of barter. For, though the Germans had appropriated a large quantity of agricultural products, one could not, in all honesty, accuse them of looting.

In my native Loire Valley, for instance, I never lacked bread. And when I went to Paris, a baker's daughter, with whom I had had a love affair, slipped me a couple of dozen sheets of ration coupons. She said that her mother had no need of them and that a farmer, under cover of darkness, had brought the corn to the mill, where it had been ground on the quiet and had then been secretly delivered to the bakery. So the baker could bake good white loaves and I, in exchange for the coupons, got myself Gauloise cigarettes and all kinds of provisions.

One saw nothing like that in Germany, where the controls were much more severe. The black market certainly existed, but on a much more limited scale, and it was almost exclusively confined to the badly bombed towns where the distribution of food supplies had been disrupted. Everywhere else, people received the necessities. Personally, I never saw a civilian collapse because of hunger, or resort to ruses to procure himself provisions. This was because a serious study had been made of what the body needed. The Germans knew both the minimum and maximum that could be eaten, as well as the right kind of food, and the distribution and composition of the rations were organized on this basis.

We suddenly had to adjust to an entirely new dietary

picture. We had to forgo the *pommes frites* without which, it seems, the French soldier does not know how to get himself killed. Our meals consisted mainly of potato and cabbage soup at midday, and sausages at five o'clock. We received two hundred grams per day of glutinous black bread, which quickly became stale and to which we had difficulty in accustoming ourselves.

Each week we drew our ration of artificial honey, hard and solid; forceful use of a penknife was necessary to get it out of the container. It was supposed to be made partly from resin. The sugar was also synthetic. As for the margarine—there was no question of butter, even the very memory of it had faded away—it was made from coal from the Ruhr, which did not prevent it from tasting delicious.

When all was said, we realized that this extremely frugal diet, which often had a strange taste, had a marvelously restorative property. Thus we easily endured the hellish training to which we were subjected and which used up all our resources without ever exceeding them. On the contrary, it gave us strength and resistance, and an exceptional physique: a precious capital, and we did not yet know to what extent we would have to draw on it in the months to come.

All the same, a point came when our French stomachs rebelled. In the heavy-arms battalion, to which my company belonged, Boudet-Gheusi looked after the food supplies well enough, which did not preclude some comic moments. Several times the soldiers invaded the kitchens and turned everything upside down. The officers were ringleaders, for, as I have said, they shared the same food as the men and between them was a common bond.

Christmas approached, and it was then above all that we longed for a less spartan menu. We had been promised packages from our beloved Führer, but to augment the usual fare it seemed more reasonable to rely on ourselves. Some smart-assed guys in my company came to me with a proposal: "You know that during maneuvers we went out to a farm? Well, we've arranged with the farmer to sell us half a pig."

"But that's forbidden."

"We'll have to sneak out one night to get it. We've taken the battalion cook into our confidence and have come to an arrangement about the sides of bacon by letting him have a little. Some pork chops on Christmas Eve wouldn't be bad. . . ."

I thought it over: "Look, do whatever you like. Get your pig, cook and serve it. But I don't know anything about it."

"Right!"

"But look out for the sentries!"

"Of course."

"I warn you, if you get yourselves caught I'll have to punish you. But if you get away with it I'll expect a share of the eats. O.K.?"

"O.K."

They pulled off their coup, and it was not child's play by any means. They had to cover quite a number of kilometers in the cold and through a biting wind over the same uneven ground where all day we had been struggling with the guns that the snow was constantly engulfing. At any moment they risked being surprised by the patrols that were supplied in turn by the different companies and that kept constant watch around the camp. Then, on the return journey, loaded down like donkeys, they had to pass the sentries once more and then climb the walls of this barracks, which was like a small, always brightly lit village.

Christmas arrived and with it the famous packages. We could hardly wait to get hold of them; when we lifted them they did not seem very heavy, though they were bulky and prettily wrapped. We returned with them to our respective quarters and I shut myself in my room. Excitedly, I opened the package and the first item I found was a photo of *le grand Jules* (another nickname for Hitler), ornamented with a mimeographed dedication. I felt my face drop at once and from the dormitories came cries of indignation: "What's this?" "It's grub we want; he's making fools of us, is Dodolf."

Underneath there was some toothpaste, a toothbrush, a piece of soap—in short, all sorts of toilet articles, which added a few pounds but almost nothing to eat. There was also a very small bottle of Schnapps, some odds and ends, and finally a packet of ten German cigarettes, which, as soon as they are lit, catch fire like hay. The guys were furious and booted the packages into the corners.

Once over the disappointment, we got ready for the evening. Monseigneur Mayol de Luppé said Mass. I let myself sink into memories of mangers and candles as if, this evening, I could recapture some of these moments from the past, something of their tenderness. In the riding school nearly two thousand of us were crowded together, for the most part ex-militiamen, those knights of the Cross who came from upright, honest backgrounds and who mixed Christ with repression. It was an astonishing sight, indeed, these members of the Waffen SS receiving Communion and singing in Latin! Krukenberg had sent his observers, who, though somewhat flabbergasted, could not but admire our Monseigneur at his good work.

Afterward, I rejoined my men. In a jiffy, they had decorated the dining hall with holly, and the room looked ready for a family party. In place of tablecloths they had covered the tables with sheets, and a better-than-usual meal began. There was a concoction made of prunes and pasta, a common dish in the German army that had become our food for special occasions; we had, indeed, acquired a taste for these sweetened noodles, which did fill a large hollow in the stomach. Under the heap we located, with the prongs of our forks, the famous pork chops and got ready to make a feast of it. Suddenly there was a commotion: "*Achtung, Achtung. Brigadeführer!*"

Krukenberg entered, accompanied by his staff and also Puaud. He had selected certain companies to visit to see how they spent Christmas Eve. Everyone stood to attention and replied with one voice: "Heil Hitler" to his greeting. He came up to me and I presented the company to him. He asked me, "What's that you're eating?"

As if we had already tasted it, I told him it was veal, but he did not look as if he believed me. He pushed aside one of the men and sat down; we gathered behind him, extremely uneasy, for he obviously smelled the pork. He took a piece, chewed, and swallowed it.

"And you tell me this is veal . . ."

"But, Brigadeführer, veal is what's on the menu."

"Well, I'm telling you it's pork."

"Impossible, Brigadeführer, quite impossible."

"Please taste it yourself."

He made a sign to me to sit down. I returned to my place, really worried, and cut a small piece of meat.

"How strange, it certainly does taste a little like pork."

He glared at me. "I want the truth."

It was then that one of the guys had an incredible inspiration. He stepped up to Krukenberg and said, "It's all right, Brigadeführer. I'm a farmer and I brought some lard with me from France. I gave it to the cooks so that they could fry the veal chops in pork fat."

Krukenberg looked at us without a word; then he smiled slightly. "I suppose no one will ever change the French."

We gave him a big "Heil Hitler!" and he departed with his entourage. We were in the process of becoming model Waffen SS while he, on his side, was learning something from us.

On November 12 the militiamen had taken the oath in the presence of Degrelle and Darnand. For them it was the big step that consecrated their entry into the Charlemagne Division, though not without occasional inner reservations and rebellions. I myself had already taken the SS oath a few days earlier with fifteen other officers and noncommissioned officers. We had, in a sense, sworn as delegates for our companies.

I still have a vivid memory of this ceremony, invested as it was with a religious solemnity. Following an old Germanic tradition, it took place between two oak trees. Swords, on which was inscribed "My honor is named fidelity," were crossed; underneath them an officer, having sworn in the name of all of us, pronounced the ritual text in German, which we repeated in French: "I swear to you, Adolf Hitler, Germanic Führer and Remaker of Europe, to be loyal and brave. I swear to obey you and the leaders you have placed over me until death. So help me God."

It only remained for us to be tattooed in order to feel fully integrated into the SS. Some men looked on this as a sort of magic sign of affiliation. It was simply the indication of the blood group to which each belonged, essential information in the case of someone wounded needing a blood transfusion. Today, practically everyone knows his own group, but this was not so then, particularly in the French army. In the Wehrmacht the soldiers had their group number inscribed on their identification tags after their serial numbers. The tattoo was peculiar to the Waffen SS. The operation was not at all complicated: a medical officer analyzed your blood and an assistant with a tattooing needle inscribed the appropriate letter on the inside of the left arm, below the armpit. This eminently practical procedure showed that we were people well worth saving, but at the same time it made us inescapably identifiable.

Not everyone was familiar with this formality; to put it mildly, it did not arouse much enthusiasm in some, who found it unpleasant. Others, more simple-minded—and among them were certain officers—I heard comment, "No, really, this is barbarous.

It's a blood marriage like the ones Red Indians practice, drawing each other's blood and mixing them."

For myself, I must admit the announcement made me stiffen; tattooing had a bad reputation where I came from. The practice had been modish in certain armed forces, but my father had referred to it with contempt. It was unknown among respectable French people, although a habit in certain royal families, such as the Danish one, where the king used to be tattooed from head to foot.

The important fact was, I told myself, that it was an incredibly obvious distinguishing mark. I had heard the Storm Brigade discussing how the Russians, when they captured the wounded, examined their arms, and if they found they were members of the Waffen SS dispatched them with a bullet in the back of the neck. Those who escaped, having managed to remove their insignia, if recaptured were made to strip naked and if they had traces of tattooing were immediately executed.

Within me, beside the man of strong conviction, there was another being who was vaguely beginning to have premonitions of the great disaster; and I knew that the only people who could survive, if such was their destiny, would be the solitary spirits, masters of their minds and bodies, capable of sufficient self-renewal never to find themselves suddenly in the situation of hunted animals. Now the tattoo would make me legitimate quarry; the Russians knew too much about the Waffen SS, these elite troops were their most formidable adversaries, and they weren't going to bestow any favors on them. "No, certainly not," I decided, "I'll have to opt out; too bad if I'm wounded."

The operation had been announced for November, but it struck me it was likely to take quite a time; there were nearly seven thousand men to be dealt with, company by company, and there were not too many medical officers. I would wait and see, and perhaps with a little luck by the time it was my turn I might have left for officers' training school.

It was the day after Christmas that I received orders to take my company to the infirmary, but, simultaneously, I was told that I had been summoned to headquarters, probably in connection with my departure. I called my men together:

"We are going to be tattooed: Take your soldier's books with you."

There were some mutterings and groans, but the majority were silent. A column was formed; I took my place at its head, and we marched off. On arrival I saluted the doctor in charge in the most formal manner and presented my unit. "Here is the PAK, all present. You can proceed."

He took a look around. "Right. I'll start with you."

That is what I had been expecting. "Look, I've been summoned urgently to headquarters. Take care of the company first, if you don't mind, and you can do me when I come back."

Then I turned to one of my noncommissioned officers and said, "If I'm not back by the time they are finished with you, take the men back to the barracks and don't worry about me; I'll attend to it later."

And I disappeared. "Fine," I thought as I walked away, "perhaps I'll manage to get out of it altogether. When the papers arrive at the administrative office and they find out I haven't been tattooed, I'll say there was a mixup and that I'll go there again. But by then there's a fair chance that I'll be gone."

At headquarters I was asked to wait in Zimmermann's reception room. I felt a little ashamed, all the same, and walked up and down, at the mercy of conflicting feelings. "It was a small act of betrayal, what you've just done! You managed to dodge your commitment; having led your guys to be tattooed, you yourself slipped away." But I also told myself, "So what? Shit, what's the good of all that! If I get a bullet or a piece of shrapnel in my left arm, who's going to be able to find my blood group in the pulp that's left?"

It was then that a bony, gangling young fellow in noncommissioned officer's uniform entered. His face had pronounced planes, his eyes were pale and he wrinkled them up at the corners ironically, he had a long, aristocratic nose, his mouth stretched at the left corner in a slight grin. With red, thinning hair, beautiful hands, and slender fingers, he certainly made an impression.

"Georges de La Buharaye."

"Christian de La Mazière."

"I'm being sent to a course for officers; you too, I think?"

"That's right."

While we talked, I studied him carefully. He was a Breton of good family. I sensed the professional soldier and was greatly taken with him.

We were not able to say very much to each other before Zimmermann suddenly called us in. "Here you have your papers. You'll go to Yanovitz near Prague. It's a school for officers and noncommissioned officers specializing in antitank combat, a hard course, as you'll soon see, but we need people like you to be trained as specialists. You must come out at the very top and come back here with your commission from headquarters; this is very important. I'm counting on you."

We were then received by Krukenberg, but Puaud, who was definitely being kept on the outside, was not there. Our Brigade-führer received us with his customary cool composure, having, however, a brief smile for me in memory of the pork chops. Above his head hung the portrait of *le grand Jules;* in front of him was a photo of himself, taken during the First World War, as a young officer, which struck me as rather strange.

He made us a little speech: "You are going to take an intensive two months' course. There you'll learn what a German school is, but you'll be among men of various nationalities as well as Germans. You have to come out on top. I want us to be talked about."

He added, referring to the bands that the Waffen SS wore on their left sleeves on which one could read the name of their division in Gothic lettering, "We have just received supplies and you can sew the name of the Charlemagne on your uniform. Go and see Zimmermann on the way out; I want them at Yanovitz to know where you come from and see to it that you establish the highest reputation for our unit. Heil Hitler!"

"Heil Hitler!"

We clicked heels and departed. We were given our papers and then, at the commissariat, some provisions, travel vouchers, and also vouchers for accommodation in the Soldatenheim, the military hostel where one could eat, read, and see movies. The Waffen SS had its own special hostels in which, unlike those of the Wehrmacht, everyone, from simple soldier to general, met socially.

Then we separated. As my room was near the camp entrance, La Buharaye said, "I'm going back to my company to pack my things and then I'll rejoin you and we'll leave together. If we don't find a vehicle of some sort we can walk. It's not all that far to the station, about three or four kilometers. We'll keep our packs light." Then, gazing at me with his pale eyes, he added, "I'm really glad to be going with you; I think we'll get on well together."

I thought so too. I watched him go off with that mixture of nonchalance and authority that I already associated with him.

Then I went to the barracks where my men were; they had all been tattooed, while I had got out of it. But I was not thinking of that anymore. I said good-bye to the officers who were there. They had heard the news and were expecting Vincenot, back from Neweklau, who would succeed me. Then I went to my room.

Having finished packing, I stood still on the threshold to fix it in my mind, with all those memories that already were crowded into it. It was not so long ago that I had entered it for the first time. What a road I had traveled since! I was no longer the same person; my destiny had been set in motion, as if it were preceding me. Where would I catch up with it, and for what awakening?

My anguish took on a face, the face of Inge. She had been here and, suddenly, she was the only person I saw. It had still been October when one day there was a message for me from the guardroom: "A young lady is here to see you." Women visitors were strictly forbidden. But I was company commander and our barracks was near the entrance to the camp; I could take a chance in ignoring the regulation. "I'm coming over; ask her to wait," I replied. I had not gone far when I met her; a well-meaning noncommissioned officer was bringing her to me. Her progress was greeted by a chorus of admiring whistles.

I was both astonished and delighted. My God, how lovely she was! But I was also uneasy. Feeling like a schoolboy committing a fantastic act of folly, I brought her to my room. She had received mobilization papers assigning her to an antiaircraft unit; her turn had come and total war had caught up with her. She was here to say good-bye and to give herself to me.

What was in her mind? I could imagine it in astonishment. It had started with that meeting in Heidelberg, those walks hand in hand when the beauty of fall seemed to defy the coming apocalypse; this Frenchman had loomed up beside her like someone out of one of her books, wearing the uniform of her own people and about to fight the same enemy. . . . And this Frenchman was not alone, he was one among thousands of these beings, who were reputed charming but superficial, among thousands of them in this camp to which she had come. Symbolized by me, it was perhaps with all of them that she was in love.

She had come to bestow on me the most solemn gift, the gift of her innocence. She is one of the very few virgins I have ever slept with in my life, and I shall never forget it.

In my room after I had locked the door—how many steps I heard behind it!—we made love, very badly, as one is apt to in such circumstances. She did not cry out but undoubtedly she suffered pain. There was such beauty in her glance, her expression, such a desire to make me understand what she was offering me, that I was perhaps more moved than I have ever been since.

We stayed together a long time, talking and holding hands. Then I unlocked the door and went with her as far as where the barracks ended. I knew that we would never see one another again; nothing of her remained but the small bloodstain on my sheet.

Inge at Wildflecken . . . that was two months ago, perhaps a little more. That happiness, snatched from the pitiless time in which I was involved, lacerated me. I shut the door, hoisted my pack on my shoulder. Downstairs La Buharaye was waiting for me.

III.
IN WHICH I GET TO KNOW
WHAT A GERMAN
TRAINING SCHOOL IS LIKE

We made our way to the station at Wildflecken. The journey we were about to take was a fairly long one. Yanovitz was about seventy kilometers from Prague, in one of the territories that after Heydrich's assassination[1] had been annexed to Germany as a reprisal measure.

Since we had not found a conveyance, we had walked to the station, and on the way La Buharaye and I had talked and got to know each other better. I told him how I had come to join the Waffen SS and then he told me about himself.

He had gone to Saint-Cyr, not with any particular enthusiasm but because in the circles he came from it was the natural thing to do. After his graduation he applied to join a unit in the Sahara. So for several years he had served in desert outposts, which is perhaps where he had acquired the air of tranquillity and quiet suppleness that was peculiar to him. He seemed to

---

[1] Reinhard Heydrich. Called "Heydrich the Executioner," he was an assistant to Himmler noted for his effective elimination of German Communists and the terrorization of Czechs after 1938. He was assassinated in Prague in 1942.

skim over the surface of the snow, whereas my jackboots sank into it. And I was soon to discover that he was equally at home at night, moving catlike, furtively but with alerted senses, catching every movement.

In 1942 he had been granted leave to return to France and his native Brittany. It was during his stay there that the Allied invasion of North Africa had taken place and the Germans had occupied the Southern Zone of France. All at once he found himself trapped in this corner, practically demobilized. As a second-lieutenant, he had to report to the police and various other authorities and had asked them what he should do. They had left him to his own devices until, in 1944, he had been called up again and drafted to the French Security Force.

He might easily have joined the Maquis, but his convictions did not run in this direction. Although, to be honest, could one speak of convictions in his case? He was a skeptic. Since he was caught in this current, hell! he might as well let it take him with it. So thoroughly did he follow his laissez-faire instinct that he ended up at Wildflecken. This amused him a lot. He lived in a state of ironic detachment, and he suited me very well indeed.

After a short wait we took the first train that came and later changed to one that would bring us to Prague. Traveling was not really fun at this period. Allied bombers were constantly over Germany and there was a continual series of air-raid alerts. The train windows were painted blue from top to bottom and after leaving a station the lights had to be extinguished.

There was a general feeling of nervousness, to say the least. German Feldgendarmerie men and plain-clothes police went up and down the corridors examining identity documents and travel permits. We began to hear tales of how some young fellows from the Wehrmacht, having had enough of it after 1941, had quietly opted out.

In the compartment of the Prague train there were some charming girls belonging to the Women's Corps, whose members were known in France as "gray mice." We soon joined them, and as they had plenty to eat we had a happy little meal together that became so animated that the Feldgendarmerie guys poked their noses in to verify that we really were from the SS. When they found out our nationality they shrugged their shoulders with an air of resignation.

The journey, however, was a long and tiring one, and it was fairly late when we reached Prague. We crossed the frontier without really being aware of it, for, in fact, at that time, there was no frontier. Czechoslovakia, Poland, Rumania, Hungary, and Germany constituted a German Confederation or greater Reich.

I only knew Prague through a film called *La Ville Doré* (*The Golden City*) that had been popular in France during the Occupation, from which one got a good impression of its bridges, churches, and multitude of steeples—a wonderful city. But when we arrived there I was struck by its quiet air; it did not feel at all like a capital.

We did not have to leave until early morning, so, with the vouchers we had been given, we settled ourselves in the Waffen SS house. It was a large and comfortable hotel that had been requisitioned, where we were given two rooms. We deposited our packs and had dinner, after which a film was being shown; but we preferred to take a stroll around the city.

We went out again into the sharp, frosty night. I kept telling myself that, for the first time, I typified an occupying enemy, a conqueror, undoubtedly a very much feared conqueror when one recalled all the reprisals that had followed Heydrich's assassination. I must say, however, that I observed scarcely any animosity toward us. The girls were pretty and smiling, but possibly this was their way of resisting, because, as one learned later, Czechoslovakia had stood together as one man. . . .

In any case, we picked up two of them without any difficulty, and after a short walk they went home. We accompanied them, making them laugh; they were certainly sweet little things. Perhaps the fact that we were French was in our favor, or perhaps they took us for police agents in disguise. There was no way of knowing. Without any fuss they let us bring them back to the Waffen SS hotel and up to our rooms, where they did not try to kill us while we slept! Nor did they ask us for any money. Uniform or no uniform, we pleased them, and obviously this was not their first adventure.

We were up early to catch a local train to Yanovitz. After a three-kilometer walk from the station, we arrived at the camp and were immediately struck by its appearance. Roofs, narrow streets, a steeple—we were in a small, snowbound village, a Czech hamlet that had been evacuated. The command post was in the school, whose classrooms were used for the theoretical courses; the church was where clothing and other items of material were stored; the camp commander lived in the schoolteacher's house.

We presented ourselves at the administrative office, where we were expected; our training course had already started some days before. Then we were introduced to the commanding officer.

He was a truly extraordinary being, a force of nature. More than six feet tall, he had an impressive-looking scar plowed down his head as if someone had attempted to cut it in two with a billhook. Starting from the right temple, it skirted the corner of the eye, where it stood out in a bulge that made a hollow in his cheek, cut across the lips, and disappeared under the chin at the top of his neck.

This Obersturmbannführer was one of the Waffen SS heroes, a warrior above all else. Nobody knew if he was married or whether he had children. He directed the training school because he had been ordered to, but he had a burning impatience to be back in the fighting line. His story could be read in the ribbons that he wore: Poland, 1939; Norway and France, 1940; Greece, Crete, Yugoslavia, Russia. His deeds were commemorated by his decorations: Iron Cross to Knight's Cross, Close Combat Medal, Gold Assault Medal, and, sewn to his sleeve, five miniature tanks, the number he had knocked out.

He did not speak a word of French. A noncommissioned officer, standing to attention, acted as interpreter. He was an Alsatian redhead, as, curiously enough, were all the Alsatians I came across in the Waffen SS. This one's hair was absolutely egg-yolk color.

The colonel interrogated us rapidly while going through our papers. At the conclusion he said, "Good. You're being assigned to us. You'll be in a room for three; as you'll see, the cadets are grouped according to nationality. You'll be equipped and given combat uniform. You understand that one doesn't eat much here, sleeps hardly at all, so that you are turned into machines for killing and commanding. I don't tolerate any show of weakness; one such, and you'll be sent back."

In short: the grand old style. . . . Once out of there—La Buharaye as ever with his little one-cornered smile—we started on our enrollment round, going first to the church to pick up our blankets and combat uniform. The place had remained just as it was after the last Mass had been celebrated, with its altar, Way of the Cross, and statues. But there were additions in the shape of placards bearing slogans. On the altar could be read: "There is only one God, our Führer." Others proclaimed: "A real man needs only to believe in himself, in his leaders, his country, and the Führer, in order to find happiness." And the typical formula: "Religion is the opium of the people," just as in Russia.

La Buharaye, who had a fair knowledge of German, translated these oracles for me. He snickered quietly, as was his habit, but I felt he was a little shocked. Not that he was a practicing Catholic. I do not suppose he had worn out the knees of his trousers on a prayer stool. When on leave he had shown up at Mass in the chapel of the family château or in the village church to please his mother. But, as he liked to put it: "The best church is the brothel; that's where one runs the smallest risks and gets the warmest welcome." His skepticism was general and he had never thought of marrying and, as they say, establishing a family. In his detachment I felt a kind of maturity that impressed me all the more because, at thirty-four, he was considerably older than I.

All the same, these German maxims clashed with his core of Breton traditionalism. Quite as an afterthought, he grumbled with a slightly haughty air, "Who are they to bore us with their philosophy?" or, more forthright still: "That's a philosophy for idiots!" It was the first time, in fact, that we had come up against an indoctrination system. At Wildflecken, as I have said, it was only a question of physical training even if some members of the Storm Brigade would have been quite capable of taking a political or ideological course; and at Yanovitz, when it came to it, it turned out the same.

Provided with our equipment, we went off to install ourselves. Beside the village, clusters of huts were arranged around a large square—Adolf Hitler Platz, as was to be expected—where the flag of the Waffen SS, and not the German one, floated. This was where the dormitories, bedrooms, and mess halls were situated. The well-paved streets were cleared of the snow that lay everywhere else. It was the habit of the German Army to keep the troops in conditions that varied between comfort and severity. On our way we noticed buildings bursting with military supplies: tanks, machine guns, and antitank weapons of a new design.

The trainees came in and we were introduced to them. They had various ranks, noncommissioned, officer candidates, and even commissioned officers. Some were there to qualify for promotion, others to receive additional antitank training. Most of the courses were taken by everyone, but those men who were to become officers—the minority, in fact—had extra sessions. I was in this category, so was La Buharaye, who at Wildflecken had not been reinstated in his rank in the French Army. He had not even been made Oberscharführer, as I had, because the company to which he had been detailed already had its full complement of officers. He was simply Unterscharführer, or sergeant.

We entered a truly cosmopolitan milieu, and mingling with the various groups was like touring Europe. There were, naturally, many Germans, as well as Poles and Russians, some Latvians, Lithuanians, and Estonians, Norwegians, Swedes, Dutch. There were only two Belgians from Degrelle's division, but the Walloons, whose unit was now at the front, had been numerous in the previous lot of promotions. And, on top of all these, there were an Italian and a Hindu in a turban preparing to become officers.

We ate lunch together and immediately afterward had our first lecture. As in the barracks, we were divided according to nationality, each group in its appointed place with an interpreter, if one was needed. Most, however, in particular the men from the East, spoke fluent German. We two, the only Frenchmen, were a bit conspicuous with our redheaded Alsatian. But the instructors soon realized that we were eager to learn.

It was, in fact, an exciting course, dealing with the whole range of antitank weapons. It was true that Wildflecken had familiarized us with the theory of the Panzerfaust and the Panzerschreck,[2] and we had already worked with the 75-mm cannon, but now we discovered new possibilities in the 88, notably that the viewfinder had an electric eye.

Two hours later we went to the training ground for firing and aiming demonstrations. Each man in turn became part of a gun crew, learning how a gun works, then how to control it—in short, an elementary course and an officers' course at one and the same time. The two hundred cadets worked at every position under the direction of the instructors, officers and noncommis-

---

[2] The Panzerfaust was an offensive antitank weapon, consisting of a hollow charge whose firing mechanism and means of propulsion were by means of a light tube that could only be used once. The Panzerschreck depended on the same principle as the bazooka and was used in the same manner. Its range was longer than the Panzerfaust's but the antitank troops preferred the latter as lighter and easier to handle in close combat, besides being much more effective.

sioned officers, young fellows who had had two or three very hard years at the front. In the biting cold we drove ourselves without respite in a truly fantastic session.

We returned to the messrooms at nightfall. After the meal I went to my room and lay down. Until then I had not had time to realize how exhausted I was. A whistle brought us to our feet— out again for night maneuvers. It had been a fitting introduction to the course.

We were back on the stroke of 2 A.M., chilled, our teeth chattering. The rooms were not heated. La Buharaye, whom nothing, not even an earthquake, could disorganize, went off nonchalantly to the toilets with toothbrush and towel. I did the same, but had he not been there I wouldn't have bothered with this ritual. Then we undressed in a jiffy, head under the sheets and blankets, and warm in no time at all!

The whistle was blown again at six in the morning: "Out!" La Buharaye calmly put his towel around his neck and started off to the washrooms with his toilet things. But he did not get far; a German noncommissioned officer barred the way: "No, no. Leave all that, and get outside. Naked!"

What? Outside? And stark naked?

Yes, indeed; the guys could be seen rushing out without a stitch on into the darkness, which was still dense and cut only by the streetlights. They began to rub each other down with snow. Finally I, too, stepped outside. Such a wave of icy harshness surged up my legs and enveloped me in biting cold that I thought I was going to die. Beside me La Buharaye kept on cursing: "No, really! What kind of idiotic goings-on are these?"

Very soon, though, we were sweating all over. This Finnish method made our blood bubble. We returned indoors at full speed, dressed, and shaved, in icy water of course, feeling full of energy with which to face the day.

The program was quite simple: antitank theory and practice in the morning; the rest of the time, physical training. There was no question, as at Wildflecken, of learning the role of infantry or the handling of small arms. We were to get to know the new 88 recoilless gun, whose infrared viewfinder could spot the movement of tanks at night and take precise aim at them. We had a varied collection of targets at our disposal: T34 and Joseph Stalin Russian tanks and the American Shermans. These machines had been divested of their cannon and their caterpillar traction did not function; they were towed by a cable behind half-track vehicles.

We were also submitted to a particularly thorough training in "man against tank." For the first time I used a Panzerfaust. One gets as close as possible and, bang! the rocket is dispatched into the tank's belly. As for handling magnetic mines, that is quite a game! The Russians, we were told, used well-trained dogs to put them in position. The dogs had learned that they were only fed on top of the "Tiger" or "Panther" German tanks. When an attack was imminent, the wretched beasts were tied up and deprived of food and, when the first enemy machines came in sight, let loose with a mine hung around their necks. The poor dogs jumped onto the turrets of the tanks in the hope of a good mash.

This ruse had not lasted long because the Germans had taken the precaution of killing all the dogs they came across on the battlefield. In any case, at Yanovitz, it was we who did the running. A mine was about the size of a wheel of Camembert cheese. Quickly one grasped hold of it, dashed from one hole in the ground to the next toward the tank, which one tried to reach from the side, jumped onto the caterpillar track, stuck the mine on the inside of the turret—where it clung like a cupping glass—and leaped off backward as one pulled the detonator. Bouncing onto the ground, one had to run like hell; it blew up in five seconds.

We kept repeating this little exploit, trying to do so in all possible conditions, for generally there are lookouts on top of the tanks, infantry men, who are there precisely to protect them against Panzerjäger, or antitank units. It was first necessary to dislodge them with our Sturmgewehr.[3]

We also had to dig cavities in the ground in which to lie in wait, called foxholes. These were a kind of funnel with a horizontal excavation at the bottom as a protection against the flame throwers with which Russian tanks were equipped. They had trapdoors at the level of the caterpillar tracks, through which they sprayed the Panzerjäger when they passed their hideouts.

That was why our instructors had the Russian tanks roll over our foxholes while we were not then allowed to attack them

[3] Offensive weapon, between a Bren gun and automatic pistol, with a curved magazine.

because they were guided by infantrymen. As they passed they released a jet of flame. If one was not well hidden, it was just an unfortunate accident.

In every class, some got burned. So it was in our own interest that we quickly assimilated the morning course during which all the tactics that we had to put into practice in the afternoon were explained to us: how to camouflage ourselves, how to approach a tank through snow, over both hard and soft terrain, how to jump onto a T34, which is far from easy sailing.

In the morning the officer candidates also had instruction at the "sandbox," a large-scale model, changed every day, of a section of the region. In rotation we were given charge of a regiment; although normally our command would be at company level, we had to be capable of instantly taking over from a superior. Thus, at Yanovitz, the training of officer candidates was carried out on a level both below and above their actual rank in the military hierarchy: below in individual instruction, above when it came to overall tactics.

In these sessions the instructors nominated one of us to the command. They would say, for instance, "Von La Mazière, today you're in charge of this regiment. Choose your assistants." I would make my choice, selecting some fellows suitable for overcoming the communications problem, and go up to the "sandbox." The instructors took the data for the day from an envelope.

It was always a problem of counterattack. The colonel had explained this circumstance to us, not without humor, and with the realism of the true military tradition. Formerly, he told us, the emphasis was only on offensive operations, on the theory that the enemy was constantly cracking and that there was no halt to our advance. But the fortunes of war being what they are, it was now necessary to reappraise the offensive in the framework of defensive tactics. The heydays of the war were over.

So it was the "reds" who did the attacking. They had a given number of tanks and were advancing over a predetermined type of terrain: forest, marsh, ice, and so on. The "blues" had so many regiments, so many battalions and antitank weapons. We had to draw up a plan quickly, issue orders for establishing a front and conducting the counterattack. I explained my decisions: "This is where the terrain is favorable," and went on to elaborate them. "I am positioning this company here with the 88 guns that I've placed like this." Then, in turn, the officer commanding the designated company continued, "As for me, this is how I'm deploying my sections." Sometimes air support was called for, but in principle it was never available.

In a word: a totally absorbing game, and much more fun than Monopoly. One piece of terrain would be lost, another gained. In the afternoon it was all reenacted on the field with reduced forces: one gun represents four, that is to say, an artillery section; four stand for a company. Then one could see which of us had been right about the theoretical plan, and verify the mistakes: one might not have taken into account that a tank could infiltrate at such and such a spot, lie in wait during the withdrawal, fire on and knock out part of our artillery.

During the whole exercise the instructors followed us through their field glasses and graded us. They watched us in our foxholes, with the Panzerfaust in our hands. They checked the quality of the orders given by the company commanders, the accuracy of their calculations, the speed of their decisions. Finally they judged the quality of our tactical procedures.

They quickly saw that La Buharaye and I were particularly gifted at the "sandbox," more so than even the German officers who had come for a refresher course. We received very good marks and knew we were on the right track. On the other hand, our enthusiasm was somewhat less when it came to camouflaging ourselves like zebras, jumping from one hole to another, keeping out of the way of flame throwers, "all these shit games," as Georges, who continued to curse them, put it.

The instructors, feeling that we were really getting our teeth into the tactical lessons, were fully behind us. They placed us at the head of increasingly large troop formations, so that the others ended by resenting these Frenchmen who were taking a little too much on themselves. The rotation of command became stricter and we were given only secondary roles.

We remained, therefore, outside the center of action and watched what our pals were doing. When their plan had been shown in action—in directing the "red" offensive, or, above all, the "blue" counteroffensive—the spectators were asked, "What do you think? How are they doing?" La Buharaye and I exchanged winks, making numerous ironic observations, joking all the time.

"It's crazy," I told Georges, "there's nothing easier than to become a great general. All you need is to have enough people to move around; no need to wait years." And he replied, "Do you know I've learned more in a month here than in two years at

Saint-Cyr and ten in the French Army. And besides, at least this is fun; marvelous, in fact."

It happened, however, that on evenings when we had nothing to do—and at a rough estimate we had almost seven hours' sleep a day—we felt our stomachs grumbling. The diet was even more restricted here than at Wildflecken, while the training was distinctly more severe. And then, too, it was terribly cold, constantly below freezing. Everything was frozen hard and the forest could be heard crackling.

La Buharaye had a lot of stuff in his pack, loose tobacco, for example. He was a moderate smoker and had given me a packet of tobacco so that I could at least roll my own cigarettes. This was a pleasure I had almost lost the habit of. Smoking was forbidden during both the indoor courses and the exercises, so only the evenings remained.

His supply, however, was not inexhaustible and he suggested going to reconnoiter some of the neighboring farms during maneuvers. The village had been taken over, but some farming estates remained. These were well-marked enclaves that our artillery spared. One evening I saw him returning from the nearby huts with a bundle on his shoulder. "What are you up to?" I asked.

"Keep quiet and don't worry."

And he disappeared into the darkness with his catlike agility, which was why, when we went out on night maneuvers, I kept close to him. Time passed; I was not too concerned. As long as we had not had to start off again after dinner and they let us go to bed, we could count on at least four tranquil hours. We would not be marched out before dawn.

He returned two hours later; I was sleeping.

"Hey, Christian!"

"What?"

"Hungry?"

"Eh?"

"Look."

He showed me bacon, homemade bread, a whole lot of provisions.

"But how did you pay for all that?" He had on his slight smile.

"I've a feeling that tonight there'll be some Latvians cursing when they can't recover their losses."

He repeated the exploit two or three times, thus making it possible for us to have a little extra food on the sly. On leaving the dining room we could have an extra snack. For this reason we were in distinctly better shape than the others.

We tried to take care of ourselves as far as possible. One afternoon at the training course, when the officer in charge of the exercise had been chosen in the morning, we found ourselves with only minor assignments. La Buharaye came up to me. "Look here, we're liaison officers; well, you know what? We'll go back indoors. It'll soon be dark, and anyhow we've had enough of their goings-on, these stupid shits. No point in freezing while waiting for a message that's unlikely to turn up."

A look through the binoculars. The others were sufficiently far away and had surely forgotten us. We turned and made off.

At a little over three kilometers from our barracks there was a concentration camp. I discovered its existence the first morning when we were rubbing ourselves down with snow: into the still dark sky the camp's searchlights projected a beam of light. Because our streetlamps only shed a dim light in comparison, there was never any shadow at any hour of the night, down there. Subsequently, during our night maneuvers we saw lookout posts and barbed wire silhouetted on the snow. But there was a regulation, displayed in the rooms and dormitories, forbidding us to go near the camp. Should we disobey, the guards had orders to fire at us.

Although they wore the same SS insignia, these guards did not have the same uniforms as ours. In fact, we had nothing in common with them. We saw some of them with the prisoners whom they brought to clean up our camp. The prisoners, who cleared away the snow, wore pajamas and striped coats. All they had on their feet were rags wound around them and thick wooden soles tied on with string.

This attire had shocked La Buharaye and me. We concluded they were convicts and left it at that. In any case, how could we find out more? We were not allowed to speak to them or, above all, let them speak to us. The number of different nationalities at Yanovitz explained this strict regulation; the prisoners would have been sure to find compatriots among us.

This prison camp, however, continued to interest us both. And when we left the scene of maneuvers, there it was. We stopped to have a look.

"There can't be that many people in there—a couple of hundred perhaps? They must pass through in rotation. Who do you think they are? Political prisoners?"

"Yes, no doubt."

"I think so too; Poles, or possibly Czechs. After the Heydrich business there were a lot of arrests."

Above each hut was a smoking chimney.

"Say what you like, it doesn't look as bad as all that. Shit! Look at us, can't even warm ourselves! Wouldn't mind sleeping in their dormitories, it can't be that bad."

A conversation, in short, that had not got very far. . . . It must be remembered that we were obsessed by the cold: the snow over which we were walking and which was incredibly hard, the countryside that seemed frozen stiff, including the air that we breathed, everything was petrified by the frost. We had the feeling that if we relaxed our tempo, however slightly, we might find ourselves suddenly changed into statues of ice. Only the water did not freeze, for the pipes were buried deep; but when we plunged our hands into it it was like a whiplash through the body. Then, all at once, the glimpse of those huts with smoke coming from them and, far away, men in a fatigue party out for wood.

Then, after a few moments, we were on our way again, talking casually and smoking; and just as we came to our quarters we ran into a batch of the prisoners. They were clearing the road, watched by a guard, rifle on his shoulder, and an unconcerned look on his face. It was one of the prisoners who seemed to be in actual control of the little group.

We continued on our way without slowing down, as the regulations demanded. In passing, we brushed against a young fellow who was scraping up the snow with a shovel, piling it into a heap that another prisoner collected in a wheelbarrow. Suddenly we heard a lowered voice: "You're French?"

We were startled. He had evidently noticed our badges. We stopped and La Buharaye replied, "Yes, and you?"

"Me too, but we can't talk. Do you have any cigarettes?"

"Yes."

"Look, I'm taking a big chance, so listen carefully: if you've some to spare, drop them on the ground as you walk and I'll pick them up."

I looked at him: a prisoner like all prisoners, looking neither sad nor happy, but just withdrawn, not his real self, thinking of nothing but his longing for a smoke. La Buharaye dug in his pocket and took out a packet of ten German cigarettes. We moved off; the packet fell on the snow.

We were hardly back an hour when we heard the rumble of tanks and the roar of engines, all the racket made by the returning armor. With it were the German Waffen SS, which was entrusted with its maintenance and also its operation in our training exercises. They came in; the day's work was finished.

We ate dinner and went to our rooms. The evening was a quiet one and we slept all night without interruption. Next morning, after the short session in the snow, we went off for the training course. But this had scarcely started before someone came and asked for us.

"The Obersturmbannführer has summoned you."

The officer who was lecturing turned to us. "Off you go."

We left. On the way La Buharaye said to me, "I bet you we're not going to finish our training and that the Charlemagne has been ordered to the front. You'll see."

Indeed, the news that had come through to us while we had been at Yanovitz had not been very good. The Russian offensive had recommenced on January 12, and in the center, near Lake Balaton in Hungary, there had been violent fighting. For a time there had been talk of sending the whole training school to the battlefield, echelon by echelon. We were assembled in Adolf Hitler Platz and our Obersturmbannführer had told us that we might be leaving for Hungary under his command. Together with the camp personnel we could have constituted a small brigade. For a few days our training was accelerated, the maneuvers became ever more exacting, and our nights shorter. Then gradually the threat blew over, but we remained under some pressure.

We arrived at the colonel's office, a fine room, lined with books—a true warrior's retreat. This man who was only happy on the battlefield, who had never spared himself anywhere, who had been through more than a few hospitals with his numerous wounds, surely must have said to himself that, inasmuch as he had the command of this training school, he might as well take the opportunity to rest and relax.

At our heels was our Alsatian. His only job was to act as our interpreter and he followed us about like a faithful dog. When we were out at the training ground without much to do, as on the previous evening, he kept busy at the camp. But in the morning he joined us again at the course. And, in fact, we really needed him. The colonel, as I have mentioned, did not speak a single word of French, and as for me, my knowledge of German remained sketchy. La Buharaye knew it better, but his accent left much to be desired.

"Heil Hitler!"

Our Obersturmbannführer was standing in front of a magnificent portrait of le grand Jules in military uniform wearing a very martial air. The colonel was obviously furious, his face flushed with anger so that, in contrast, the disfiguring scar made a while groove across it.

Our entry was greeted with a roar of abuse, a regular Niagara flowed down on us; we turned white as a sheet. Dumbfounded and fascinated at the same time, I only understood some odds and ends such as that the "Franzosen" were "Sweinereien": swine and bastards. . . .

Then all at once he stopped and turned to the interpreter. "Translate."

Our redhead began to speak in a neutral tone while the colonel banged the table with his fist. "This is what the Obersturmbannführer says: 'Yesterday, you returned earlier from the maneuvers. On the way back you stopped and talked to a prisoner, although this is strictly forbidden—as you have read and has been told you again and again. What's more, you gave him a packet of cigarettes; it's useless to deny it, because the Kapo [a trusty among the prisoners] saw the whole incident and on his return to the prison camp reported it to the guards. This morning I had a message from the camp commandant telling me of the affair and that it was two Frenchmen who were implicated."

Our Alsatian had made a résumé and had spared us the insults. When he finished, La Buharaye immediately began to speak in a reserved tone and with a somewhat haughty smile. "Please translate carefully to the Obersturmbannführer everything that I am about to say. Firstly, perhaps we are French swine; you didn't translate that, but I want you to tell him this. Possibly we don't know what discipline is. But I should like you to remind him that we aren't here to waste our time over trifles; we're not here to defend French territory, but we're here to defend German territory, because it just so happens that the Germans can't bloody well defend it on their own and need others to give them a hand. So that's the first point; our gesture in coming here should at least be respected. The second is we know the rule and are very well aware of what it prohibits. But, just the same, I want to get things straight; does the Obersturmbann-führer give the word of a Kapo, a type of prisoner that I have little doubt he despises, more weight than that of one of his Waffen SS? I want you to put this question to him. Should he say yes, there's no point in continuing."

The Alsatian translated the speech phrase by phrase with a slight smile. I was thinking, "This is great, though Georges is completely crazy." But he was off again, standing straight as a ramrod to his full height, after the colonel had interjected, "Continue."

"It's true we came back earlier and that on the way someone spoke to us and asked if we were Frenchmen. Quite instinctively we stopped and said yes, because it was a compatriot of ours. We didn't want to know why he'd been arrested—presumably for political reasons. But we're here in Czechoslovakia in a military training camp and if we run into a Frenchman, whether he's a prisoner or not, if he asks for cigarettes, we'll give him some. And now, Obersturmbannführer, you may do as you wish with us. You can send us to a concentration camp, since that is the punishment, as we well know. It only remains to say that, whatever the uniform, to us a Frenchman remains a Frenchman, first and foremost. If he is unhappy and one can perhaps do something for him, one does it, even if one's opinions are the very opposite of his. That's how we have been brought up."

I prepared myself for the worst. "They'll make an example of us," I said to myself, "it's the only solution in the army: the spirit must be broken. We will be stripped of our ranks and sent to the nearby camp." But the colonel had calmed down, and his face cleared.

"I know who you are and how you are making out in the course; I'm aware that you're among our most brilliant pupils." And he complimented us on our intelligence, our qualities as technicians and tacticians.

"This business has upset me. But now I believe it should be treated with scorn, and forgotten. I am not going to challenge the attitude of men like you who have come to fight at our side; you belong to the new Europe."

La Buharaye had touched the colonel's pride in the Waffen SS and, without a doubt, he had been won over by this blond, tall Celt. I myself, although a Mediterranean type, was also a respectable height; and he was appreciative of the fervor with which we had set ourselves to learn.

"We'll say no more about it," he concluded. "But I have one request: give me your word as an officer that even if a prisoner speaks to you again, you won't answer."

It was difficult for us to do other than comply; we had already scored a major point, so we gave our word, and it proved the less of a restriction because events began to move fast.

Our term had still almost a month left to run. Since the plan to send us to the front had not materialized, our training had been intensified. But all the same, La Buharaye found time to get some pickings from our neighbors with which to barter food from the few peasants in the surrounding district. The great cold had not abated; but we grew used to it and became tanned.

Then, two weeks later, toward the middle of February, telegrams arrived from each of the divisions, German, French, Belgian, Latvian, and so on, urgently recalling their respective officer candidates. Headquarters had decided to proceed without further delay in ranking them according to the reports and grades of the instructors. But before we left we were allowed to stage a gala maneuver, using real bullets and shells. This was a tradition whose object was to inure us to combat by submitting us to the test of fire. The guys had to face up to the MG 42's, the Sturmgewehr, and the big guns, to advance under machine-gun fire and leap onto the tanks. On each occasion there were casualties, sometimes even fatal ones.

The evening before, we had pored over the "sandbox," concocting a very carefully thought out plan of campaign. And on the day itself there were fabulous fireworks. There had been one serious casualty, a young German officer hit by a hail of bullets. As for La Buharaye and me, though by right we should have been shot several times over, we came out of it without a scratch. Besides, since we were among the top students, we had the advantage of having a share in commanding the operation and had issued orders not to fire on those in full view but around them, to teach them to conceal themselves. So it was safer to expose ourselves systematically to the enemy's fire than amuse ourselves by playing at heroes.

The following day was given over to resting and feasting. We got ready to leave and, above all, for the next day's ceremonial announcement of how we had done. We knew from information we had had that La Buharaye and I had won our officers' epaulettes, but did not yet know that we would be among the top five, though we had certainly done less to deserve it than the others. We had the best marks for the "sandbox" classes; we owed this a little to trickery and more to a taste, which was natural to us, for films with tactical scenes.

The great day arrived. The snow had been carefully cleared from Adolf Hitler Platz. From the flagpole floated the flags of all the countries represented at the training school. Filled with emotion, I gazed at this burst of color, in which the last moments of a great dream blossomed. Our colonel stepped forward, surrounded by his staff. He called the cadets one by one, handing each his diploma.

"Christian von La Mazière."

"Yes."

"You have won your epaulettes as Untersturmführer."

I had graduated second for the first time in my life! La Buharaye was number three. The top man was a young German. So now we were officers of the Waffen SS, and it was only a matter of the ranks being confirmed by our divisions.

The list of honors completed, the Obersturmbannführer gave us a little speech: "You have all been recalled and for that reason we have cut the course short. I hope that our Führer will be proud of you and that you will be true to your oath. The school will be closed down and I myself am being given a command on the eastern front. Perhaps we shall meet again. We are living through a difficult period, but there will be victory in the end. Germany is about to make use of certain scientific discoveries. I can tell you without betraying a secret confided to me: Germany has weapons that are going to astound the world."

The leaders of the Waffen SS knew, indeed, that research scientists in the Reich were on the track of the atom bomb. Churchill too, better informed on this score than the German people, was to tell the House of Commons: "England was never so close to defeat as in the last two months of the war." It was these two months of delay that destroyed Hitler's hopes.

After the ceremony, there was a little celebration and Schnapps was distributed. Those who had become officers were as happy as kids. Others, who had only been sergeants, had won the rank of adjutant and had the possibility of returning to training school, provided they survived. Finally, there were those who had not been promoted. They looked depressed and a little envious, but the general atmosphere was joyful.

At the end of the afternoon La Buharaye and I packed. As the camp was closing, we could take our camouflage uniforms and training equipment. We were wearing our new epaulettes and, with our long-visored caps pulled down on our heads, we felt like different men.

Next day buses deposited us at Yanovitz station and we were back again in camouflaged trains with little German girls in uniform ready for fun. We went through Prague, this time without stopping. As we were coming to Munich La Buharaye said to me, "We really ought to make a trip to Sigmaringen before rejoining the Charlemagne and going to the front. It seems that there's a provisional French government there, with the Marshal and Laval."

"O.K."

We changed trains, made inquiries, took another, made further inquiries. In short, we did not worry over wasting a couple of days, with no idea whatsoever of the way events were accelerating, and one morning we got out at Sigmaringen.

We were in a beautiful countryside, full of a gentle peacefulness. The town was two or three kilometers from the station and we started to walk. Along the road we met middle-aged Frenchmen, wearing, for the most part, Basque berets, typical of the war veteran. They looked worried and threw gloomy, unsympathetic glances at our badges.

We came to the small town through which the Danube flows.

La Buharaye stopped. "Let's ask for an audience with the Marshal. He has to tell us what he thinks of all this."

We took a road that led to the castle. In front of it were both French and German sentries; Georges went up to one of them: "We want to see the Marshal of France, Philippe Pétain, or, if that isn't possible, Premier Pierre Laval."

"You have an appointment?"

"What do you mean, an appointment? We've just come from Czechoslovakia and are about to leave for the eastern front. So surely we're entitled to a short talk with the Marshal. . . ."

Guards were sent off; they came back: "The Marshal cannot receive you."

"He can't receive us though we're going to get ourselves killed? What about Premier Laval?"

Half an hour of these palavers followed. The truth was that we and they did not speak the same language. Finally the guys went off again; in ten minutes they were back: "Premier Laval can't see you either."

La Buharaye straightened up. "That is just what we wanted to find out. Thank you, gentlemen." Then, pointing to their empty holsters, he added, "You're right not to take any risks, it might turn out badly. We're going to defend your peace and quiet." Then, turning to me: "Let's have lunch; and then the train again."

We walked back into Sigmaringen, where there were several *Gasthaüse* where the French congregated. With us, feeding time is a sacred hour, but here it was first come, first served. We saw Rebatet, Céline with his wife, and Le Vigan pass by in the street.[4] I wanted to speak to them but La Buharaye, who had not got over his anger, told me to forget it.

We entered a restaurant that was already jammed full, so we went back to the kitchen and found the owner.

"We're taking a train to the front, but first we have to eat."

She was a German and knew what war was. She made some civilians move over, not without grumbling on their part: "What on earth are they doing in German uniforms. It's sad for a French person to see such things!"

Disaster was about to fall, and these political refugees began to look on us as dangerously compromising. They were only here to save their skins, which would not have been safe in their French towns or provinces. But they were, as was well known, Frenchmen beyond reproach who had only the tip of their big toe in the collaboration morass, and our uniforms offended them.

Some people, however, mostly women, came up to us with a photo: "Do you know him? He's my son, he's in the Charlemagne." There one was, face to face with the mother who cared nothing for nationalities or political parties, but worried about the son she had accompanied as far as the railroad cars in which the occupying power had sent him off. The others did not speak a word to us, contenting themselves with making remarks to each other in a loud voice.

The atmosphere became still more tense when these patriots

---

[4] Lucien Rebatet was a French journalist who worked for the Germans. Louis-Ferdinand Céline, the well-known novelist, was a fanatic anti-Semite; and Robert Le Vigan was a friend of his.

noticed that the owner gave us the best of what she had, and that we were served a meat dish while they were not. Envy seemed the common denominator of their little world. Aside from food, they were only concerned with their petty squabbles and were constantly betraying each other. In a few hours pseudo-governments were formed and then dismissed.

Their ultimate goal, if things turned really bad, was to take refuge in Switzerland and wait there for the situation to settle down. As if by chance, the French, with the Germans' approval, had chosen to establish themselves in the Lake Constance district, the most Latin part of Germany and the one nearest Switzerland. What these poor people did not know was that the Swiss were only taking in the rich. Those with plenty of money or who were lugging a treasure of some kind with them—whether it belonged to them or they had stolen it—were let in. The others could either disappear or get themselves nabbed. We were quite disgusted, La Buharaye and I, when we boarded the afternoon train. We had to change once again. Our morale was really low when we reached the Wildflecken Station.

With its buildings half buried in snow, it looked like a winter sports resort. A military train was waiting with steam up. We were on our way toward the station exit with the intention of returning to the camp, where we were looking forward to having our epaulettes and our camouflaged combat suits admired, when we met Hauptsturmführer Bassompierre, surrounded by several of his men, in the waiting room. We presented ourselves at attention. "Heil Hitler!"

He stared at us somewhat absentmindedly from behind his gold-rimmed glasses. "Where are you going? Where have you been?"

We told him and he smiled a little cynically.

"Your comrades left four days ago, so, like myself, you haven't a command. You know, perhaps, Krukenberg never approved of my loyalty to Darnand; and he wanted me to intervene with those of the militia who refused to take the SS oath. Now I have the task of leading the last Charlemagne detachment—but I can't yet tell you where. No point in your going back to the camp; I'll keep you with me."

We looked at each other. So be it; too bad, though, about the belongings we had left at Wildflecken. We were disappointed; some of the guys were getting into the cars without much enthusiasm, others were lying down in them, smoking. Amid the hubbub, voices demanding the evening meal were raised; it did not seem to be materializing. Georges shook his head. "It looks nasty; I told you we might find ourselves in the same sort of mess as France in 1940. The engine's beginning to seize up."

We waited in a corner, buffeted by icy gusts. From time to time we stamped our feet to try to warm ourselves, and the snow that fell from our boots turned to dirty slush on the platform. Only a few days ago we had been at Yanovitz, proud of having succeeded, hopeful of being given real responsibility. Now we were at the mercy of no matter what decision. . . . I turned to La Buharaye: "If we cut loose, and join Degrelle?" The Walloonia Division: that was the great temptation. It was magnificently equipped and it was French-speaking; moreover, it had distinguished itself in several of the principal battles on the eastern front. Its training and its morale were exemplary, and, almost constantly in the line of fire, it had constant need of recruits.

Degrelle liked to entice the French; we had seen him at Wildflecken among the men of the Storm Brigade. The Belgian leader's prestige stood high among a large number of us. The esteem shown him by Hitler had intensified his ambition to become one of the principal leaders in a new National Socialist Europe. In Belgium, before the war, when only twenty-seven, he had proved himself a political leader of stature. Received by the king, he had, at the elections, seen his party returned with some thirty seats to parliament, and their number would have been increased in the next. At the outbreak of hostilities he had been close to gaining power and swinging his country over to Fascism.

Our detour to Sigmaringen, on the other hand, had taught me the fallacy of relying on the French, among whom political power was completely fragmented. We knew that henceforth we would only be fighting for the Germans and to defend their territory. It was from them, and through them alone, that the fraternal hope that we had shared at Yanovitz had a reality. Even more clearly than at Wildflecken, it was there that I suddenly realized what a decisive step I had taken. So I was burning to get back among men animated by a spirit similar to mine.

La Buharaye, however, by nature more of a pessimist, did not share my feelings.

"No, old boy, you're crazy. We have made our choice, and we've got to go through with it. It'll be interesting to see how this shit business ends. In disaster, that's for sure, but let's meet it with elegance." Then, with a change of tone: "And now, let's see about a snack."

He walked off again with his springy step, his arms dangling. While waiting, I thought about the companies that we would not command and of our success, which was not going to benefit anyone. Night fell; the lamps and the windowpanes, all painted a dark blue, shone with a dusky light. It would be sad to die.

Then Bassompierre, who was directing the loading of supplies and the last hundred and fifty men to leave, appeared.

"You and your friend will travel in the first car, which I'm using both as office and dormitory. We're leaving tonight in the hope of getting through the railroad junctions, which are under constant bombardment, without too much trouble. I heard yesterday, by chance, that the first Charlemagne convoy came in for a mauling a hundred kilometers from here. It was standing in a siding, alongside a fuel train. There was a lot of damage and quite a number of dead."

A moment later he added, "These are the first; we don't even know where they are buried."

It was as if he were talking to himself. I kept thinking that the Charlemagne after all had not such a steely morale; until then I had convinced myself that during our absence the division had found itself united in a common spirit. . . .

Bassompierre went off, and Georges reappeared, a steaming plate in his hand, a big loaf under each arm, his knapsack full to bursting. I told him that we were to go to the first car; I picked up our two packs and we went to settle ourselves in our crib.

It was a cozily appointed freight car. Hurricane lamps, hanging from each of the four corners, gave off a faint glow. The small arms were hanging on the walls and the ammunition cases served as a desk. On the floor, alongside the neatly laid out packs, was the straw and bedding. A brazier made from an old gasoline drum radiated a gentle warmth; Bassompierre's orderly was rewarming the contents of his mess kit over it.

We took possession of our corner and started on our dinner.

"Where the devil did you find all this?"

"At a restaurant a kilometer from the station; I haggled with the owner and her daughter. They don't much care for the French, but finally I won them over. The man is at the front and they haven't heard from him for a month. So they prepared me a dish and gave me some tinned food, honey, substitute coffee, sugar, and a couple of packets of cigarettes. With our own rations added, we're all right for a few days."

After the meal we treated ourselves to a small shot of Schnapps and then decided to have a look over the convoy. Behind the very old locomotive came a flat-top car with two antiaircraft guns mounted on it; the freezing gunners were jumping up and down beating their arms. We then went the length of the train. The men were crowded into cattle cars, their belongings strewn around. At the rear of the train there was a second FLAK flat-car platform with its guns in the firing position. We did not see any military supplies, so we went up to Bassompierre, who was walking up and down the platform.

"Where's our armament? We haven't seen a single Panzer-faust—nothing but training equipment."

"Don't worry; that's the German method. They don't want to overload the convoys and make them more vulnerable. We are going to a camp near the front where there's a stock of tanks, artillery, light equipment, and combat uniforms. Since the Waffen SS has priority, we should draw the best of these . . . at least in theory."

He looked at his watch.

"Come on, we leave in ten minutes."

We climbed in again; on the platform the Reichsbahn employees were busily swinging their lamps. A shrill whistle, and we lurched forward to an unknown destination. The engine driver would get his directions at each station. Only the officer in charge had the full itinerary, which was in an envelope that he was forbidden to open until the train started.

Leaning against the siding door, I watched the countryside, in which I had spent some absorbing hours, disappear in the darkness. Now the real adventure was beginning: I thought of France and of my father. He did not know where I was and could never have imagined what I was committed to. La Buharaye also seemed to be meditating in his corner. Then he began making up our straw bed. He was right: What was there to do except sleep? We stretched out, side by side, and exchanged a few sentences. The train moved slowly along and its rumble soon made us drowsy.

The cold awoke me next day, or, rather, an abrupt halt. We were in open country, the snow stretched as far as one could see; nothing moved, the stillness was deathly. It seemed an air-raid warning had been given. We listened: not a sound. Fine, where were we? Nobody knew and Bassompierre was silent. We got ready to jump down onto the embankment if the bombers showed up. Then, in the distance, we heard the sirens.

Behind a hill in front of us a small station nestled and from it emerged a half-track vehicle. It climbed onto the railway line and stopped at our car, and a German officer got out. He explained the position to Bassompierre while we listened to the interpreter we had with us.

No, it was not an air-raid attack. A trainload of victims of the bombing of Hamburg was about to pass, its occupants suffering from phosphorus burns. The sight was so appalling that the sirens had been sounded to send people living beside the line to their cellars, so that they should not have to see it. We were told not to move.

Slowly the train came in sight, soldiers, with submachine guns hanging from their necks, standing at some of the doors to repel the curious. We watched in distress as the train took forever to pass. Its noise could not smother the groans and cries that came from the compartments. Through the windows, over which pieces of wood were crisscrossed, we glimpsed women, children, old people. The phosphorus with which they had been sprayed continued to burn in them; they had become living wicks. I saw the horror reflected on the nurses' faces.

We felt ourselves freeze; this was our first real acquaintance with fear. Questions flew from one car to another, but those who had seen were silent. The convoy moved off again, one village followed another, but before our eyes was still the vision of the ghost train.

I was not conscious of time passing; a feeling inside me was caught somewhere between anger and despondency, and suddenly I was aware how alone we were. La Buharaye shared my disquiet. At a large station we got out and mingled with the civilians waiting for a local train to take them to work. We needed to feel liked a little and included. They were astonished to see Frenchmen and offered us food and cigarettes. Their kindness touched us and also their conviction that "nothing was yet lost."

We got back on the train and it was then that Bassompierre told us where we were going. He spread out a map of Pomerania and showed us, circled in red, the small market town of Hammerstein. We were in a hurry to get there before it was too late. The radio news bulletins were not good, and from the ambiguity of the communiqués we could guess that the Russians were trying to seal up a huge pocket of resistance and that it was there we were going to be rushed.

We arrived at the immense steel bridge in Stettin spanning the Oder as some Russian bombers were attacking it. The train stopped while the German FLAK let hell loose from the bank. We saw young women wearing helmets in their foxholes, while, shells in their hands, they were servicing the guns. The whole nation was mobilized.

The enemy aircraft finally disappeared and a convoy passed us coming from the front loaded with ripped-open tanks. Beside them were men covered in mud, unshaved, with feverish eyes. We waved to each other as we passed and then our train moved onto the bridge. On the other side was the war.

IV.
IN THE HELL OF POMERANIA

We were like actors crowded together in the wings, busy making last-minute adjustments to their costumes. It was not yet our turn, but our scene would soon be staged. A new seriousness took hold of us.

The monotonous landscape had not changed, but it did not look the same. Those snowy fields and woods emanated a kind of agony that gradually intensified as we advanced.

The train moved at walking pace, stopping and restarting, like a caterpillar on a branch that the slight ripples in the bark slows down. We had gathered together our belongings, put our papers in order, checked the revolvers that were our only weapons. I was an officer with neither troops nor equipment. I had certainly not imagined my arrival at the front this way.

We had become aware of a dull, continuous rumbling and on the horizon rose the first columns of smoke. Aircraft were flying in the distance; we could distinguish the roar of artillery and of bombing. "That's already the front," I said to myself, and those of our guys who had received their equipment were there in the thick of it. But where the devil was Hammerstein? La Buharaye, beside me, grimaced slightly.

"Things are moving pretty fast. If you want to know what I think, old fellow, we've been fucked!"

I struggled against this fatalism of his and clung to the idea that the Charlemagne, whose advance units had reached Hammerstein five days previously, was waiting for us to join the battle in which it was engaged. However, the seeds of doubt had been sown in me. The communiqués announced that the fronts in Pomerania and East Prussia had been stabilized, but this was one among many optimistic generalizations, and what we were finding out little by little did not tally with them.

We were lost in conjectures without having any definite information to go on. The situation was obviously changing very rapidly; the nearer we came to the battlefield, the more fragmentary were the reports. All we knew was that General Zhukov, in the center, and Rokossovski, in the north, had received orders to sweep down on Peenemünde, where the secret weapons were being made, then on to Berlin, bypassing the remainder of the German Army that they had not been able to defeat. It was therefore against Rokossovski's army that we were being thrown in.

We came to a junction and read the name of a fairly large town: Neustettin. Hammerstein was a little farther away to the southeast. We were barely at the station when the sound of explosions grew louder; we thought they were coming from Russian bombers.

I was among the first to jump onto the tracks and came face to face with two "Ivans," who made me put up my hands. I was a prisoner. These soldiers were wonderfully well equipped and were carrying submachine guns. They shoved me toward a small shed, the station lamp room, where I found myself against a wall, shocked and stunned. But my comrades in the freight car, seeing what had happened, fired and killed the two Russians. I had evidently been saved thanks to my officer's epaulettes; if the Ivans had not killed me on the spot it was undoubtedly because they wanted to question me. Thus, brutally, we were discovering what mobile warfare meant. I learned later that this small detachment was an advance party carried forward by the impetus of the Russian offensive. For them the arrival of our convoy had been an unlucky surprise. Now it was a matter of hiding ourselves and moving quickly.

On the flatcars, however, the FLAK was getting ready to go

into action against the tanks that the Russians had with them. A shell hit a T34, setting it on fire. Having taken cover, I watched the guys at the rear of the train who alone were in a position to take effective action. It was quite extraordinary to see how these men, with the minimum training, at the first attempt took the right action to defend themselves, launch an attack, and inflict death. At the same moment an Ilyushin aircraft, part of a formation that had just bombed the station, loomed above us. A large number of refugees who were waiting for a problematical train had been killed and corpses were strewn over the platform. The plane swooped down on us and discharged a bomb with incredibly bad aim, which it was just about to remedy when our FLAK scored a direct hit; it was our first aircraft. As for the surviving Russians, they made off as fast as they could.

All this had only lasted some minutes, long enough for us to grasp that the front had been pierced. Attracted by the noise of this brief skirmish, the guys from the Charlemagne Division that had gone ahead appeared on the scene. We jumped on them: "What on earth are you doing here?"

"We fell back."

"And what about Hammerstein?"

"There's been fighting there since early afternoon. It must be over by now."

"But what about our equipment?"

"You won't see it any more than we will. We haven't even any trucks. When we arrived, the Russians were only a few kilometers away and we were immediately sent into action."

Since February 25, that is to say, for the previous two days, the Charlemagne had been fighting around Hammerstein, but had had to give way in face of superior numbers. The survivors had been ordered to regroup at Neustettin. Although deprived of their honor guard, they had broken through the enemy's lines in the northeast, in the direction of the encircled Danzig. A large number of Russian tanks had been destroyed, but we had lost about a thousand dead and another thousand missing, almost a third of the division's fighting strength. Some units were completely disorganized and had not a gun left. Our battalion commander, Boudet-Gheusi, was missing, and Oberjunker Vincenot, who had taken over the command of my company at Wildflecken, had been wounded and evacuated.

What should we do? We unloaded the equipment we had with us and then we waited. Night fell and we were cut by icy blasts. La Buharaye and I wandered about in all directions among the helpless civilians. The Charlemagne survivors were turning up in bunches. But I did not come across a single familiar face, anyone from my own unit. There was nothing for me to do but to attach myself to the staff headquarters, wherever that was. And where were the Russians? And what about the division? Did it still exist as such? It looked, in the end, as if we were going to be stupidly captured: in short, there was utter disorder.

The next day, however, Zimmermann arrived. He assembled us.

"Don't worry; you are going to be given your orders. The units will be re-formed and commands redistributed, and soon you'll be given new objectives."

Nothing happened until the end of the afternoon. The guys were divided up into provisional companies, mine consisting of around fifty men, when theoretically it should have totaled at least one hundred sixty. La Buharaye and I listened, fascinated, to these people who had just been through the mill; they knew the score already.

Finally the order was given to withdraw; it looked more like a rout. It meant a hurried retreat of no less than eighty kilometers northward, without a breathing space, with the object of joining up at the village of Belgard where a German mechanized division was stationed. There we would finally be regrouped.

During the night, the Russians attempted to surround Neustettin, so a battalion was formed to protect our withdrawal route for at least another day. It was to be covered by a dozen antiaircraft guns, the ones we had brought on our convoy. Lacking tractors to tow them, they were left on their railway trucks and the whole train, with the empty cars, moved off again to a position north of the town. We said good-bye to all these guys whom we would never see again and then got ready for our adventure. We had already been here twenty-four hours.

We left, I with my company, La Buharaye, a little farther up the column, with his. A snowstorm set in as night began to fall. The expedition might well seem like madness, but the conditions made it quite the reverse, as Krukenberg well knew, and allowed us to evade the Russian tanks. In the darkness their armor was immobilized because they were easily located. The noise of their caterpillar chains carried better at night, and if they turned on their headlights they immediately gave themselves away. Moreover, irrespective of the weather, we had to make the most of the respite afforded us. The Russians had suffered such heavy losses that they needed time to catch their breath, but this would not last long.

We were on foot, loaded principally with munitions. We had equipped ourselves in a hurry, drawing on the supplies that were lying around here and there. I for one had retrieved a Sturmgewehr. Some carts, drawn by horses of Arab-Russian origin, followed, piled with heavier equipment. It was far from the imposing division that was to have arrived at the front impressively, complete with guns and tanks in full battle array! On the road to Belgard we were more of a herd than a troop. It was still some time before I got to know my own men—I did not even always know their names.

The road was crowded with thousands of refugees and I recalled France in 1940. It's incredible, I said to myself, everything repeats itself. They had fled from the battle zone but were being inexorably overtaken: two or three days' start, and then events, which were moving more swiftly than their wretched convoy of horses and handcarts, caught up with them. They were all those who had managed to escape from East Prussia and the annexed territories, old people, women, and children, and like us they were heading for Belgard. Some hoped to reach the port of Kolberg on the Baltic and board a ship there; others were trying to go westward to Stettin.

What struck me about this interminable and dogged procession was its silence, a heavy, oppressive one. The only sounds were occasional cries to the horses; these people did not talk anymore, not even with one another, but tramped along with a fixed stare, some with babies in their arms. They ate little, although their carts were piled high with provisions, for they had taken all they could from their farms before fleeing. But they had neither the inclination nor, above all, the time to prepare meals.

We marched along beside them with scarcely any exchange of words—a smile for a kid, a caress, a piece of chocolate when we had some. Our column and theirs flowed side by side like two streams of liquid that do not mix. One idea, however, obsessed us all: not to be caught, to save our skins. We were like those animals that flee together in one body when the forest is on fire.

Once we were overtaken by German motorized units. We looked enviously at their trucks; at this time there was a great shortage of mechanized vehicles in Germany. Gasoline, on the other hand, though scarce at the front, was not short here, since the storage tanks had been filled from the Russo-Rumanian oil reservoirs. But there was no question of getting a lift; there was no room and, besides, these units had their own objectives. So we were forced to walk like tourists, who go ashore and find their buses have left.

A little earlier we had passed by a concentration camp that was being evacuated at the outskirts of Neustettin. A train was supposed to be waiting for it somewhere. It was a very brief encounter. The prisoners, in striped pajamas, joked and jeered at us. They walked with a lively enough step and, I must say, seemed in good condition.

We also encountered some prisoners of war being taken farther into Germany. What was extraordinary was that some of them, though they knew they would soon be liberated by the Russians, wanted to join us. I saw two or three of them leave their companions and quickly put on uniforms and arm themselves. They evidently had an unsatisfied appetite for fighting; in France in 1940 the Germans had marched them off without their having time to consider changing sides, and they had been thinking, ever since, of the battles they had never fought. I heard that about ten of them had come over to us.

Later I was told how in other localities, at Kolberg in particular, prisoners had fired on the Russians without even changing uniforms. Many of them had worked on German farms in East Prussia and had chosen to stay on with the families where they had lived for four years. With these refugees they had set off by small paths through the fields, avoiding the main roads where they might meet the armored columns. But on the way they had been overtaken at one time by the Russians and had had to see the women whom they had admired or hated, no doubt desired and perhaps loved, raped. And it had made their blood boil.

Gnawed by cold, lashed by snow and sleet, we marched interminably on. We could hardly breathe in the storm and were tormented by a constant desire to urinate. And alongside us all the time, in a similar plight, moved the silent crowd of refugees. There was not even the sound of a child crying; they were like phantoms, automatons. As we went along, we passed debris left by the Wehrmacht, tracked vehicles, some Tiger tanks.

The sun rose, thawing the frost, and mud clung to our boots. I took a look around at Pomerania, a landscape without softness but with an honest air of dignity; a regular granary, the well-tilled earth black and sensuous. The wide plain was undulating with small valleys that, though deeper, reminded me at times of the Loire Valley. There were magnificent forests with trees as strictly aligned as the regiments on parade at Nuremberg. And from south to north, leading, they said, to the sea—less often from east to west—there were long roads bordered by poplars.

We passed through very tidy villages, with prettily grouped houses, the railroad station a little distance away. The same air of sadness was here as in northern France but in a more beautiful, spacious setting. It was a very prosperous region.

One could say it was also a region made for war. There were hardly any art treasures, apart from some castles taken over, in the best tradition of conquerors, by German staff officers as rest houses and to keep up the impression that this was an occupied country, even in defeat. There were many isolated farmsteads, keeping a jealous eye on their acres, but as we went on we found them abandoned. The peasants had fled and mingled with the flood streaming out of East Prussia.

By day the conditions of the march were made even worse by the Russian aircraft that constantly machine-gunned us. Luckily they did not go about it very well, taking aim from fore or aft, whereas the road wound gently and was well protected by trees.

During the morning we came to Bad Polzin. A little earlier I had seen La Buharaye again; I did not know it was to be for the last time. Squatting down, he had taken off one of his boots and was darning a sock. He was in fine form; he had some wool and a sewing kit with him and I saw that he had shaved, something I had not managed to do for the last thirty-six hours. We looked at each other and I told him, "Till Belgard, then." This was the last sight I had of my friend, my big brother. He disappeared and must have been killed. He had entered my life with a smile, his cold blue Viking eyes; the unlucky Breton, he went out of it with another smile. . . .

Puaud went up and down the column with a word for each of us: "I led you into this but I'll lead you out again, you can be sure of that." He saw that many of us were exhausted; there were around three hundred disabled, either sick or with broken morale. They were dragging their feet and would have to be evacuated. And Puaud realized that what lay in front of us was terrible. His bearing, however admirable, was disquieting. He behaved like a regimental commander rather than a general; you could almost say that he would have liked to get killed.

With Krukenberg it was altogether different. He was the real boss, the one we needed. He was not a man to give way to subjective states of mind. On the contrary, he spoke of having all deserters shot—though, in fact, there were scarcely any. Some of the guys, more or less left behind, had tried to mingle with the refugees or with the wounded being sent to Kolberg; physically they were all right, but their spirits flinched. But they were being subjected to a severe test: a division without armor sent against an army with superior equipment. I think that Krukenberg must have just then felt the gravest doubts about us and said to himself, "My French Waffen SS will be back in Aix-la-Chapelle before I can say Jack Robinson." But, in the end, things turned out in our favor: in forty-eight hours the Russian armor had been stopped, more than forty tanks of the T34 and Joseph Stalin class, the pride of the Red Army, weighing almost seventy tons, as well as guns of the 126/127 type, had been set ablaze with the Panzerfaust. The "Ivans," according to preliminary estimates, had lost two or three thousand men, and our withdrawal, though hasty, was not a rout.

Night was falling when we reached the outskirts of Belgard. We had covered eighty kilometers in twenty-four hours! At last came the order to halt. We were in a forest, completely numbed by the cold; we soon threw ourselves down in the snow. Some still had their tents, which they pitched. For a few minutes there was absolute immobility, but hunger kept rousing us out of our torpor.

We had very few supplies with us; like our weapons, our provisions had remained at Hammerstein. All that was left were our individual rations, which were pretty inadequate after our marathon march. We had to manage as best we could. I heard the story of a guy who had gone hunting, guessing that the area was full of game. He pushed his way through the thickets where signs announced that shooting was forbidden. But the French do not take notice of the German "*Verboten*"; besides, at the rate the war was moving . . . Would the "Ivans" read the signs?

Before long he bagged a doe, but Krukenberg had learned about it and became violently angry. He had the wretched boy arrested and ordered him to be shot, a command that caused a loud chorus of laughter to echo through the camp. A dummy was substituted, and as soon as Krukenberg had departed, the executed man had been brought to life and had shared the doe with the execution squad.

As for me, I decided to make an expedition into Belgard with some of my men. We were well received by the few civilians who remained in the virtually dead town. There was no activity apart from the barracks, where a motorized Wehrmacht unit was stationed along with ground staff belonging to the Luftwaffe. It was reassuring to see German troops at last. We also found some Latvian SS who were regrouping themselves. They were extraordinary soldiers, infused with deep anger, hating the Russians, who in 1939, at the time of the Finnish affair, had annexed their country. They regarded the Germans as their liberators. Latvia, in fact, contributed two divisions to the Waffen SS, which were bled white.

We did not delay, however. I was impatient to receive a command, and on returning to our forest I found that a semblance of administrative order had been resumed. New commands were distributed. I clung to Bassompierre's coattails. Except for two guys, I had not found anyone from my old antitank unit. So I launched a recruiting campaign to form a new one, which was not too easy. This one knew an officer and wanted to serve under him, that one had a friend already fixed up and did not want to be separated from him. One might as well have been in a school-yard choosing sides for a game.

All the same, after a lot of talk, I found myself at the head of a rather disparate band. A spirit would be forged in it little by little, but just then my own morale was not too high. It was all the worse because I had been making futile efforts to find Georges.

Finally our objectives were revealed to us. While we had been in Neustettin, Krukenberg had gone to the headquarters of General Steiner, who commanded the German forces in Pomerania. Krukenberg had rejoined us at Belgard, furnished with strict instructions. We were to take part in the defense of a line protecting the Baltic coast, denying the enemy access to the mouth of the Oder. This was to be achieved whatever the cost. In short: a sacrificial assignment, like all those given to the Waffen SS divisions.

Soon Bassompierre sent for me. "I'm leading a battalion and taking you with me," he said. "We're going to Körlin, twenty kilometers or so northwest of Belgard; it's the last town before Kolberg. We'll establish ourselves there, taking advantage of its special geographic situation at the confluence of the Persante and Radüe rivers."

A little later we were on the road again—our halt had been a short one. We were around five hundred men, in two battalions, one commanded by Bassompierre, the other by Captain Fenet. A reserve battalion led by Captain de Bourmont was to deploy northeast of Körlin. Some of our troops had remained at Belgard with the Germans who were preparing to defend the town; others had gone to Kolberg, to which the wounded had already been evacuated. Thus the fragmentation of the Charlemagne was in full swing.

We were carrying a maximum of light arms; rifles and Sturmgewehr knocked against our chests, making us bend our necks forward. The heaviest weapons were the MG 42 machine guns, which, with their ammunition belts, weighed all of twenty kilos. On the previous march I had seen Puaud take one from a guy who was stumbling along and carry it for several kilometers. We helped each other; there was no longer any question of rank. And we still lacked vehicles and heavy armament, a large part of which was in Russian hands, and which we would never see.

Körlin, situated northwest of Belgard, was a market town with a population of around five thousand, on the banks of two rivers: the Persante, which flows into the Baltic about thirty kilometers farther on, and its tributary, the Radüe. Thus access to the town is by way of several bridges, which in itself made it an obvious strategic position, commanding the road to Kolberg at the mouth of the Persante. The place was a rather sprawling built-up area, neat, with no historic past. But on this night of March 1 we found it almost empty, except for the crowd of refugees filling the main street.

Krukenberg and his staff were billeted nearby, in the castle of Kerstin. We in turn divided responsibility for various sectors. Bassompierre took the east sector and handed over to me the defense of a bridge that commanded an important trunk road at the entrance to the town. I set up my control post in an abandoned house, assembled my men, after having tried to get hold of some extra men, and made an attempt to get to know them better.

I did not have much time, however. The terrain had to be surveyed and prepared right away and machine-gun positions selected. While German sappers mined the bridge, we cut down trees to form antitank barricades at its exit, arranging them with narrow openings to allow the flow of civilians, with their wagons and carts, through. After that, we tried to stock up with a few provisions.

Facing us, beyond the bridge, the road stretched straight for a kilometer and then disappeared between two hills. It was black with refugees for whom the sea was the only hope, like Dunkirk in 1940. From time to time, in the midst of the exodus, we saw German soldiers. We had been told to stop them, interrogate them, and if possible make use of them. That was how we were able to recover a Tiger tank that arrived all on its own.

The crew made no objections about staying with us but their morale was at a low ebb. What remained was the discipline that the German soldier never loses, even in the most critical circumstances. They belonged to an army made for attack and victory, and now they knew that it was all over. For four years they had been the masters of Europe, buoyed up by illustrious feats on all fronts. When they had had to make strategic withdrawals, they were orderly ones, after heavy losses had been inflicted on the enemy. They had experienced only one real defeat, at Stalingrad, and it could be said that before 1945 the vital spirit of the Wehrmacht had not suffered. Then suddenly everything had swung in the opposite direction, one man was faced with ten Russians, one tank against fifty. There was no longer any kind of parity.

Some troops with mortars, belonging to a reserve unit of the Charlemagne stationed at Greifenberg fifty kilometers to the west, also came to reinforce us. A stocky young noncommissioned officer presented himself to me: "Arnaut."

I thought for a moment. "But I know the name, it strikes a bell. . . ."

"Yours too."

I asked him, "Your father?"

"Army."

"What branch?"

"Cavalry."

Something clicked. His father had been in the army of the Rhine during the First World War and had left it at the end of the French occupation. That was where he had got to know my father. They had taken part in military horse shows together and had remained close friends.

While we walked about, issuing various orders, we talked.

His father, he told me, was an active member of the Resistance, an agent for London. He himself had passed the examination for appointment to the police, but one day, in Paris, his inspection squad had been assigned to the Department of Jewish Affairs. Not wishing to take part in these activities, he had joined the Waffen SS at the period just after the battles of August, 1944. He had been sent to Greifenberg, then to Wildflecken, then back to Greifenberg. In the meantime his father had been arrested, sent to Fresnes prison, and then probably deported to Germany.

At once I felt less alone. Through our fathers' friendship a warm understanding developed between us. Arnaut, too, was under Bassompierre, who had give him precise instructions about the disposition of his guns, and we met frequently.

All day we were busy positioning our available forces. Toward evening two more soldiers arrived from Greifenberg with magnetic mines, to be placed, at the appropriate time, at the antitank barricade. Enemy armor that tried to break through would probably attract the mines by their tracks. A certain doubt crossed my mind, and I asked the young officer in charge if his devices were deactivated. He assured me they were. Then he placed them alongside the highway, close to the bridge.

There was nothing to do but to watch and wait, field glasses in use. The defenses of the town had been established, even if in rather a makeshift fashion. . . . Our means were restricted, though somebody had rescued one or two 75 guns, and there was the Tiger tank. What news came through remained sketchy. Headquarters, or so we hoped, had a complete grasp of the situation. But since the briefing to which the battalion leaders had been summoned, news only filtered through insofar as it affected the respective sectors.

Night fell, and we were able to wash and eat. I had begun to get to know my men: first their names, where they were from, and then I tried to question them more closely. How many of them were there? Fifty, perhaps; I hardly had time to make an exact count. In any case, it did not much matter. I knew that the paper strength of our units was largely imaginary. Our first concern was to keep watch and prepare ourselves. We could load the belts of the MG 42's, arrange piles of ammunition where they would be protected. The patrols and sentries succeeded each other, we waited, for the time being all was quiet.

Day dawned, and it was then that, in the sky, in the air, everything began to change. In the distance there was a heavy, dull sound like the rolling of drums or a storm. The front was coming closer. To dispel our anxiety we gave way to all kinds of optimistic suppositions. The German divisions, from the other side of Belgard, were disengaging themselves perhaps, and falling back on a second line where we would join them. . . . The pocket was shrinking but its breaches were being sealed off, the Russians were driving us back but had not broken through. . . . Though there was this gap farther down, the Wehrmacht would finally close it.

The flow of refugees suddenly stopped, and, in spite of the intermittent rumble, a deep quiet settled over the countryside. The weather improved, the snow melted, and a thaw set in. This seemed a good omen, since most of the men were not equipped for the cold they had had to endure. As was happening in nature, something revived in us too, a kind of serenity, that suddenly recovered self-control that precedes a confrontation.

We waited and, abruptly, toward noon the refugees again began to stream toward us. But these were a different type. Even more crushed by fatigue, they had come a longer distance, from behind the front, and jostled by the Russians in their path. They said there had been some brief skirmishes at Belgard but that the enemy had not delayed there. I went to Bassompierre. "What are we to do about all these civilians with the Russian tanks among them?"

"Let as many through as you can."

"But suppose the tanks are right in the middle of them?"

"Then it's up to you. You'll have to fire."

A short time elapsed and then the first Russians appeared. They spread out and took up positions behind the hills, just to feel us out and get an idea of what we were doing. Then the first artillery fire, the first automatic fire, nothing much, falling short of Körlin. My sector was free of the enemy, disengaged. I had a clear kilometer in front of me—no point in sending out patrols. To left and right in the open country, Bassompierre had mobile units posted. They would hold the advance enemy parties and then withdraw to better positions.

A little later, the enemy was getting the range and beginning to rake the bridge with automatic fire. This was the moment chosen by Krukenberg to inspect the sector, while his chief of staff, Bassompierre, Fenet, and I looked on. He stood erect and motionless on the bridge with bullets whistling past. To me it was rather ridiculous; a direct hit from a shell and the whole thing would have been blown to bits.

There followed the first engagements, nothing very serious. The Russian light units were obviously waiting for reinforcements. They stayed away from the high road and let the flood of refugees pass, evidently wanting us to be saddled with as many of them as possible. Indeed, after the first explosions, the civilians were rushing toward the town, where they dug in, hoping to be able to resume their flight to Kolberg.

The Russians now arrived in force and began to probe our defenses in the east; these held firmly. We expected them, however, to try from the southeast, as we had heard that the troops defending Belgard had surrendered. The French units that had been fighting alongside the Germans had fallen back toward Stettin and would not be coming to reinforce us. So we were isolated and would soon be caught in a vise.

Through binoculars, we followed the movements of the first enemy armor. It fired on the town but the overall plan seemed uncertain. Then what we feared happened: the enemy decided to attack the town along the road through the civilians. The Russians literally forced their way into the midst of the thousands of refugees that were still passing along it. I was forward at the other side of the bridge behind the barricades, and two tanks were pushing on behind the refugees, shelling the sector over their heads; to open a way through, soldiers were machine-gunning the crowd from tanks. It was chaos. The terrified civilians scattered, many dropping into the river.

We did not fire yet, waiting for the last possible moment. . . . We had no radio, so I hurried to where Bassompierre was, to inform him of the situation, returning just as quickly. I reached the bridge with one of my noncommissioned officers and was about to cross it just as a heavily loaded farmcart appeared, at the other end, followed by a Mercedes. One of the cart's shafts banged against the tree trunks balanced on each other, so that some toppled down and rolled away, crushing the mines that, as I had rightly feared, were already primed, and exploding them one after another with a frightful din, hollowing out a huge crater.

The smoke cleared, revealing a disastrous calamity. Havoc had been wreaked; the barricades had been shifted. The Russians redoubled their shelling of the entrance to the bridge. The civilians scattered, and in front of me, all alone on the bridge, was the Mercedes, completely gutted. A body lay alongside with something that moved in its arms.

We ran over to it. It was a young woman with a child of about three whom she had protected as she fell and who had escaped injury. She, on the other hand, had rivulets of blood running from all over her body. I picked up the child and two guys carried the woman. At my control post, where we undressed her, we discovered that she was riddled through and through and was losing all her blood. The medical orderly said she would not last long. She could still speak and begged for the little girl, whom we gave her. She then asked us to go and look for her things in the car, and I agreed, at least in principle. I told them at the control post to look after the kid and, if the mother died, to dig a grave for her in the garden. We would try to find someone to take over the child.

Then I went quickly back to my sector, where the skirmishing continued until nightfall. Then things quietened down somewhat. The Russian tanks were wary, having advanced so far they had come under fire from our Panzerfäuste, and had to pull back a kilometer, not daring to expose themselves. The enemy, however, had surrounded the town; forces coming from Kolberg had attacked in the northeast while others from Belgard arrived from the southeast. Still others—and this was the worst surprise—emerged from the southwest on the road from Stettin. And now the Russians turned northward in order to cut the Körlin-Kolberg link. Things certainly began to look bad. All that remained was a narrow corridor to the northwest leading toward Krukenberg's headquarters.

The second night came, and we were very serious, tense, disillusioned, thinking about the blow the Russians were preparing to deliver and the divisions at their disposal. We checked and repaired our defenses, not knowing very clearly anymore who was under one's command and whom one was obeying. I had my small core of fifty men and I held on to them.

The Russians had brought up their artillery and were shelling the town; houses were collapsing. I had to leave my control post on the ground floor, and we went underground like the civilians trapped here, who were crammed into cellars. Their abandoned carts clogged the streets. The horses strayed but we brought them to safety; we would need them later.

Our first concern was not to lose contact with the Russian

infantry, because we knew that the enemy would use the infantry to try to infiltrate. One of their patrols, which had come slightly too far forward, had already tried to cross the river; it was our first brush with them. We killed half of them and captured two prisoners, one of them seriously wounded. They were taken to Bassompierre's control post to be interrogated. The wounded man's abdominal cavity had been torn open and he was holding in his stomach with both hands. Naturally we had no surgical instruments and could only undertake the simpler medical tasks, for which our own wounded had priority. However, near Krukenberg's headquarters there was an M.O. and male nurses, and some beds had been set up in requisitioned houses, where the more seriously wounded were treated before they were to have been evacuated. Now, however, we had no way of getting them out; they were as good as lost.

We took our wounded Russian there, but he did not want to speak. We had no ambulance, so he had to walk in order to have his stomach sewn up. We questioned the other one and he told us of large forces, of hundreds of tanks.

Morning dawned. There was a short period of calm and then a renewal of activity, though not in my sector, which was too open for the Russians. They were not going to repeat their attack of the previous day. We were subjected to no more than some artillery shelling and bursts of automatic fire, resulting in a number of wounded. We held on as best we could under cover and economized on ammunition.

Then a curious incident took place. Bassompierre's control post was not far from the church. A courier emerged from it, took a few steps, and collapsed. There was no shell burst. Strange! We were about to hurry to the body when a sniper fired from the top of the belfry; and we guessed at once that some Russians had slipped in among the refugees. Snipers—something we had not anticipated. Since the church was close to my sector, Bassompierre turned to me. "Go see what's going on there."

I approached the church with some of my men. The door was locked, but I blew it open. We saw men running behind pillars and hiding in the choir loft; then they fired at us from above. We hurled a Panzerfaust and blew up the altar. A fire started. There was agitated movement inside the belfry. We let loose some bursts of machine-gun fire and threw a Panzerfaust into the organ; it blew up with a roar and bodies crashed down at our feet. There were some ten snipers, who, with their weapons hidden, had got into the town with the civilians and taken up positions in the church at the risk of being shelled by their comrades. We now understood why the Russian artillery had seemed to neglect this sector. The survivors came out with raised hands; among them were two Frenchmen, former prisoners of the Germans. That was some surprise.

I took these two to Bassompierre, who interrogated them. They were two militant workers. Liberated by the Russians, they had wanted to fight alongside them; one of them had even been with the partisans behind the German lines for some time. I felt that Bassompierre was torn in two: two snipers, but, at the same time, two Frenchmen. To have sent them to Krukenberg would have been to deliver them to the firing squad. What was the good of that? In any case, we were fighting our last battle. But what of the so-called rules of war? A partisan is not a soldier, and the officer who has him shot cannot be charged; this is according to the Hague Convention. We were engaged in pitiless warfare and snipers were shooting us in the back; whether they were Germans, Russians, Poles, or French, it was all the same. The German army, which had in particular suffered from them, took none of them prisoner. Nor had the Russians; if German civilians attacked them behind their lines they would have shot them without a moment's hesitation.

"You should be shot." One of the two was weeping quietly.

"What a crazy mess," he sighed. "Getting ourselves into the same kind of shit just because the 1940 war was loused up."

Bassompierre suddenly turned to me. "Take these two men to one of the underground shelters where they can be guarded by German refugees."

Then he told them, "If you're ever stupid enough to appear again and play smart guys, if you're caught as much as putting your nose outside, then, no more pity, you'll be shot. I'm sparing your lives. If you get back to France one day and if we're defeated, I hope you'll testify to what we did. Because you'll certainly hear about us, and I hope you'll have the courage to give your own account."

I took them to a shelter and turned them over to two elderly members of the German Volksturm. This organization had suddenly appeared when Goebbels proclaimed total war. It included men over the age of sixty, many of them retired officials, until then considered useless. They wore various uniforms, with a swastika on their left arms. Like us, most of them wore the

Norwegian long-peaked caps, which were much more practical than helmets. And, operating with them, we came across the Hitlerjugend: kids of twelve to fourteen, proud of their little uniforms, the getup of the complete soldier boy. In a last wave of enthusiasm, the two age extremes had come together. They had arms of a sort and took part in defending the town.

We therefore had the heavy responsibility to hold the front around Körlin, while inside the town itself were possible partisans—the business of the church had taught us a lesson—the Volksturm people, and kids in uniform. And, on top of this, there were the refugees trapped in the cellars anxiously asking if they would ever be able to get away. We did not really know how many there were: in my sector alone, one hundred and fifty to two hundred, many of them completely exhausted and some very ill. What could be done for them; how could we feed them? We had already very few provisions for ourselves, except for what we had collected as a result of some very fruitful expeditions in the well-stocked German houses, where the fleeing occupants had left behind tins of food, chickens, rabbits. . . .

The civilians stared at us in astonishment: Frenchmen taking charge of an entire German town. As for me, I was observing these Prussians about whom I had heard so much. When my father had wanted to personify a particularly rough or rugged type of soldier he had taken the Prussian officer as an illustration. Well, here they were, those famous Prussians, the proud bulwark of the German nation, a self-possessed people, but tough, with splendid-looking children, robust old men, and magnificent women. A people singled out, too, by destiny. When the Russians advanced into their territory, or into the part of Poland they occupied, they knew at once what to expect.

The women, in particular, were aware of what was in store for them. The victorious "Ivans" had the right to twenty-four or forty-eight hours of pillage and rape, a rule that they took full advantage of. The women in Körlin, and especially those with daughters between eighteen and twenty, had quickly grasped that it was the end of the road. And then to see the French suddenly appear to defend the Eastern Marches, to defend all their past greatness, aroused their admiration, a spontaneous love for us. And we witnessed an astonishing event: they offered us their daughters. The girls, obviously, were almost all virgins. They were terrified at the thought of being violated by Mongols or Kalmuks; some, in fact, unable to endure the prospect, had committed suicide. Women who had already been in Russian hands had told them what it was like to be raped by men covered in grease and eaten up by lice.

Our brothers the "Ivans" did not in fact much like water. They only washed when the sun shone and it was very warm. To keep out the cold, many of them kept their bodies greased all winter, so that they were rather gamy, so much so, that the Germans could often spot Russian patrols by the smell.

Those women who had no daughters offered themselves. There was a return to the great tradition of the cities of antiquity where the women were the warriors' reward. I hope that there were some of us who honored and accepted these self-oblations. As for me and those men in my immediate circle, we were, alas, hardly in the right mood. There were, however, some really lovely girls, and the Russians must have enjoyed themselves later, that is, if they had taken the trouble to have a look at them. Generally speaking, they raped en bloc, anyone from ten to seventy, without differentiating.

Meanwhile, as we had feared, the woman rescued from alongside the Mercedes had died, and we buried her in a large garden close to some of our comrades. I was now suddenly obsessed by the feeling that we were done for, that the Russians would soon begin a house-by-house assault and that we could never get out of this rattrap, that we were all going to die. I said to myself, nobody knows that I am here in a corner of Pomerania which no one in France ever heard of. I can't disappear just like that. Perhaps I can give a signal, find a way of communication.

We went to the wrecked car and recovered some papers. Three corpses still lay there, the grandparents of the little girl, perhaps, and the driver. No doubt the father was at the front in the east or west. We wrapped up the documents and then turned over the child to a German woman who had several children of her own, including a daughter of seventeen. Then, by the light of a hurricane lamp—there was no electricity, the Russian artillery had seen to that—I wrote a short letter to my father, devoid of inessentials, as from officer to officer. I told him, "If this letter reaches you, you will not see me again, because I don't have much chance of escaping from this inferno. It will be accompanied by a little girl who will be handed over to you by the person I have confided her to, provided they escape from the battle zone. I should like you to care for her until she finds her father again, if she ever finds him. I should like her to be the last link between us. I have chosen her as the youngest and smallest of messengers and the one who perhaps will be luckiest. I ask you to take her in and bring her up as if she was my own daughter."

When I was later sent back to France, it was with a heavy heart that I wondered if an adopted daughter was waiting for me, if she had reached my family by the means I had imagined. I sent word to my father and asked for news, but I never knew what became of that child.

Back to March 5 and the battle that raged. A certain number of Russian tanks had succeeded in infiltrating into Körlin but had been stopped by our Panzerfäuste. While the machine-gunning and shelling went on, Krukenberg distributed our first Iron Crosses. He then left us for General Steiner's headquarters.

As he departed, he ordered the evacuation of the town. The battalions under Fenet and Bourmont were to try to escape by way of Belgard to the Oder. Bassompierre's battalion would remain where it was to hold up the enemy a little longer. "Twenty-four hours," Krukenberg suggested. "Two days," shouted Puaud, outbidding him.

Fenet and Bourmont left when night fell; a group of their men managed to reach the German lines, but a larger number were never heard of again. As for us, now definitely surrounded, we shut ourselves in the ruined town. With seven hundred fifty men we were supposed to hold a front of almost ten kilometers. Bassompierre assembled his officers and noncommissioned officers. "We're going to try to do our best, and, for a start, we'll have to seal off the gaps left by the departure of Fenet's battalion."

We withdrew the advance posts that we had established on the other side of the two rivers. Next morning, in my sector, the Russians launched a violent attack. On the road I was defending, two of their tanks advanced to the entrance to the bridge. We set the first on fire, then the second as it started to cross the bridge. Finally we blew up the bridge itself. To the south and the east there was not another bridge left by which the "Ivans" could enter Körlin, except the railroad bridge. But this was a suspension bridge and the tanks could not take that chance. Neither was there question of the enemy constructing pontoon bridges—the river was too narrow for that. The tanks were thus immobilized on the opposite bank, while their guns reinforced the artillery. To this running fire we could only reply with our last mortars.

Some infantrymen tried to swim across, and in the dark a few even risked using inflatable boats. But, since the day before, the main threat came from troops that had crossed the Persante upstream from the town and were attacking us from the west. They advanced inexorably, though constantly slowed down by our isolated units, who fought desperately. They were squeezing us together in fact, cutting off our pockets of resistance, which were wedged between the two main enemy formations: those advancing and those holding their ground. Having harassed the Russian flanks and rear, our troops fell back while keeping contact with the advancing enemy. The result was complete confusion; at night it was hard to distinguish friend from enemy. Only the sound of the tank treads enabled us to recognize the "Ivans."

Six hours, twelve hours, twenty-four hours . . . we still held out. It was an intoxicating and desperate show. We hurled grenades over our heads, we vied with each other in machine-gunning. Clinging to the ruins, each of us fought his own fight; we were far beyond forming an organized group. We were all sorts of people scattered over too large a battlefield. We had, however, a real leader in Bassompierre: the last to arrive, he was the last to leave.

The Russian corpses piled up, but they were continually replaced by new waves of attackers. Our determination must have astonished them. There was one period during the day when they had ceased their shelling and through loudspeakers announced that General de Gaulle had signed an agreement with Stalin. "Surrender, Frenchmen," they appealed to us, "and come and join your Russian comrades; you will be able to go back to France and won't be regarded as German SS. You are friends." They repeated this announcement once, but not twice. We gave our answer with mortar and machine guns. There was not a single defection. We had pledged ourselves to the death, and that was it.

As evening approached, however, we knew that the end was near. The Russians, attacking from all sides simultaneously, would overrun us the next day. Our fighting strength had suffered bloody losses; of seven hundred fifty men, only about three hundred fifty remained. We had to try to break out. In each sector those responsible took stock of the situation, and we then considered the general position. Bassompierre thought over our findings and then made his decision. "We'll get out tonight, at whatever time seems most favorable: say about two or three in the morning when the Russian artillery quietens down. We'll move from north to southeast, in other words, toward the large Russian reinforcements, turning our back on their assault troops."

The orders were precise: no provisions, nothing but our individual ammunition, each man to carry thirty to forty kilos all told. We would take the least seriously wounded with us.

We got hold of some of the horses that we had penned and covered their shoes to prevent them making a noise. We then fastened rudimentary stretchers to them, on which we placed the wounded. Finally we drew lots to determine which company should head the march and which close it. Mine was at the rear.

V.
THREE WEEKS BEHIND THE RUSSIAN LINES

The night was calm, but a bright moon and the burning buildings lit up Körlin; it might have been the middle of the day.
"We'll never get through," I thought. Walking stealthily, the
advance party started the retreat. As they proceeded they received instructions; I had assembled my group near the almost
totally destroyed bridge. We were going to make our way
through the ruins and join up with the rear units in order to
cover the breakout maneuver.

This was all the more tricky in that it involved following the
railroad track. For a hundred or a hundred fifty meters the line
crossed the river on the suspension bridge and for another
kilometer the track remained raised so that we could not march
more than two or three abreast. We would be marching past as if
on an elevated plateau, and it would be a real massacre if the
Russians, who were everywhere, spotted us.

For the moment, however, the quiet was broken only by
some sporadic firing. My men let off some bursts at random to
make the enemy suppose we still held the sector. The head of the

column, with Bassompierre, had reached the station. We followed furtively and in our wake the silence intensified. Surprised civilians peered from their shelters. "We're taking advantage of the lull to mount a counterattack," we explained to them. But by their look we could tell they did not believe us. They grasped that they were being left to their fate and that the next day they would be in Russian hands.

When we, in turn, arrived at the station the sky was becoming overcast. Heavy clouds from the east gave promise of snow. The cold again became intense. "Provided there's no hitch, provided a Russian patrol doesn't come strolling round a corner . . ." The locality was a natural defensive position, so the Russians had not bothered much about it; but they could always send out a reconnaissance party.

We advanced meter by meter, keeping close in the shadows, and came to the railroad bridge. I could see the last of the men who were crossing it, the horses following, noiselessly. Now it was our turn and I vowed that I was not going to wait the agreed time before we followed. The last of the column had just disappeared when I told the men to advance in groups of five or six. I remained behind with a party of ten, and we crossed over; we traversed this seemingly endless kilometer without a shot being fired, without anything happening. From time to time the Russians sent a shell into the town at random and were probably surprised at there being no reply. But they were evidently reserving their strength for daybreak.

We reached the place where we were to regroup. This was the zone where the enemy had assembled his tanks and where it was going to be almost impossible to avoid them. From there, according to Bassompierre's plan, we were to move off to the southeast, toward Belgard, the way we had come some days before, and only beyond Belgard were we to branch off to the northwest in the direction of the Oder. But the Oder was still far away. . . .

We assembled and, fanning out, formed a short front. Then we spread ourselves farther, little by little. Still nothing. Then, without hiding ourselves, just as on the training ground, we ran for it. And, of course, we ran into the Russians quickly enough, infantry and armored units from the assault contingent. They were completely taken by surprise just as Bassompierre, with fantastic intuition, had foreseen. They were for the most part Mongolians and were sleeping; they needed sleep, even if it was with tommy guns in their arms. They must have thought that they were being attacked from the rear, not imagining that it could be the Körlin garrison that had been standing up to them for three days. As for us, we wanted to get out as quickly as possible; there was no question of using our weapons or amusing ourselves blowing up the tanks shrouded in the darkness. The whole thing lasted less than half an hour. The astonished "Ivans" did not know where to fire and were afraid of attacking each other.

We hardly believed our luck. By forced marches we plunged on to Belgard, where all resistance had ceased and which was bristling with Russian tanks and infantry. We skirted the town and halted in the forest. Then, navigating by guesswork—we had no staff maps, only the general post-office maps—we made our way to the Persante in order to recross it. There were some brief skirmishes on the way, and we killed a certain number of the enemy who were not expecting us; for our part, we got away with a minimum of casualties. We came to a small bridge still intact, but we were wary. For safety's sake half the men dived into the icy water (during the night the thermometer fell to minus three), swimming to the other bank. The others used the foot-bridge after having blown sky-high the "Ivans" who were guarding it. Then we entered the vast Pomeranian forest that, as we imagined, meant security.

At this time we still numbered about three hundred strong, even though there had been some men killed, some captured, and some wounded, and we were to suffer more losses during the period of guerrilla warfare that was beginning for us. For suddenly we became like partisans, who live in the shadows and operate in bands. Coming from the most modernized of armies, we were going to fight as in the Middle Ages.

At one stroke we had a new image. The only confirmed command was Bassompierre's. Below him a natural hierarchy took the place of the recognized one. We split up into small cells where those with the strongest personality stood out as leaders, those with sufficient endurance and experience to be able to assume responsibility for the lives of others. It was individual qualities that counted now, qualities that had been singularly developed by the training we had been through. No troops without that background could have fought and held out in the conditions awaiting us.

We had among us a remarkable character, Adjutant Walter, very probably an Alsatian but from the interior of France; the

Alsatians who stayed in their own home areas had been called up into German divisions. He had already become a hero of the Storm Brigade; his courage and instinct had proved invaluable to us. There were also two other adjutants who had come from the LVF and for more than two years had been fighting on the eastern front against the partisans who attacked lines of communication in the rear. Thus they knew how to cover the ground like well-trained hunting dogs.

Our plan, as I have said, was to follow the attacking Russian troops to the Oder where, as far as we knew, the Germans were stabilizing the front. Since we had bypassed Belgard, we had, in fact, found ourselves as if in a sponge unevenly soaked in water; the Russians were using the main arteries through the territory they had captured but had not spread out over the countryside in general. All the withdrawal routes were therefore cut, while Danzig, Königsberg, and Kolberg still held out and the German Navy in the Baltic was evacuating the last survivors. But large districts between the main roads along which the enemy supplies and reinforcements rolled toward the west remained unoccupied. Elated by their success, the Russians were mustering their forces in forward positions. This was our chance; we considered that the only risk was to come up against enemy infantry units whose task was to occupy the captured territory, village by village. They operated methodically and in a relaxed atmosphere, so that up to now we had the surprise element in our favor. Whenever they had occupied a hamlet in our path we fell on them unexpectedly and they were speedily dispatched. This had become almost routine and we felt that the worst was over—a grave illusion.

Accordingly we gathered in a forest and took stock of our supplies, tying up our remaining horses that carried the wounded. And then we took a short rest. There was no more sound of shelling or bombing. "The front must still be far away," we told each other, "the 'Ivans' have evidently made a large-scale break-through." The occupation of and pacification operations in the rear zones explained the rumbling of passing columns and, at night, the shifting beams of their lights. Even the weather improved in one of those sudden variations typical of the climate of these eastern regions, and a thaw set in.

We continued the march while it was still dark. The forest was like a cathedral, with the trees well and regularly spaced, the blocks of felled timber neatly piled in squares. A little later we stopped once more and set up a temporary camp. We fell asleep as the snow started softly falling. When we woke in the early morning we were covered by it. All was gray and padded, and in this solitude we had a deep feeling of security, almost a sort of happiness. We set about lighting a fire and with the help of melted snow preparing a brew from a coffeelike substance that some of us had brought with us.

Suddenly a Russian patrol loomed up. Just time to regret the lost tranquillity as the fusillade broke out. It would have been merely another skirmish if the noise had not attracted troops skirting the forest on their way to the front. They investigated and evidently concluded that we were a large German contingent. For them it was a complete surprise; and also, this time, for us, and more than we had bargained for. In our ignorance we had set up camp in a forest that was a storehouse for the German artillery, and the cubic-centimeter blocks of wood concealed with diabolic skill piles of 88-mm shells.

There followed a fireworks display such as one seldom sees. The Russians attacked us with mortars, since their tanks could not penetrate the forest, and when the shells hit the wood piles, the hidden ammunition exploded. They must have thought they had come up against an entire army: they knew nothing of the real situation, and luckily for us, this is what stopped them following up the attack. We defended ourselves energetically while edging ourselves bit by bit out of the hell's kitchen. There were explosions left, right, in front, and behind us. Absolutely deafened, we took our wounded and zigzagged around the damned piles, which, covered with peaceful-looking snow, were exploding one after another.

We finally extricated ourselves and pushed on into the wood. Now we imagined Russians everywhere, and that their patrols were pretending to ignore us in order to surround us more effectively. The falling snow covered our tracks, but it also slowed up our march, made everything look the same, and thus disorientated us. In fact, we were more or less lost. We had lost our maps and the compass was our sole guide. We moved northwestward—more west than north—avoiding the narrow roads that ran through the forest and keeping to the small paths. We advanced laboriously, then in the quiet of nightfall we bivouacked once more.

We were hungry and at last resolved to eat our two remaining horses. We shot them with a pistol wrapped in cloth and devoured their raw flesh This, however, made it necessary for us to abandon our seriously wounded. We lay them on the ground with a gun beside them so that they could kill themselves. Many would not use this expedient, recalling the promises broadcast by the Russians at Körlin and continuing to hope. Then sleep overcame us.

We had our tents, but our fatigue was so great that we bedded down in the snow. Who could imagine a better blanket? After the first moment it enveloped us warmly, taking on the body's temperature; we slept in its embrace and in a lassitude reminiscent of a slight drunkenness. One felt one would never get up again, which is why the old mistrust the snow.

Next day we moved on again and came to the edge of the forest. A vast, rolling plain lay before us, crossed on the horizon by a major highway. Through binoculars we could see Russian convoys moving along it and decided to remain where we were until nightfall. Once again, the weather improved and the snow melted. As evening fell, we hoisted our packs on our backs and made our way along a minor road that seemed to be clear. We reached the main highway on the stroke of two in the morning. It was a major artery with three lanes leading to Stettin and Frankfort-on-the-Oder. Beyond, there was still a kilometer of open plain that we simply had to cross before coming to the wooded valleys.

We were fifty meters from the highway, advancing quietly in Indian file. At the right of our narrow road, as on each side of the main one, was an imposing line of trees. On our left was a ditch surmounted by a wire fence, belonging to a small house situated at the crossroads and from which came voices, bits of Russian. At once we dropped down in the ditch and waited. Two or three light convoys passed, then silence. We watched Bassompierre for a signal.

Then suddenly the most fantastic column I have ever seen appeared on the highway, made up of T34 and Stalin tanks, and trucks crammed with infantrymen. They drove with all lights on and the noise gradually swelled to an uproar, cries, songs, the rumble of tank treads, and the stridencies of accordions mingling in the intoxication of victory. Recovering from the impact of this appalling hubbub, we huddled together in the ditch, one on top of the other. Just in front of the house there was a slight bend in the road that allowed the headlight beams to catch some of the guys crouching in the front rows almost at the crossroads.

We were petrified, our hearts throbbing with anxiety. How long could this last? Then, little by little, we began to get used to it. A half hour, three quarters of an hour . . . would it never end? The more exhausted dozed in snatches, heavy heads weighed down, helmets against arms. Then back up with a start. The waiting was becoming harder and harder, we were afraid of being spotted. As a precaution, Panzerfäuste were distributed to those at the front of our column.

Things seemed to be working out, though, and the Russians were going to pass without spotting us. It was then that the column suddenly halted about thirty meters beyond the small house. A Stalin tank placed itself across the roadway while the vehicles in front of it continued on their way. All the lights were extinguished and in the frighteningly total darkness I could make out its turret, which turned slowly until it soon pointed toward us. But Adjutant Walter, with his wonderfully quick power of reaction, jumped up, ran fifty meters through the bursts of fire—the antiaircraft machine guns on the tanks went into action immediately, even before their cannon—loading his Panzerfaust. The turret blew up just as it had finished its rotation, its gun collapsing, powerless.

In one rush our spirits rose again. Some of the guys who had been asleep got up so suddenly that they bounced off the wire fence like rabbits chased by hunters. We were cornered; the enemy armor swept our road with their terrible .20 bullets. They sent up flares and the battle began.

We had been discovered by the "Ivans" in the little house at the very moment we had heard them. The Russians were aware that here and there throughout the conquered territory were fragments of the German Army trying to reach the Oder. They had placed small lookout posts along the main roads. We had been spotted by this one, whose soldiers had continued to talk in loud voices as if they had noticed nothing, while giving the alarm.

Those of us who had Panzerfäuste ran toward the tanks, and in a few moments three of them were in flames. The Russian infantrymen jumped from the turrets and threw themselves on us, among them women equipped with the "chapkas" and the so-called camembert submachine guns. They were tough customers. They were as furious as the men, and I remember I had to shoot down one of them without a moment's thought. We fought hand to hand and even with bayonets. The road, blocked by the three turning tanks, which were exploding, looked impassable. I was opposite the first tank; to get across I ran through its burning shell, after an encounter with several "Ivans" who had got out of it.

The Russians fired like madmen, trying to regain control of the situation. There was a quarter, perhaps a half hour—how could one retain any idea of time—of savage confusion. We benefited from the light flares sent up by the enemy, a good kilometer of fireworks, knowing that anything that moved and looked well-equipped was an "Ivan" to be shot at. We had flushed out the fellows from the sentry post, blown up the tanks that were in our way, and carved a path through the mob attacking us. We were not yet finished with them, however, for the Russian officers, anticipating our next move, had deployed some of their men beyond the road onto the plain.

Luckily for us, they evidently supposed that a hundred or so of us had managed to get through this far, a number that hardly counted, and that the important part of the force, which they apparently estimated at three thousand, must be in the rear. We had seen by the way they had reacted and blindly pounded a sector where no troops were left, that they took us for an ordinary advance guard. Thus they must have supposed they were in a trap, when, having got ahead of the last Russian infantry, not without some trouble, we had suddenly turned around to attack them from behind. The total confusion among them was what finally allowed us to reach the forest.

The cost to us had been heavy. It is true we had shown maximum effectiveness in minimum time: hence the enemy's surprise and error of judgment. By dint of staring at this interminable column, we finished, in fact, by getting an idea of the topography of the place. In less than half an hour we had set three tanks on fire, as well as trucks and all kinds of vehicles including armored cars. All our Panzerfäuste had been expended: a wonderful and fearsome weapon when a man finds himself alone face to face with armored vehicles, especially if he is in the dark and can operate only by guesswork. But we had been more than two hundred, of which a certain number were slightly wounded; and we left around a hundred men there on the ground, dead or seriously wounded.

Day dawned, and the snow was a huge film of delicately joined crystals glittering in the sun. As it melted on top, little rivulets formed underneath. We had seen the Russian infantry moving in the distance, back from where we had come; the "Ivans" obviously thought they had isolated an important detachment. Another column advanced in our direction. The armored vehicles—and to us this was a miracle—proceeded on their way; never had we witnessed such a vast deployment; it was hellish. They were heading for Berlin, but we did not know that at the time. We thought the front was nearer, and that was why, the night before, we had been astonished to see the convoys roll past with their lights on. Now we began to realize we were already deep in the rear, and the troops that we ran into were those assigned to mopping-up operations, while along the supply lines there was an inexhaustible forward flow.

After having dressed the wounds of our casualties and regrouped, it was necessary to move on farther into this new forest and find cover. Coming to a clearing, we allowed ourselves a short rest. Heavy clouds were gathering and a fine snow began to fall again. There seemed no end to the alternation of snow and thaw.

Soon, however, we were spotted by the Russian patrols and involved in a harassing chase. We held our ground, we fought, we disengaged ourselves. Another plain, other Russians. These were in tanks and fired directly at us, a shell per man. We ran till we had no more breath, with the sensation of not moving an inch, as if our boots had lead soles; the nearer we came to the safety of the valley, the more it seemed to recede. Again another forest and another short period of relaxation. We were worn out; our number, which was dwindling before our eyes, was now about a hundred and fifty. Arnaut had vanished. We realized that we had all the time been going around and around as in a trap, confused by the harassing Russians who never relaxed their pursuit. Aircraft came over, looking for us. Deceived by our speed and fighting prowess, the enemy imagined that they were after a much larger force than we actually were.

The sun came out and we were dying of thirst. Some sucked the melting snow, but we had to stop them: the snow burns certain parts of the system and increases one's thirst. I myself was holding up well enough. We were vainly searching for water, and an event that took place then is one of my most painful memories. In a clearing we found a pile of SS corpses. They were frozen when those at the head of our column first discovered them. I was at the rear end and by the time I arrived on the scene the thaw was causing them to move and wiggle like worms.

But they were dead, all right. . . . There were around twenty of them, all with a bullet in the back of the neck. They had been wounded and taken prisoner; then the Russians had shot them. There was now less question than ever of our giving ourselves up. On the contrary, we had to hold out at all costs and this sight renewed our energy.

By now it was several days since we had left Körlin. We were starving, with no food left. We had to do something about it: mount a surprise attack, which would not be easy as we had no maps. While on the march we had noticed from a hill a hamlet consisting of a few farms. We studied the lay of the land and found it favorable. With the hope of eating, life took on a rosier hue. We holed down to wait for dark.

The shadows lengthened. We moved forward slowly, by fits and starts, keeping an eye out for prowling aircraft. In the distance there was the ceaseless rumble of trucks and tanks. It was almost night when we came in sight of the small village, but we had to wait until the early morning hours, the best time for our operation, when tiredness overtakes those who keep watch, work, or mount guard. And meanwhile we could recuperate a little.

We slept, curled up in the biting cold. Occasionally, opening my eyes, I took a look at my companions. We certainly were no great sight! We had not washed for days and had begun to be infected by lice. Our eyes had dark circles under them and were feverish and bloodshot from the harsh sun and snow glare, as well as the strain of trying to pierce the darkness at night. Our exhausted faces were like masks, our black-nailed hands filthy and calloused; we had become automatons propelled by fatigue and I have no idea what else: no one thought about it.

Our weapons were no longer oiled, but what mattered was that they functioned. We had become still more vulnerable since our fight with the Russian convoy in which we had used up all our Panzerfäuste. We certainly felt lighter without them but, all the same, we asked ourselves anxiously what would happen if we had to cross another major highway and found ourselves face to face with tanks. . . .

The dawn came, and through vegetation all fresh in the early dew we sneaked toward the village. We had noticed two farms still inhabited by the Germans, but, as luck would have it, someone had got there ahead of us. Russian patrols on the loose in the district had also noticed and overrun them. The peasants fled to the forest. I still remember an old German bowed under a burden that had a human shape. The wraps suddenly fell and two thin and stiff little legs stuck out—those, no doubt, of a paralyzed child. From the houses came the cries of women being raped by the soldiers.

We decided to intervene and in no time were involved in a very rough fight. It was then that a very young guy who had been with me since the start was cut down by a burst fired right into his stomach. He called out like a small boy; I made a half turn and went to him; he really had a child's mug and tears ran down the layers of dirt on his face. In his street-urchin's eyes I saw an immense astonishment in face of death: he knew it only as it had affected others and suddenly it was his turn. "Stay by me," he said. I wanted to know something of his story. "Where are you from?" I asked.

So he told me. He was nineteen and had been an apprentice in the Renault factory where his father, an old militant Communist, worked. They lived near Paris, at Boulogne-Billancourt, in a small suburban house such as was common at the time. They were a happy family. He was also politically militant since, from an early age, he had been brought up on the Marxist ideology. Then, in 1944, during an Allied air raid, his house had been destroyed, his parents, his elder brother, and younger sister killed. He managed to escape but emerged from the shelter to stumble over corpses in the debris. . . .

Pain made his voice jerky and he was losing a lot of blood. My hand on his stomach was sticky and warm drops trickled between my fingers. His trousers and uniform jacket became soaked and stiff. What he had not been able to get over, he said, was seeing a cat carrying a bit of brain to a corner to eat: his father's, mother's, brother's? That had made him so furious that he had vowed to get revenge. And that was how he came to die on the eastern plains.

I often asked myself why there were so many working-class people in the Charlemagne. The proportion, in fact, was a third, with another third students, and the final third made up of aristocrats, members of the upper middle class, and adventurers: but virtually no peasants. A strange mixture. Most of the young workers had come by way of Doriot, that is, from a Communist background, and their ideological education was superior to mine. Yet when they enlisted it was not as a result of mature reflection, but rather a matter of impulse and anger which were part of the paradox of our particular adventure.

So it was with this kid, who died while begging me to leave him a grenade with which to kill himself. I stayed as long as I could beside him, then I took his papers. For some days I had been given the task of recovering documents from the dead. If we managed to reach the German lines the families would thus have a chance of being told. I had already quite a number of soliders' books on me.

My companions, meanwhile, had occupied the hamlet. The old German who had fled with his daughter had been killed by a stray bullet, victim of the settling of accounts that was no more than a comic opera story, as well as, for the Russians, a question of women. The Germans, I believe, had done the same in Russia and it was an eye for an eye. Suddenly I had a feeling of nausea faced with the absurdity of it all. Since the boy's death I had the feeling that everything was finished and that we would all be killed one after the other. I no longer knew if I was hungry, thirsty, or anything else. I tore up the soldiers' books I had on me; what earthly use was all that?

I felt emotionally worn out when I joined the others, who had already discovered milk cans, and cows in the stables to milk. Only an hour ago the villagers had been living here as if they thought they could preserve some semblance of the days of peace. War had raged around them, waves of occupation had passed over them, and they had remained, carrying on their lives as peasants, considering it pointless to leave, prepared to welcome the new conquerors with all the risks that this implied. We threw ourselves on the food to the point where we made ourselves ill, but, at least, we had been saved. We cared nothing about being filthy or feeling sick; we had become like animals.

Of the three hundred of us that had got out of Körlin, no more than eighty remained. In our wake were strewn dead, wounded, weapons, and supplies. We had lost everything that could still keep us together as a troop. What remained was a gang, a collection of people determined to save their skins, possessing only their lives and the weapons to defend them.

Bassompierre called us together: "It's impossible for us to remain together any longer. We're going to split into groups of ten and rejoin the German lines as best we can."

So we separated and said our good-byes. I did not see Bassompierre again until Fresnes prison, before his execution. Arnaut, who to some extent had taken Georges's place as my constant companion, had disappeared, as I have mentioned, and so had Adjutant Walter. We dispersed into the countryside.

A new kind of existence began, that of the lone guerrilla, isolated and without hope. So far we had made little progress toward the west: in a little over a week, eighty kilometers at most. I no longer had even a compass, having had to throw away my knapsack during a skirmish. To orientate ourselves, my handful of men and I had to rely on the stars and the distant advance of the Red Army, whose itinerary indicated our direction.

Most of the Russians, however, had already passed through, and the occupation forces were largely operating behind the troops preparing along the Oder for the great Berlin assault. We were surrounded by an enemy intent on other things and there would be no more confrontations except those we ourselves provoked. We had to take the risk of replenishing our supplies of food and ammunition. Avoiding the main, well-guarded highways, we would live and move through the woods like the bandits of old.

The cold relented and it was suddenly spring. And in that region once that happens it is soon very warm. The earth became loose and greasy, sticking to our feet. Absolutely parched, we marched on painfully in search of a stream and did not find one.

Finally we came to a pond full of decomposing corpses. Approaching it by a woodland path we saw, near the bank, the floating body of a Russian soldier. The heat had inflated it like a goatskin bottle. We tried to shove it away, but it burst and slowly sank, making huge bubbles and turning the water pink.

I thought we were all going to vomit, but thirst was the stronger impulse. Some of us still had our helmets, which we filled and drank from, our stomachs heaving to our mouth. However, we were only drinking polluted water, which did nothing worse than give us diarrhea.

There was the worse threat of typhus on account of the lice that devoured us. I had them under my jersey, under my camouflage outfit; I was crawling with them. They preferred the most sensitive parts, such as the neck and waist. When it was cold they kept you warm, but the sweat irritated them and they became vicious. We would have had to strip naked in order to dig them out and kill them. In the end they shared our body with us. When I looked at myself I seemed like an ox covered with flies or a horse tormented by them.

They were enormous lice, military lice, so to speak. The Germans maintained they had been brought by the Russians, but I think that all campaigning armies, in which hygiene is nonexistent, are the natural prey of parasites. When the troops came from the front their clothes were disinfected in steam fumigators, but for us there was no way of even washing; we could not find enough water and in the forests where we lived the snow had disappeared. At first one felt the need to change one's underclothes, but then one very quickly fell into a state of stinking squalor and horrible indifference.

There was a diminution both in body and in spirit. We had obviously lost pounds and pounds, we had got rid of most of our belongings, including my field glasses, which I had thrown into a ditch. What use were they now? We were not going to maneuver anymore or study the territorial layout.

In the early days of our march we still exchanged thoughts such as "The Russian assault troops seem strangely far away now"; "If we get ourselves taken, we might save our lives; we'd be put in a prison camp but at least we'd have something to eat." We subsisted on such commonplace conversations. For us, the prisoner-of-war camps in Russia were similar to the French camps in Germany. Then a time came when, like sleepwalkers, our conversation was limited to such mechanical and hackneyed phrases as "Let's stop," "I've had enough of it," "We'll never get anywhere!" Beyond that we hardly spoke.

With our wild heads—I had a comb I had not used for two weeks—dirty beards, bloodshot, feverish, angry eyes, we were more like beasts of prey than soldiers. Thus we struck real terror into some peasants who had remained on their farms and whom we were going to ransom, so to speak: to us they represented food supplies. Trembling, they kept insisting that the Russians had taken everything; we had to press a tommy gun to their stomachs, saying that what the "Ivan" brothers had not done to them we would make up for without further delay.

In spite of our appearance, however, we had no wish to fight. The time was long gone when we said to ourselves, "Fine! I've just laid out three Russians!" or "There, we've set their rotten vehicle on fire, that'll teach them to come slinking around in little groups!" We were hunted animals with only our instinct to survive.

We moved mostly at night, locating isolated farmhouses. Very rarely we found Germans in them, but often small detachments of Russians camping there before continuing on their way. We had to dislodge them; after taking them by surprise and killing them, we got hold of their weapons. We ended by having only Russian revolvers, submachine guns, and ammunition.

The next thing was to make a clean sweep of all their food, carrying away a minimum of it. There were seldom eggs, but almost always we found salted pork, which increased our thirst; and sometimes milk, in those farms where work had been carried on irrespective. But gradually we found only abandoned buildings, already ransacked by the Russians, who had a passion, goodness knows why, for turning everything upside down.

The cows were often wandering the fields or loose in the sheds, mooing desperately in great pain from not having been milked for days and days. It was difficult for us to draw milk from them and, even more so, to slaughter them. No trouble, on the other hand, strangling a chicken, plucking, cleaning, and cooking it. We collected what we found in the way of food and then cleared out.

We also made use of these raids to attack our lice, which bred at an astonishing rate, and we would put on peasants' shirts when the wardrobes were not empty. Then there were the bed sheets, even the dirty ones, which we tore up as bandages for the guys who had been wounded, for whom we did the best we could. But we lacked medicaments and in particular sulfonamides, which we had been given when we went to the front and which, at that time, were the miracle drug.

One man had a badly infected left shoulder that constantly suppurated. A bullet had apparently fractured the collarbone. His dressings had a foul smell and were black. Since we had made him an arm sling, he could use only his right arm. When we got into fights, he wedged his submachine gun against his hip and did the rest with one hand.

As for me, part of my left foot had been frostbitten before our outfit had been broken up, when the cold had still been intense. I had gone to sleep once at the edge of a marsh and had been so exhausted I had not noticed that in my sleep my body had slid or that my legs were lying in water. During the night the marsh had frozen and I had begun to freeze with it. When one is exhausted one does not react to cold; on the contrary, it feels comforting and death overtakes one quite easily. Luckily, a guy had quickly roused me.

It was only later with the return of warmth to the body that

I took off my boot and found that my left foot was affected, the big toe being completely black with third-degree frostbite. I was going to continue the march without my boot but one of the others, who knew something about it, had shouted to me to put it back on at once. The foot must be kept warm and well wrapped.

For this purpose there was nothing like a Russian sock, which is simply a square piece of material. The foot is placed on it, the toes are first covered, then the sides are folded over with a vigorous tug, likewise the back. The boot is then pulled on while keeping both side flaps of the cloth firmly crossed between index and middle finger. The more the subsequent movement, the better the cloth, stiffened with dirt and sweat, keeps in place, while the foot is warm and well protected without being constricted. Mine wore well because I used a dishcloth, and though it hurt a bit at first, that soon wore off. The device derived from the foot bands worn in ancient times and we all made use of it.

Adapting oneself to circumstances in order to survive: our instincts drove us to this. In this context the Russians were our masters and it was strange how, little by little, we became Russianized. We used their weapons and smoked their tobacco. Whenever we shot one of them, we searched him for his *maorka,* a very coarse kind of tobacco in which the leaves and ribs are cut up together. Ordinary cigarette paper punctures if rolled around it, which is why the Russians used newspaper. The tobacco is spread along the center and rolled in it loosely, for even such tough paper risks being torn. Before sealing, the edges are lightly chewed, then a few blobs of saliva and it is ready to light. But we were always looking for matches because our lighters had gone dry long ago and we had thrown them away.

Looters, that's what we had turned into, but joyless ones, looters by reflex, in self-defense. It was as if an inner mechanism was dictating our actions. We no longer thought, we had lost the power to think. Or rather, our minds were no longer wed to our bodies; we were at times merely uninvolved spectators of our own struggle. When we emerged from a wood and descended on a farm and it crossed our minds we might be captured, it was all the same to us. "We're going to get killed," we told ourselves. "Well, too bad; it doesn't matter."

At times I felt I should make an effort to think of other things. I mused on my adolescence, recalled a traditional provincial existence, immersed myself in family memories. The events of 1936 came back to me; it was the year of the Popular Front, with the threat of an uprising. I had escorted a van taking arms to the peasants in the Saumur district. Rifles and ammunition had disappeared, as if by chance, from army stores under the charge of Madelin, nephew of the Academician and regional head of the Camelots du Roi—a right-wing royalist movement.

It was rumored that the railroad workers from Saint-Pierre-des-Corps would descend on Saumur and attack the cavalry school, which had been placed on a war footing. My father had not come home. The high school students, belonging to both Right and Left, were on the alert, but not for the same reasons. I knew that Léon Blum was seeking power and was told that if he did not succeed in gaining it, there would be a Red revolt.

I recalled that night of the convoy between Fontevrault and Villebernier, a very short night during which a lot of things that I am still not clear about happened. It was the first time that I acted in what I thought of as a revolutionary manner. Then there were other memories: of holidays, of a girl, of the defeat of 1940—that, above all, had plunged me into confusion. I tried to recognize some links between the past and the battered creature that I was on the way to becoming. It seemed I had taken an interior leap. "No," I said to myself, "there's no reasoning about it; hold on, and you'll come out of it."

We moved forward at a ridiculously slow pace, in the heat, and past corpses and abandoned equipment. At most we covered five kilometers a day, guiding ourselves as best we could. We marched a kilometer, then halted a couple of hours, utterly exhausted, while two or three kept watch, and the others slept. Our one fixed idea: eat in order to live, which meant: kill in order to live.

Things had gone on like this for a week; the ten of us had remained together. And then one day about six in the evening, as we were lying down to rest, we heard voices in the distance. We were completely exhausted and also fed up with sleeping in woods, and on the ground, at that, having long ago abandoned knapsacks and tents. As for the voices, they could be those of German peasants.

We descended on the farm and came face to face with some Russian cooks laughing and talking at a field kitchen from which came a pleasant smell of pork and potato stew. We machine-gunned the "Ivans" and threw ourselves on the pots like madmen, standing over the bodies of the men we had just killed, gratuitously and brutally.

We heard yells; we had not stopped to think that a field kitchen with so much food was not intended just for the few guys who had been tending it. There were soldiers stationed a little farther away on the other side of the slope, a whole column that we had not seen because they were hidden from us by the woods.

This time we were trapped. We behaved like panicking rats, flinging away the pots and pans, firing in all directions, rushing toward the protection of the forest. But once again, as in a bad dream, one felt one was hardly moving. The couple of minutes that the flight lasted stretched into ages. We were terrified, spent animals contending with well-fed guys in top condition just out of their trucks.

We had lost three of our group by the time we reached the thickets, our hearts thumping as if they would burst, while keeping an anxious eye on the Russians. The shouts lasted a moment or two and then faded in the distance as the "Ivans" decided not to persist in the chase, evidently guessing that it was only a question of a few isolated stragglers. But they were certainly furious at the unexpected losses we had inflicted on them.

We remained for hours in the underbrush, totally prostrate. The thought of putting an end to it had begun to enter our minds. "Either we give ourselves up or get ourselves killed, but it can't go on much longer like this." All the same, we tried to struggle on and to regain our courage. We managed for another two days and then were at the very end of our strength.

On the third day—it was March 27, the date is engraved in my mind—we caught sight of a farm.

"Come on," someone said, "let's dig in there and we'll fire our last ammunition and get ourselves killed." We were convinced that the Russians would not take us prisoner but simply shoot us. We belonged to the Waffen SS, many of our comrades had already been shot, and, besides, the "Ivans" had a score to settle with us and we would have to pay everything that was due.

We entered the farmhouse and settled ourselves there, having firmly decided not to move out again. We were soon enjoying a wonderful sense of relaxation, keeping house as if we could stay there as long as we liked. It had not been looted, the Russians not having come this way. We lit a fire, heated water, washed. I found a big, old-fashioned razor but did not know how to use it, so one of the guys shaved me, using some German wartime soap. We rummaged around for a change of linen. Now that we began to look like human beings again, our love of life returned.

We were happy as kids in this farmhouse, laughing at anything and nothing: seeing ourselves in a mirror, discovering what we looked like. There were now only five of us, including the guy with the infected shoulder; we had lost two on the way, but that did not seem particularly important. We called each other by our first names, abandoning the use of ranks; we might have been a group of friends on holiday.

The house seemed to have been awaiting our arrival to bring it back to life. The hens ran around, the pigs grunted; we dived into the comfortable beds. And then, all the food! We gorged ourselves to the point of sickness.

It was during the afternoon, as we were eating and dozing in the sun, that a Land-Rover loomed on the horizon headed for the farm. We grabbed our guns, cursing. "O.K., here goes; it's beginning again!"

Clean and shaved, we felt our energy return, and with it, our morale. We let the vehicle approach and opened fire when it was not more than fifty meters away. It at once reversed, the men got out of it and returned our fire. I heard their cries of command and turned to the boys. "They're Poles."

Poland . . . a whole chapter of my childhood, from the age of three to seven. My father had resigned from the French Army of the Rhine in 1918 and had volunteered to go and fight there. It was at the time when the Russians under Budyenny tried to recapture the territory that had been lost when the new state of Poland was created. Under the leadership of General Maxime Weygand, my father was one of those who had helped to build the Polish Army; he had been on Marshal Pilsudski's staff, with another young captain, Charles de Gaulle. He had taken Tarnopol from the Russians. A monument there, now destroyed by them, had commemorated his name.

He became a kind of national hero in Poland and received the highest decorations. Later, he taught at the Military Training College in Warsaw, drawing on his experiences in his own campaign. His theories had thus become part of military history there, continuing to be taught after his departure, so that the name de La Mazière was familiar to young officers.

I had been brought up to speak the Polish language and on our return to France did so fluently, which annoyed my mother, who forbade it at home. I thought I had forgotten it, but in the heat of the moment it came back.

I thought, There's a chance for us, since they're not Russians. I shouted, "Are you Poles?"

"Yes."

"We're French."

"Don't fire and stay where you are, and we won't harm you."

I translated to my companions.

"What do you think?"

"We've had enough of it; we're through."

"No regrets?"

"No regrets, we've had enough."

So we flung down our weapons, came out of the house, and surrendered to the soldiers. Our war was over.

VI.
THE SURPRISES OF
CAPTIVITY

The Poles advanced to meet us, led by a blond young officer who spoke a little French. "What are you doing here?"

I told him we belonged to the Charlemagne Division. He took a long, reflective look at us and finally said, "You'd better take off those SS badges right away. If the Russians catch sight of you you're finished. The best thing you can do is to get hold of ordinary clothes and disappear. You can pass yourselves off as French civilian workers."

Then, turning to me and a noncommissioned officer standing beside me, he said, "But you two can't do that. I'll have to bring you back to be interrogated by our regimental commissar."

He told us of Germany's defeat, of the great Russian attack along the line of the Oder, and of the Red Army's advance on Berlin. In regard to what concerned us personally, we heard that we were a few kilometers from the town of Greifenberg.

Greifenberg! A place that had some real links with the French, for it was there that the LVF and certain units of the Storm Brigade had been regrouped and where, later, some elements of the Charlemagne had been held in reserve. It was also the place where our division had stored its arms. As it was situated only a little west of Körlin, we had indeed been walking in circles.

The Poles treated our wounds, and then our guys made a search through the house for civilian clothes, emerging in rather shabby-looking suits. Meanwhile I had torn off my insignia and the epaulettes of which I had once been so proud, while all the time regarding our situation and these precautions as something of a joke. Now we no longer looked like anything at all and suddenly this wrenched us.

We tore up our papers; I kept only those showing my French nationality. The Polish lieutenant spoke to three of our men: "Stay at the farm for a while and then try to get to Greifenberg under your own steam. Along the way, you'll come across foreign workers and French prisoners that we're rounding up."

He then made me and the noncommissioned officer get into his vehicle, and during the drive he began to question me, partly in French and partly in his own language. I explained to him how it was I had some knowledge of Polish and, in doing so, mentioned the part played by my father. He asked for dates and nodded at my answers, offering me a cigarette—it was nothing great, but all the same an improvement on the *maorka*.

"Normally I should take you to Russian HQ, but that would never do. I'll bring you to Polish HQ and we'll discuss all this there."

We came out on the road to Greifenberg. The dividing up of Germany had started and Pomerania was being given back to Poland. The Russians had granted the sector to the Polish Liberation Army. This had been formed in the USSR and was made up of Poles from the territory annexed by Russia in 1940—at that time the object had been to undercut Sikorski's army in the west—and, in addition, those whom the "Ivans" had liberated in the course of their advance. Some of the officers were pro-Russian, but the majority of the troops had hardly any more use for the Russians than for the Germans. Besides, as I learned later, the Red Army had made little distinction between Polish and Prussian women.

At the outskirts of the town I received a shock. I realized, all at once, the measure of our defeat and the enormous power of the forces to which I was being handed over. Squadrons of Ilyushin aircraft flew across the sky as we overtook columns of guns mounted on caterpillar tracks, and all sorts of cars and supplies. We also passed trucks full of Russian and Polish troops, and I imagined that everyone was staring at me.

There were also vast multitudes of people: captured Wehrmacht soldiers and other prisoners of war, and liberated civilian workers, a varied assortment of people that the victorious troops suddenly had on their hands. I had the feeling of an organization that was enormous and yet constantly overflowing at the same time, and of my own personal pain in the midst of this oppressive universe.

We drove into the half-ruined town and came to a Polish command post, where I was separated from my noncommissioned officer. I do not know what became of him. I was taken to a room where there were some Polish staff officers who received me with great civility, asking if I was hungry and offering me vodka. This augured well.

We conversed; they were particularly interested in the Charlemagne Division and asked me a lot of questions on the subject. Finally, a high-ranking officer said, "In any case, we can't keep you here very long. But what are we going to do with you? If we hand you over to the Russians, there's no saying what might happen. So I shall have to think it over. While waiting, you'll remain in one of our billets nearby. I'll see what I can do for you tomorrow. I won't let you down. Your father fought for Poland's independence, you've lived among us and know how we love France, which for us is the land of liberty. Then, too, many of our brother Poles fought on the German side, which makes it all very complicated. No, I'm not going to hand you over to the Russians."

Turning to another officer, he said, "Take him away."

I was taken to a house crammed with soldiers where the atmosphere was very gay, and in no time a drinking bout, such as only the Slavs can organize, was under way. These Poles were overflowing with happiness, their country was free, victory was theirs. I drank with them and joined in the shindig, and what a shindig! At nightfall they lit hurricane lamps to continue the party, the singing and laughing.

When I closed my eyes for a moment the voices and the music recalled to me other voices and music. I was five years old and in bed in my room in the French Embassy in Warsaw. It was late at night and the noisy echoes of a reception prevented me from sleeping. So I had got up, descended the staircase, and opened the door of the big drawing room. The room was filled by members of the fashionable world, women in evening gowns, crowned with jewels, civilians, and decorated officers, French and Polish.

Smiling faces were turned to this child with ringlets who had drifted in in his nightdress, signaling to him not to make any noise. Seated at a grand piano in the middle of the room a man with a white mane of hair was playing Chopin. My father came over to me and gently placed his hand on my shoulder. "Take a good look; that is one of the greatest pianists and statesmen in the world, Paderewski."

The piece ended and I was presented to him. I made a little tour of the room, bowed to certain gentlemen, and kissed the hands of some of the women. Then I was led back to my room.

Now I was far from that elegant insulated atmosphere, but it was a long time since I had laughed so heartily. We drank and talked of Paris and I ended up by forgetting my own predicament.

Just then a Russian patrol, having heard the noise, came in to see what was going on. I was spotted and its leader asked who I was. There were no officers in the room, only ordinary soldiers. Embarrassed, and with uncertain voices, they replied, "He's a French prisoner."

The Russians saw my camouflage uniform. The leader came toward me, noted that my epaulettes had been removed from it, took hold of me, and pulled me to my feet.

"SS?"

"Niet."

He had a look at my boots.

"Officer?"

"Niet."

The upshot was, after all these "niets," he made me come with him.

I was full of alcohol and was staggering. He pushed me into an American jeep. The Poles tried to argue with him but without insisting too much. I said to myself, "They're going to have my skin."

We came to a big building with sentries in front of it: a Russian command post. Watched by the sentries, the patrol hustled me out of the car and into the guardroom, where it started all over again.

"SS?"

"Niet."

"Fransuski?"

"Fransuski."

"Officer?"

"Niet."

An impeccable Russian officer, wearing red epaulettes with stars, must have said that I was to be left alone and that I would be interrogated later. I was put in a corner with my arms raised and whenever they drooped, the soldiers yelled at me and stuck the muzzles of their tommy guns under my nose. Women soldiers passed through, looking at me derisively. My arms were getting heavier and heavier . . . and what made it worse was all the alcohol in my stomach.

I kept thinking, "If only they'd do something: shoot me, it doesn't matter what." It lasted perhaps an hour but it seemed an eternity. Then a noncommissioned officer appeared. "Come along."

He led me upstairs and into an office where some officers were seated.

"Your papers."

I took them out. They examined my identity card and my tricolor press card. And suddenly I had a brainstorm: of course, the press card, that could be my salvation! Keep your head, old soldier, say you belong to the Propaganda Kommandos and that you were reporting from the eastern front. Keep cool.

An officer told me to sit down and the session began.

The Propaganda Kommandos consisted of journalists and photographers with the German Army, and it is thanks to them that we have so much documentation on the war. Among them were Frenchmen, Robert Brasillach[1] for one, who worked on the eastern front. Brasillach paid for it with his life, de Gaulle maintaining he had been executed for wearing German uniform, as if one could arrive at the front in a business suit! Recently in Vietnam, journalists with the American troops wore American uniforms, and those with the Vietcong, Vietcong clothes.

The important fact was that members of the Propaganda Kommandos did not carry weapons, only pen and camera. With my press card there was nothing to prevent me from passing myself off as a journalist. There had been some in the Charle-

[1] An extreme right-wing collaborationist writer, executed by the French after the war.

magne and I doubted if the Russians had a list either of war correspondents or of the active members of the division. My special status would furthermore enable me to explain my uniform, which was better than that of an ordinary soldier.

Like all self-respecting administrations, civilian or military, the Russians started by compiling a dossier on me. They did everything short of taking my physical measurements. Then the interrogation started: "How did you get here?"

"We marched."

"How long have you been in the district?"

"About three weeks."

"But the Charlemagne Division was defeated between Hammerstein and Kolberg. . . ."

"That's right, we were badly mauled, but most of the division managed to cross the Oder." (This sounded good.)

This dialogue was carried on in matter-of-fact military language and very calmly.

"You're a journalist?"

"Yes."

"You didn't bear arms against the Russian Army?"

"Certainly not. Besides, as you see, I was attached to the air force and had nothing to do with the ground forces."

"You swear it?"

"I do."

For the sake of a reprieve one will swear anything.

"If you're lying, you'll be shot."

"I know."

But in the back of my mind I did not believe they would execute me even if they found out I had lied. On the battlefield I would have been shot at once, but by now the moment had passed and, besides, there was the agreement with de Gaulle. No, they would not shoot me, but I would surely be beaten up, which is no more than the recognized lot of the defeated. They wanted to scare the hell out of me because they had found the SS nasty customers, and they always liked to have some of them as prisoners. Their sudden furies were soon followed by a cooling down; I knew how the Russians behaved and that, basically, they were not bad sorts.

There was a good chance, on the other hand, of finding myself in a Wehrmacht prisoner-of-war camp . . . but at the moment my morale was high. This officer and his colleagues were now convinced that I was a journalist. What a piece of luck that they had asked for my papers! My story was coherent, it was only necessary to stick to it. Things were going well. . . .

The Russians were somewhat bewildered. As a journalist, I had nothing to do with the army; I was a different kind of bird altogether and would have to be put through a particular kind of interrogation. I was led through the building, which resounded animatedly with happy shouts and songs and was full of women soldiers hurrying about with piles of papers. I was taken to a shadowy office, dimly lit by hurricane lamps. At first I saw only a guard with submachine gun hanging from his neck, and *chapka* well down over his eyes. Then, at a table, I noticed a soberly dressed individual, without insignia or, in fact, anything to distinguish his rank, in a simple Russian blouse, on the left side of which was fastened the red star. I realized right away that he was one of the political commissars—I had heard about them from members of the LVF who had escaped from Russian captivity. An important person, in fact. After the reverses of 1941, Stalin had extended their powers and even generals feared them, as we had learned from prisoners. They reminded one a little of the republican commissars attached to the Rhine Army in 1790.

He was of average build, the sort of man one would hardly notice. He had an intellectual's face, with penetrating eyes behind steel-rimmed glasses, and looked about forty. He spoke a very good French with a slight Russian accent; I heard later that he had studied for a time in France.

"Kindly be seated."

This was quite a new piece of politeness, somewhat disquieting. I was aware of the guard behind me with the tommy gun. I tried to concentrate but found it hard to do so. In joining with the Poles in their celebrations I had somewhat recovered from the immense exhaustion of the last three weeks, but the vodka was pulsing through my temples. My mind was obsessed by my press card, which was lying on the desk. It represented my salvation.

The commissar looked through the notes of my previous interrogation. "So you're a journalist?"

"That's right."

"What paper did you work for?"

"*Le Pays Libre.*"

"Edited by Pierre Clementi?"

I was astonished. It seemed he knew all about the collaborationist press down to the last details.

"And what were you doing with the Charlemagne Division?"

"I was sent to report on the Waffen SS. Then the Americans occupied France and I couldn't get back."

"You offered, then, to work for the French papers that were circulating in Germany?"

"Exactly, and that's how I became a member of the Propaganda Kommandos."

He raised his head abruptly and shouted, "You're lying!"

"No, it's the truth."

"You were undoubtedly an officer in the Waffen SS."

"Certainly not. I'm wearing the uniform because, as you well know, the P.K. men wear it. But my fighting was done with a pen and pad."

"You're lying!"

"No."

Another change of tone, and his voice grew calm. He was very shrewd, like an examining magistrate playing with the accused. In a conversational tone he broached another subject. "Do you have personal convictions? Were you a Fascist?"

Be careful; to deny it would be stupid. "Yes, in fact, I was."

He inquired into my family background, asking me a whole number of questions. "Your father was at the cavalry school at Saumur?"

"Yes."

Suddenly he adopted a cold and impersonal tone, explaining that I belonged to a corrupt and decadent class, condemned by history, and that I had been an Establishment lackey. . . .

"Oh no, for me Fascism offered a revolutionary alternative."

His face flushed angrily and he told me that Fascism was the product of capitalism, that it was a counterrevolutionary doctrine directed against Communism and Marxism, that by a fitting reversal it had started by turning against the capitalism that had spawned it but that now the Russian Army, after having destroyed Fascism and Naziism, would settle accounts with capitalism too and put a little order into European affairs.

I let him talk and kept my replies to a minimum. Once more, he turned in another direction. "How many of there were you in the Charlemagne Division?"

He was taking notes.

"Seven thousand."

"Oh no, you weren't that many. There couldn't have been so many Frenchmen."

"I'm sorry, we were seven thousand."

"But we destroyed you."

"That's right."

"Really, you know, I'm beginning to believe you; you talk as if you were actually there. Your press card proves nothing; I'm sure you fired on Russian troops."

"I swear I did not. You can ask the Poles; I had no weapons on me."

"That's true; I asked them for a report a little while ago and they confirmed what you've said. One might say they're favorably disposed toward you. Your father, it seems, spent a long time in Poland?"

"He did, in fact, and furthermore fought against Soviet troops there."

"Ah, yes, in 1920; he was with Pilsudski?"

"Exactly."

He looked at me intently, picking his words. "People like you should be done away with, eliminated like vermin." Then, loud and brusquely: "Undress."

I did so.

"Keep on your shirt."

That made me feel even more ridiculous. Total nakedness has its own defense against sarcasm and brutality; in nothing but a shirt one feels completely helpless.

He gave the guard an order in Russian and the latter opened the door and called down the stairs. Two other guards appeared.

"You are to go downstairs."

We went down two floors. The women I passed made jokes about my attire. Then I was taken into a cellar; the guards had flashlights and hurricane lamps. We came to a large, vaulted room. The commissar turned to me: "You're going to be hung. You don't even deserve to be shot. Have you anything you'd like to say?"

"Nothing."

"Nothing at all?"

He gave some orders and the men hastened to obey, returning with a rope that they passed through a ring that hung from the ceiling, making a running knot in it and putting it around my neck. I thought of my native Touraine. As kids we loved Westerns with executions in them and mock hangings. But this rough rope that scraped the throat was something very different.

I was on the other side of fear, however, by now, in that no-man's-land where there is nothing more to hope for except that they would get it over quickly. What I began to dread was the prolonged pain. I stood still, hands tied behind my back. I waited as I heard the commissar give an order. One of the men came over and took away the rope. I thought to myself, "It's a game that amuses them, but it'll end badly."

"Upstairs."

Back to the office, still in nothing but my shirt, to the laughter and jeers of those we met on the way. The commissar did not ask me to sit down again; I stood stiffly beside the chair piled with my things. He explained Marxism to me, the scientific truths that proceeded from it and the hope it represented. But I was tired out and the alcoholic exaltation had vanished. His words were a sound that rustled past my ears and swiftly faded.

"Finally," he was saying, "people like you are retrievable; they have been taken in, but it doesn't take much to set them back on the right road."

Then he spoke of Paris and his studies there, as well as many other things which I could not take in and which sounded merely like stock phrases.

I felt my legs would not support me much longer; my left calf, in which some shell splinters had lodged, was hurting. The dressing was blackish where the blood had congealed and, with dirt and sweat, formed a kind of scab. The bandage the Poles had put on my frozen foot was also filthy from the dust and debris that lay about the building, for it had been shelled and the Russians used only the undamaged rooms. After a few moments the commissar became aware that he might as well have been talking to a half-dead dog. His anger returned. "No, there's nothing to be done with you; it's impossible. This business is over; we're going to shoot you."

We went downstairs again and into the yard, where I was put against the wall. Some guys appeared with tommy guns. This is it, I thought. They've had their fun and now they're going to kill me for real. A short time ago I had felt indifferent, now I suddenly experienced an intense will to live—it was extraordinary. And I realized the frightful anguish felt by a man led to the scaffold. I trembled inside and tears came to my eyes.

Once more, however, the commissar interrupted the act.

Again I went back upstairs, still clad only in my shirt, my legs weak. This time he had me sit down and resumed his questions. He asked me about my youth and I replied with unfinished sentences in a faint, broken voice, so exhausted was I. I told him of my studies at college in Saumur and described the atmosphere at the cavalry school. The Spanish war was mentioned and many other subjects. He was much calmer.

Finally, he seemed to be reflecting; then he said, "Yes, I believe you can be saved; something can be done with you. But first you must undergo a test. Are you ready to come over to us?"

The fact was, I was ready to do anything that would put an end to these games. No one had really touched me, except for an occasional jostle. I would have been better able to resist had I actually been beaten up. But I had had a bellyful of words, was sick of them. They had absorbed my last resources.

Down we went, once again. I was brought through the large, vaulted room where they had pretended they were going to hang me. We stopped a little farther on, beside a coal cellar; I noticed coal dust seeping from under the door. At the commissar's command, I leaned forward, lifted the latch, and opened the door. Squatting on the coal were two high-ranking Wehrmacht officers in dress uniforms that were stained and black. They glanced up at me with a hunted look.

The commissar told me, "There you have a couple of war criminals who've killed a lot of Russian soldiers and tortured women and children. They're awaiting trial."

Then he gave an order to one of the guards, who cocked his revolver and handed it to me.

"But they don't deserve to be tried. You are going to shoot them."

The revolver lay flat in my hands; without my attempting to grip it, I turned to the commissar. "I don't want to shoot these men; they've done nothing to me. Besides, I've never fired a weapon."

He then took out his own gun and I heard the click as he released the safety catch.

"If you don't execute these two criminals, I'll shoot you myself."

I pleaded, "I don't know how to fire a gun, I can't do it. . . ."

He gave a new order and the guard took back the weapon that was still lying in the palms of my hands. The door was shut on the two officers, frozen with fear. They had certainly thought their last hour had arrived when they saw this hairy individual wild-eyed and half-naked, thrust before them and given a loaded gun.

The commissar took me upstairs again. Smiling and relaxed, he said, "If you had fired, I'd have killed you like a dog. Of course, there's no question of shooting these Germans. They have to be interrogated."

I answered, "How could I have shot them when, as I've told you, I can't fire a revolver?"

"I still don't believe you. But that doesn't matter. In any case, it's my duty to take you prisoner."

He explained what the Russians had already made known to us in the hell of Körlin. General de Gaulle, accompanied by his Foreign Minister, Georges Bidault, had signed an agreement with Stalin under the terms of which the French prisoners of war and civilian workers in the Russian occupied zone, including all those who had collaborated with the Germans, were to be collected and sent to France. In exchange, the French were to hand over their Russian prisoners, in particular those belonging to Vlassov's army.

"So you've nothing to fear here," he concluded. "You'll be tried in France. Having told you that, I'll make you a proposal: that you work for us. You can have forty-eight hours to think it over."

I came back to life: "I've won," I thought. "Now I'll be left in peace; it's all over."

He made me put on a simple Russian uniform. In a few moments I was transformed into a perfect "Ivan": blouse, cord and linen belt, forage cap, an old pair of boots, and wide trousers that looked rather ridiculous. No insignia, of course.

"I'll have your injuries taken care of," the commissar said. Then, looking at me with his penetrating glance before he let me go: "We'll meet again in the morning."

It was beginning to get light as two guards conducted me to an infirmary a little distance away. There were a number of military doctors there and Russian nurses wearing the Red Cross. For the first time my frostbitten foot, which had burst open like a grenade, was treated with sulfonamide. I was given water for shaving, a safety razor with an old blade, and a huge piece of soap of even worse quality than the greasy stuff distributed in

France during the Occupation. Except for my black nails, I was soon almost presentable.

I had a mattress in a corner and was brought a plate of food, which I started on without delay. Although I had feasted with the Poles, I was hungry again. Then I stretched out like a satisfied animal.

I took a look around: there were only slightly wounded cases in the room. The surgical hospital was evidently elsewhere, and the seriously wounded were evacuated to the interior. The Russians here seemed friendly and happy, in the knowledge of the victory about which the commissar had left me in no doubt. With the exception of certain pockets of resistance such as Danzig, the German front had collapsed everywhere.

I slept. Daylight was filtering in when I awoke. They brought me coffee made from barley, as unappetizing as what I had drunk in the German Army, and with it a piece of rye bread. It was not properly leavened and I chewed a mixture of barley and rye grains. But I had a good appetite and had all the more need of it because I felt stiff and bruised all over. Some of the tension of the previous night had returned; I felt drained.

A sentry came looking for me and as we walked along he offered me a cigarette, my first. It was then that I began to appreciate the Russian from his prisoner's viewpoint. Between him and you a kind of complicity is soon established, soldier to soldier. And since I wore a Russian uniform, I was not in the same category as the other detainees. We marched in warm sunlight through the ruins of Greifenberg. And when we arrived at the building that for me had been a torture chamber, it seemed much less sinister.

I was taken once again to the commissar's office; he was already at work, talking on a field telephone on his desk. He looked refreshed and his movements were brisk. I asked myself when and how he slept. There was a different guard on duty in the room.

The commissar politely asked me to be seated, handing me a cigarette, not the kind the troops smoked, but one with a long cardboard tip. It had a peculiarly acrid taste, but I smoked it with pleasure.

"As I have to go off on an inspection tour, I'll take you with me."

"Fine."

"So you can go back to the infirmary now. We'll be leaving this afternoon for Posen."

On my return I lay down on my mattress and did not leave it. The Russians tried to converse with me, and in order to talk to them I racked my brain for all the Polish phrases I could recall. They treated me with great kindness; at lunch I was given the same food as the wounded. Then a guard came to get me, taking me to a jeep that was waiting before the administrative building, with a soldier at the wheel. Beside him sat a guard with a submachine gun, in the back was the commissar, and I got in beside him.

We headed for Küstrin, which meant a fairly long detour, and we passed a continuous line of convoys going to the front. I now had an even better idea of my commissar's importance; he controlled the movements of the Russian forces. When a column was stationary he stopped the jeep and went to talk to its commanding officers. They all received him standing to attention; they might call each other "comrade" but discipline in the Red Army is as strict as in the German. As for me, I was stared at with curiosity.

At the end of the afternoon we reached a village where we were to spend the night. It was overflowing with soldiers, a veritable human flood. Trucks and convoys of artillery continued as far as one could see, regiment was added to regiment. I seemed to be in the center of the largest concentration of troops ever assembled.

We stopped in front of one of the houses, and I entered it, followed by the guard who had sat with the driver and who kept an eye on me from ten meters behind. In the main room I recall that a soldier, a Mongolian, I think, was fiddling with a radio set, an outdated model, on the floor. The electricity did not function and the set was not even plugged in. He was listening intently, turning the knobs this way and that; not a sound came from it and his face grew progressively longer. It was probably the first set he had ever had in his hands. Suddenly furious, he started kicking it with his boots, trampling it to pieces.

Night fell, and we sat down for a meal at the table; the commissar made use of these periods of relaxation to explain to me the aims of the Russian Revolution, the difficulties it had had to overcome, and the future it planned for. He spoke constantly of the dignity of man, which made me smile to myself after what

I had seen in Pomerania. All the time we were eating, soldiers and officers kept coming and going, talking together.

A cuckoo clock hung on the dining-room wall. I noticed it because I had no watch, in fact I had nothing of my own, not even a handkerchief. The Russians were particularly partial to cigarette lighters, rings, watches—some soldiers wore one above the other all up their arms—watches being very scarce at that time in the USSR. Besides rape, loot constituted their highest reward.

Suddenly the cuckoo emerged from its shelter to chime the hour just as a soldier was passing. He gave a start and cried, "The devil!" and with a burst of machine-gun fire brought it down. The commissar had to reassure him, explaining how the mechanism worked. These soldiers obviously came from the outer ends of the earth; they had been taken from their primitive existence to be turned into killing machines.

Next day, when we left, the sun shone brighter than ever. The thaw had accelerated, the fields were spongy, and one sank into the humid earth. After we had driven a few kilometers we came on a column of German prisoners of war guarded by no more than about twenty Russians, some on bicycles. The prisoners were in rags, with nothing on their feet except the Russian-style socks tied with string, the "Ivans" having also stolen their boots. With a fixed and absentminded stare, weighed down under the sudden heat, they dragged their nightmare with them as they marched. Fighting for months on end, they had invaded Russia in triumph, and were returning with everything finished. Now here they were once again on the road that had led to Russia, which would be, from now on, a road of misery.

Seeing them, I thanked my lucky stars. I was washed and shaved, I had sharpened a small piece of wood with which to clean my nails, in short I was in luxury. We kept slowly overtaking the constant convoys on the road; then, at a fork, we left them and turned more westward.

Just at that moment we heard the noise of an armored column; it consisted of fresh troops from the farthest regions of Russia, complete with brand-new war material, including Sherman tanks. When the men riding outside of the first tanks caught sight of the prisoners they were about to pass, they aimed their machine guns at them and got ready to fire.

At the first shots our jeep turned round and accelerated with a jerk. The Germans—there were more than a thousand of them—scattered into the fields, and we saw some fall. The three leading tanks left the road to pursue them, and I saw one of them overtake a prisoner who was running as well as he could, sinking into the mud up to his knees. It ran over him, the man fell under its track, and the machine continued on its way. Then, slowly, the earth began to heave and to swell, and the guy emerged from it and started running again.

The guards fired on their compatriots. There were yells from all sides and the commissar, who had jumped from the jeep, did not do the least of the shouting. He quickly summoned the officers in charge of the armored unit, who all looked as if turned to stone at one blow. They were dead drunk; the Russians will swallow anything: aviation gasoline, alcohol distilled from pine resin or from birch tree bark. . . .

Order was reestablished in no time. The tanks were brought back from the open country to the road and the Germans stood still, dazed. In the distance there was a small wood and that is certainly where they should have made for, but they had not the perception or the strength. At the shouts of their captors they had returned, dragging pounds of mud on each foot. The commissar vigorously reprimanded the officers and I do not suppose he weighed his words. There were around a hundred German dead. The Russians left them there, as well, presumably, as the wounded. The armored unit and the column of prisoners continued their respective ways, and we went ours.

We arrived in the famous front sector: Küstrin–Frankfort-on-the-Oder, and in front of us was spread the most gigantic and awe-inspiring battlefield I have ever seen. It was there that the two hundred thousand men of Vlassov's army had been thrown in combat against the advancing Russians and for several days had fought fiercely against their fellow countrymen. When they had no guns or armor left, they killed with cold steel.

A foul stench hung over the place. Disemboweled tanks and charred, twisted guns were entangled—it was a veritable metal graveyard. And, swollen by sun and moisture, there were bodies as far as one could see, that would never be buried. Some days later, the Russians cleaned up this open-air charnel house with flame throwers.

Finally, in the afternoon, we came out on the Oder, the river I had so longed for! I was beside it at last, but in Russian uniform. We stopped overnight in rather less primitive quarters than the previous day. My guardian angel never left my side and I sensed the moment approaching when he would require an answer from me.

Next day our trip came to an end. We had made an early start, this time eastward in the direction of Posen, and drove all morning as far as a village where we stopped for lunch. Inevitably, it was full of troops. Scores of tanks and trucks were parked there. In the village center smoke rose from several field kitchens. The commissar left me in the jeep and went to meet various officers, who had been summoned by radio.

As I began to get hungry and was looking forward to his returning to take me to eat, I suddenly saw around a hundred horsemen who, as I heard later, had come straight from Outer Mongolia. They rode small horses with long manes and tails; for saddles a piece of material was placed directly on the animal, and instead of stirrups they used plaited cord, the ends of which formed loops for the feet. Slung across their back they carried old-fashioned rifles that must have dated from the beginning of the century.

They were looking for some place to eat, but did not speak Russian and were finding it hard to make themselves understood. Besides, the Russian cooks had not been expecting them and refused to serve them. They made a truly comic impression: these people who reminded me of my childhood picture books, seemingly from another planet, who had strayed into the midst of an ultramodern army.

The Mongolians took their rifles and opened fire on the cooks. The soldiers who were there grabbed their tommy guns and there was a real brawl. In no time I was underneath the jeep. The commissar came running from his conference at HQ and sent out a radio appeal for somebody to act as interpreter. He managed to stop the shooting and calm everybody down; he then ordered food to be distributed to the new arrivals.

A little later as we were having our own lunch, I took the liberty of asking a question: "Who are these people? Where on earth are they from?"

It was then that the commissar made his first confidence. "There've been serious difficulties in the Russian Army," he admitted, "because of the continued use of various dialects. Because of them, it's been impossible to modernize certain of our troops, to assign them to tanks, for instance. They wouldn't understand commands transmitted by radio."

Pointing to the Mongolians, who had dismounted and were

eating, he went on, "When the Germans invaded Russia, all tribes were alerted. They belong to a tribe that were informed in 1941 of the attack on the mother country. They jumped on their horses and have just now arrived."

Thus these men knew nothing of war but had hurried to take part in it, impelled by hopes of conquest. They had come a long, long way, slowed down by the intense cold and snows of winter, fed by the Russian authorities en route. At last they had got near the front, but the front had moved forward, and no doubt they would only reach the outskirts of Berlin when the war was over.

Some hours later we reached a devastated Posen. Since the time given me to make up my mind had expired, as we got out at Russian HQ, the commissar turned to me. "Well, what's your decision?"

I had thought it over during the journey. "Somehow or other, you've saved your skin," I said to myself. "Why stay in Russia, go through I don't know what new training, and, from having been a perfect little Waffen SS pupil, be made into a perfect little militant Communist?" Certain of us, I knew, had chosen to remain and the Russians had recruited guys from all nations. But I had stopped dreaming and for me the time of uniforms was past. My one desire was to see France again.

I explained all this frankly to the commissar. He listened attentively and without any sign of hostility. Our mutual understanding had evolved, even some kind of sympathy had been established between us, as often happens in extreme and dangerous situations. And it was evident that his ideological convictions had not stifled an openmindedness.

I gave him my reasons, purely emotional ones. I now had the possibility of shortly returning to my own country. Once hostilities ended, I would be repatriated; meanwhile I preferred to remain a prisoner. He understood.

"Right," he told me, "I will see to it that you're transferred to a camp."

I waited a short time and then a car arrived with orders to take me away. I saluted the commissar, who responded somewhat absentmindedly; he had other things to do, and I was no longer of interest to him.

We drove through Posen and my guards treated me with consideration. We passed what had been the station; it was there that the Russian tracks ended. As they advanced, the Russians had replaced the railroad network of the Reich. They had retrieved a number of railroad cars whose axles they had lengthened to adapt them for use on their own gauge; and, without letup, they were sending back to the interior of Russia not only the captured German soldiers but civilians as well, who had been converted to Communism and joined the National Committee for a Free Germany that Stalin had formed in the USSR. (No reciprocal organization had been established in the West.)

The convoys departed from a point close to a huge camp apparently set up under Hitler. It consisted of two adjoining sections, one for men, the other for women and children, who now found themselves crowded out by prisoners of war, foreign workers in process of being identified—the Soviet authorities, very punctilious in this respect, were afraid that wanted persons would hide among the latter—and masses of refugees like those we had marched alongside some time earlier on the roads of our retreat. The war was not yet over, but the USSR was already busy establishing order in the conquered territories. I saw that everything was functioning like an immense factory; at dusk, powerful searchlights were turned on: night was the same as day.

This was the first time I had set foot in this sort of place. On entry, I was taken to the administrative offices, where the formalities dragged on endlessly. The Russians, who use a different script from ours, had to employ Germans to keep their records. I was then taken to the infirmary to be deloused. Although I was wearing new clothes, I had to have them fumigated in the disinfecting oven. From there I was sent on to a woman barber. The "Ivans" had a passion for the cue-ball style, and they usually had shaven heads.

Thus spruced up, and in my Russian attire, I was asked by the detainees what I was doing in the camp. But very soon my appearance was to be of help to me.

There were in the camp two French prisoners of war of Polish origin, one a sergeant, the other a corporal. The Russians, whether by an oversight or not, I do not know, had shipped them there with German prisoners. They had protested angrily, and since they spoke Polish fluently they had managed to make themselves understood. But in vain; in spite of all they could do, they remained there, always locked up. As soon as they saw my uniform they threw themselves on me; they were astonished to discover that I was French like them. And for me, I suddenly felt

I had a duty not to let them down. If there are two guys, I said to myself, who ought to be out of this camp, it's surely these.

Four days went by and I began to lose hope. Freight trains full of prisoners being sent to Russia for the labor camps were leaving every day. My Franco-Poles were making fruitless applications for regrading, and I was not letting them out of my sight.

It was a dog's life there: mess tin at noon, soup at seven, and that was it. There was, though, one attraction: one heard yells from the women's compound next door every night. The troops bound for the front visited them regularly, sorting the girls into groups of ten or twenty—they had the decency not to have intercourse with them in their own camp—after which the women were sent to the Russians' camp, which, in the end, was turned into a huge brothel. It was evident that not all the women were willing, but the Russians had hit on an odd trick. In their pockets they had small pieces of wood, pointed at both ends, which they inserted between the thighs of the recalcitrant ones. The women clenched their legs in defense, but since the sticks caused them considerable pain, they instinctively reopened them, and the way was free. For those women this was a truly eventful period. And it would be interesting to hear the stories of some of them who now live in East Germany.

Finally, on the fifth day, my two guys, who having spent four years in a German prisoner-of-war camp had some experience to call on, managed to get hold of an officer whose job was to sort out the foreign workers. Now there were Frenchmen among them and he needed an interpreter. The two guys jumped at the opportunity, seeing it as a step in the right direction. I immediately took them aside. "Look, I don't want to have to tell them my story all over again. They took away all my papers, including my press card. Just put me down on the list of STO workers."[2]

"All right."

The screening process had taken all day, as there were a lot of French workers, and I was placed on the right list. The "Ivans" examined me suspiciously, but cursorily, and once again I congratulated myself at having escaped the tattooing. My two pals winked at me: "That's it, we've been through it, we'll get out."

[2] French nationals taken to work in Germany.

The Russians put our group in a special compound and then called us together.

"You've been accorded prisoner-of-war status and accordingly you'll be taken to a camp for French prisoners not far away. From there you'll be sent to Russia and then repatriated by way of Odessa to Marseilles."

Luck was decidedly on my side. We were at once loaded into trucks and after a drive of fifty kilometers found ourselves with French ex-prisoners of war.

They had the feeling of having only left their German camp for another and had long faces. Among them were a certain number of officers released from officers' prison camps. And all these men who after three weeks' fighting had surrendered to the Germans were already decorated with the Cross of Lorraine. In this patriotic atmosphere our convoy was rather out of it, especially as the French prisoners—though one wonders why—had always pretended to look down on the STO people.

My first concern was to have my foot treated, since it continued to pain me. Luckily there was an infirmary supervised by a naval doctor who had volunteered to go to a German prisoner-of-war camp in 1942 as one of the *Relève*,[3] so that an imprisoned doctor there could return to France. He was considered a traitor by the others and was blacklisted. But since he was the only one capable of attending the sick, they came imploring his help when they did not feel well.

A kind of unspoken complicity developed between us. He sensed that mine, too, was a somewhat singular case. The attitude of the prisoners gave me a presentiment of the kind of justice I would be faced with on my return home and, judging by them, I began to fear what might await me.

After some days, we were loaded into cattle trucks and set off in the direction of Moscow. It was an endless journey, being for the most part along a single-track line, so that when a military train was approaching we were left stagnating on a siding. We kept eating in order to kill time; there was a distribution of decent food. Most of the prisoners carried a small lunch box, with a lock and key, where they kept the chocolate and canned meat from the Red Cross packages they had been receiving. They

---

[3] A system by which Frenchmen were allowed to take the place of other Frenchmen in German prisoner-of-war camps.

also stored their packets of letters and yellowed photos, including those of the Gretchens they had seduced in the fields.

They were almost all from the country. We are accustomed to sing the praises of the French peasant, but it is preferable not to be one of their fellow prisoners. They stole away to open their little treasure boxes and quietly nibbled away on the sly. There was no generosity to be expected from them, and their mediocre world rather disgusted me.

My two Franco-Poles, however, had swiftly adapted themselves to this world that was familiar to them and in which I felt isolated. At the same time I noticed a fellow who kept himself apart, as did I. His clothes were something out of the ordinary. I was in Russian uniform, but my khaki ended by being unnoticeable among the others, whereas this fellow's attire had obviously been stolen. It was difficult to believe that he had belonged to the STO, as he claimed. I spoke to him during the train journey and he replied readily enough. I asked him where he was from and he mentioned a town in Pomerania. This intrigued me.

We arrived in Moscow and I was struck by the appalling dirt, and then our train was switched to a branch line. We left it sixty kilometers farther on at a village on the Moskva River. There we were installed in clean, well-kept barracks that the Russians had turned over for the use of French prisoners. But we were not allowed out; once again one camp had been traded for another. At first the guys took a poor view of it. They had expected special trains, even brass bands, not realizing that the Russians had the greatest contempt for prisoners. In 1941 some three million of theirs had been behind barbed wire, and Stalin had considered them more or less as deserters. When set free, they had all been sent back to the Soviet Union, to be taken in hand. Among them had been many Ukrainians in particular, and they had not been allowed to return to their native district. They had been sent elsewhere while other guys had been sent to the Ukraine in their place. Next to those who had been in concentration camps, the liberated prisoners of war had been undoubtedly the worst-treated people in Russia.

It was early May and very beautiful. Every evening the sound of singing and accordions came from the nearby *Kolkhozes*. The war was over and I breathed an air full of the sweetness of living that the camp restrictions made unbearable. If one can't go out, I thought, I'll have to make my frostbitten foot an excuse for at least a slight change of scene.

I went to see my naval doctor. "I can't walk; something must be done."

He thought for a while. "All right. Tomorrow we're having a visit from some Russian doctors; we'll let them have a look at it."

The next day these doctors sent me to a hospital in a neighboring village. I arrived with two other guys of our camp and underwent a complete physical examination—it was meticulous, down to X rays—and then was put in a ward. This was very well kept, and pretty nurses moved among the beds to talk and let themselves be teased.

The slightly wounded had a physical culture session in the mornings in which we participated enthusiastically, including those who had lost a leg. We were lined up in the courtyard and an accordionist encouraged our movements. It was a gay and friendly atmosphere and I began to feel really happy among these Russians who drank their spirits neat but always wanted everyone to be happy.

I remained there a full week. My foot had healed and there was no longer any justification for prolonging my stay in the hospital. But they kept me on because I was French, because they liked me, and because I felt at home there. It was there that I regained my health; and then it became really time I returned to the camp. The war had ended, and all sorts of contradictory news and rumors were circulating: we were leaving the next day, the next week, officials were coming from the French Embassy to make certain important announcements, etc.

I tried to renew acquaintance with the fellow I had met in the train. After searching the barracks for him I found him, alone as always in his corner. The others sensed that he was not one of them; I told him I wanted to talk to him and took him into the courtyard.

"You never belonged to the STO, did you? I'm going to be frank with you: nor did I."

He looked at me without replying.

"Listen, you're taking your bearings, which, if it comes to it, is what I'm doing too. The Russians took my clothes and gave me one of their own uniforms. But the suit you're wearing looks as if it had belonged to some old German; you must have found it in an abandoned house, and believe me, that fact is fairly obvious."

He did not want to admit it; but my curiosity had been aroused. Most of us stripped when we washed. I purposely took my place beside him in the washrooms and raised my arms as high as I could. "If he's from the Waffen SS," I thought, "he'll try to take a look under my left arm to see if I'm tattooed, and he'll be surprised to find nothing." As for him, he never stripped, which itself was significant. But he kept his mouth firmly shut and, in the end, I left him to himself.

Some more time passed and then, one morning, there was a great to-do in the camp. The Russians assembled us: "You're going to have a visitor from the French Embassy—a good sign; your repatriation can't be far off."

And there it was, one of the happiest sights I had ever seen. Two cars driving up—the ambassador's, followed by another. Mme Catroux, the ambassador's wife, stepped out of the first car. She wore the complete military outfit: uniform jacket with skirt, braided epaulettes, three rows of medals including the Croix de Guerre and British and Australian regimental badges. On her necktie was the Russian red star. I took a good look at her and said to myself, "Well, with the help of a person like that you should manage to extricate yourself."

She joined us and started to speak: "My children, as you know, the war is now over. My husband, General Catroux, French Ambassador to the Union of Soviet Socialist Republics, is doing everything to speed your return to our beloved country. This makes me very happy for I know how much you have suffered. . . ."

There followed a discourse fit to make one die laughing. One could hardly believe one's ears listening to this society lady from the fashionable XVIᵉ Paris *arrondissement*, the much-publicized ambulance driver who had risked her life rescuing two wounded men from under a collapsed house, as well as the indefatigable bridge player who chattered away between every other trick. During this comic opera performance I was reminded of everything that, over the years, had made the French Army an object of fun.

". . . Quick, my children, write letters to your dear families, they'll be sent by diplomatic courier."

All those poor innocents grabbed their pencils. As for me, I told myself that the general's wife was not going to send off seven hundred letters all at once. As she waited, I went up to her and bowed. "Christian de La Mazière, member of the STO deportees."

She was astonished to see so completely shaved a head.

"Ah, my poor little one. . . ."

"Your husband, General Catroux, knew my father well."

"Why, yes, your name rings a bell . . . write it down for me. Have you any particular problem?"

"Well, it's like this: I'm very anxious to return home. Now, I've the impression that we'll be sent off in groups, those who have been here the longest first, and those like me will be left to the last. . . ."

Actually, what I wanted above all was to be separated from the STO contingent and to come immediately after the prisoners of war in order of repatriation. I thought that they would receive special welcomes in France, with speeches and music, and that I might be able to take advantage of the festivities to slip away and get lost. My Russian attire attracted attention and dated from the time I had been faced with execution. Now I was in a new phase and had no desire to arouse curiosity. The best solution would certainly have been to exchange my uniform for one belonging to a prisoner of war with an impeccable past, but these people had not much imagination and clung to the uniform of defeat.

I quickly wrote down my name. The Embassy secretaries and an aide-de-camp collected the letters, which were never to leave Moscow. Standing at the door of her car, the general's wife had a final word for us: "I'll come back to visit you, my children, if I can. In any case, don't worry, I'll be busy on your behalf."

We saw her again forty-eight hours later, bringing packages. She asked for me, and I showed up in no time.

"My boy, I have got permission to bring you to the Embassy to see my husband."

Not bad for a start, I thought, but now I'll have to be doubly wary. As I moved up to higher circles the risks will be greater.

On my arrival I was presented to General Catroux, who remembered my father very well.

"I'll see that you're repatriated as soon as possible," he told me. "Meanwhile you'll stay here with us. Try and make yourself useful."

Thus I became an office boy at the French Embassy, while continuing to wear my Russian uniform, which emanated plenty of local color.

I had a camp bed in an office on the top floor and I put together a little toilet kit of soap, toothbrush, and razor. I also discovered the wonderful American products, such as their toothpaste. Nescafé, chewing gum, chocolate. . . . Occasionally I thought of the prisoners I had left. "They're stagnating there, those poor jerks, while I'll certainly leave before them. Isn't it marvelous?"

Life at the Embassy had not much variety; there were none of the receptions that generally embellish diplomatic life. After that terrible war, austerity was the order of the day and it was the military who set the tone. The civil servants from the Quai d'Orsay, some of whom had spent the entire war in Russia, lived with the former on less than the warmest terms. This made for a curious atmosphere. Moreover, one was only grudgingly given the right to move about the city. Cars could not leave the Embassy without a special permit from Molotov; foreign ambassadors could still not travel about freely.

I went from office to office, perfectly happy. I often came across one of those rare French officers who was an open Communist sympathizer, General Petit. He was an elusive character who had taken a dislike to me from my arrival. He claimed to have been the first to have addressed an appeal to the French people, before June 18, 1940, to continue to fight, but since he had addressed them from Cordillera in the Andes, no one had heard him. I saw quite a lot of Mme Catroux; she was charming and ever ready to be of help. She talked incessantly, recounting, among other things, her memories of the Syrian campaign, and the general watched her a little uneasily.

The Embassy's main business was the repatriation of the French, a task that gave it many headaches. Five hundred thousand prisoners of war, or thereabouts, had been handed over by the Russians, as well as almost as many STO workers, plus quite a number of petty criminals. There were camps everywhere. The Soviet authorities tried to sort out all those who had fallen into their hands, but General Catroux was having great difficulty in obtaining information about the French nationals, who, to make matters worse, often got mixed up among German prisoners.

Some had been scattered to remote corners of the country and were fearful of being forgotten. In order to draw attention to themselves some of these French prisoners, lost in some region such as the former Baltic states, resorted to a desperate stratagem. On May Day they had sent a telegram to the Russian authorities: "Felicitations to the great and friendly nation. Long live its inspired leader, Stalin! Long live the glorious Red Army!" The flattered Russians had passed on the message and it had ended up in Molotov's office; and he, in proper administrative style, had sent a copy to Catroux.

One day Mme Catroux summoned me.

"Good news, Christian, you're going home. How happy your father will be, indeed all your family. Incidentally, I can tell you that your letter to them was sent off."

At her request, I had, in fact, written to my father, in noncommittal terms, for I was afraid of possible censorship: "I am at our Embassy in Moscow and General Catroux asks me to send you his best regards. Things are not at all bad and I managed to survive the air raids." Anyhow, this letter was never delivered.

The morning for saying good-bye arrived. As each batch of repriates left, the Embassy staff drove to the station to see them off, and I went too. We were at a Moscow station and I got out beside a freight train full of ex-prisoners, two-thirds of them officers. They turned discreet glances at this strange individual in a Russian uniform who appeared to be under official patronage. I had not had any chance of exchanging my clothes. The general had promised me a French uniform but there had been none at the Embassy and no one to let me have his.

I was given a place in an officers' car. They had brought out their whole display of ribbons and medals and had put on their Croix de Lorraine armbands. They also had their little boxes but preferred to talk and exchange memories. I was reminded of *La Grande Illusion*.[4]

As the train started, I saw again in my mind's eye the very similar railroad car in which I had left Wildflecken for the eastern front, only some months previously. "It's ridiculous," I was thinking, "that having experienced so much in so short a time I still don't know what will happen to me."

Our engine looked like something out of the Old West, with a snowplow in front. We traveled at the speed of a slow train under a hot July sun. From time to time we were visited by one of the Russian officers assigned to escort the train as far as the frontier of the Soviet Zone. Across the landscape one saw life returning to normal and the gentle rebirth of peace. At the train stops peasants came to offer us their wares.

We had been traveling for almost four days. Some were ill, and the naval doctor whom I encountered again in the convoy had few means of treating them. One officer died from a throat abscess that burst and suffocated him. At last we arrived at the

[4] A reference to the attitudes displayed by the officers in Jean Renoir's great anti-war film.

British Zone, not far from Hannover, where the exchange of command was effected.

The train remained stationary. French and British officers stood on the platform. These were joined by the Russian officers who had escorted us and a discussion began. We were ordered out of the train; trucks that were to take us to another train at another station were waiting outside.

It was then that I became aware of a kind of uneasiness in the air. We waited on the platform in small groups while the French officers who had met the train talked among themselves and cast glances at us. Finally they came over, saluting the liberated officers rather coldly. They came either from London or Algeria, and the displaying of the Croix de Lorraine was not much to their liking. A lieutenant called my name and I presented myself.

"Will you come with me."

"Why?"

"Don't worry. It's just to answer some questions."

The others had turned their heads and were whispering. They were probably thinking I was somebody a bit off-color. A car was waiting and the lieutenant gestured. "Get in; we're going to Hannover."

We drove about forty kilometers. The officer occasionally gave me an English cigarette without speaking. Anxiety overcame me. We came to the city and drove through it to the prison. The heavy gates opened and then shut for good behind me.

PART TWO

VII.
OTHER MORNINGS,
OTHER TUNES

Prisons, like churches, always escape the bombings. The one at Hannover was in the solid, Bismarckian tradition, with guards who seemed to have lived through the various regimes and seen, since 1943, all kinds of individuals pass through. Nothing could disconcert them, not even the arrival of a Frenchman in Russian uniform.

Completely bewildered, I was getting my first glimpse of the penitentiary system: one enters, writes down one's name and date of birth, and is searched, a simple operation in my case as I had practically nothing with me. This was a more humiliating search than those that prisoners of war undergo; a finger is even inserted in the anus to make sure nothing is hidden there. In short, regulations are rigorously adhered to. I tried to find out why I was there, but received no answers to my questions. I was then conducted through all sorts of rooms separated by iron grilles and quickly became accustomed to the noise made by the huge bunch of keys. During this stroll, I recalled scenes from a film I had seen in my youth, *La Citadelle du Silence*.

It was the time of day when the prisoners returned from exercise and I heard them as they marched in step. I was taken to one of the first buildings, along gangways and across connecting bridges, and, without more ado, locked into a cell. And then I was alone with a spoon and a messtin that had just been given to me, my soap, toothbrush, and tube of toothpaste, which had also been investigated with a piece of wire.

Alone, above all, with my anxiety. I would have felt less crushed if I had had some companions. On the walls were scribbles in German and Polish, but nothing in French. And in the corners of the walls, the strokes each of which represented a day, six in a row and, at the seventh, they were crossed out as another week had been completed.

That is when one becomes fully aware of the frightening consistency of the penitentiary mind. There is no freedom of movement and everything is fastened down. My cell was of the classic type: toilet, chair, iron bed, which folded back, with covers and mattress. The bed, like the chair, was chained to the wall. I suppose they could easily have supplied a flimsy chair that would have broken at the first blow so that it could not have served as a weapon . . . but no, it was huge and heavy.

In the shortest wall, opposite the door, there was a narrow window, by means of which one could gauge its thickness; there is no economizing when it comes to building prisons. And in front of the window, which opened on a chain and was made of some kind of unbreakable glass, were the bars, the famous symbol of incarceration. Bright sunlight shone through them and dazzled me. One would have had to be an old hand to have settled down there right away. . . . I wanted to see what was on the other side. I dragged the chair toward the window but, since it was chained, I could not move it far enough. I turned around and tried to hoist myself up, but the bars were out of reach. I heard occasional bursts of firing and my heart pounded as I wondered whom they were shooting.

I tried to understand what had happened. I had left Moscow in very favorable circumstances, with the Embassy's blessing and in the company of repatriated officers. Finally, on leaving the Russian zone I had enjoyed comparative liberty and had been received, like the others, by a French delegation. They were looking for someone and it happened to be precisely me. So now I was here, fifty kilometers away, in prison in a half-ruined city. Doubtless they were well informed about those they wanted to lay charges against, and I would not be left to vegetate here; I would soon be interrogated and handed over to the French authorities.

While waiting, I had to sort things out inside me and learn how to survive. I had nothing to read and I looked forward to the evening soup, which was served early, at seven o'clock. This was a thin broth, quite drinkable; the Pomeranian hardships had taught me to be Spartan, and I had had to swallow such unnamable things. Then I washed my messtin: above the toilet there was a tap with a big copper knob. My cell was opened, I was ordered to put my boots outside the door, I brought out my messtin and spoon, and furtively looked to see if I could catch sight of other prisoners. Then I lay down on the bed and my first night in prison began.

I turned over all sorts of things in my mind: the successive humiliations, confinements, interrogations, trials that awaited me. I imagined the series of degradations suffered by an individual caught in the judicial machine and awaiting trial and the announcement of his fate. I missed the conditions in which I had existed in a prisoner-of-war camp where the humiliation is only temporary and the prisoner's spirit is not undermined by the inexorable and cunning process of the law. This was worse than any horrors I had known so far, worse than when each moment had brought me into promiscuous contact with pain and death. I even came to regret that I had not been killed in Pomerania.

Next morning, after reveille, I folded my blanket into quarters, swallowed the bread and coffee, both equally unappetizing, that I was given, and then waited for the time for exercise. I heard taps on the walls exchanged between the cells; from window to window people were talking to one another in German. I was in a strange world that I would have to learn to know, a silent world where everything had to be instantly grasped at a glance to right or left, through the implacable automatism of the opening and shutting of doors. All this was done very quickly. When it was time for a meal the door was half-opened, the large containers full of food ranged on a cart pushed by a prisoner appeared, you drew your ration, and, before the guard closed the door, the cart was at the next cell and it was all over.

We went down for exercise in Indian file and it was then I discovered the kind of humanity that existed in prison. There was everything: military, police, civilians who had wielded authority in the Third Reich and who were now sequestered here. The screws constantly shouted at us to be silent, we were treated as if we were already convicts. All the same, I tried to carry on some conversation. I asked a guard if there were other Frenchmen, in the hope of being transferred to a cell with them. He did not know; in any case, in the building where I was, the prisoners were in solitary confinement, this evidently being the political division. In fact, I might well be the only one of my kind, and I sensed that I aroused a certain suspicion among the groups instinctively formed by the other prisoners.

Time began slipping by. On the third day I told myself: well, they'll soon come to get you; the fourth: well no, it looks as if you're staying here; the fifth: this is where you'll be tried; the military tribunals are sitting in Germany, so they have to find something to do. I was not allowed to get in touch with anyone, to write a letter—I had asked, but they had pretended not to understand—there was nothing for it but to wait.

Gradually I hit on ways of passing the time. These are not things one had learned, but I discovered them, alone in my cell. I started walking, and when I had made what I considered the most perfect circuit of the cell, both the longest and the least monotonous, I counted the number of steps, calculating them exactly in order to arrive, after several days, at perfectly equal strides, each of about eighteen inches. It was essential to move about to keep in shape. I became like an animal that constructs its burrow, I found myself digging my hole, picking the best position on this mattress on which so many others had tossed, thinking of things that reunited them to the world outside.

I tried also to control my thoughts, but how can one still the ferment in a brain? At first, you speak aloud to yourself, needing to hear your own voice. Then you only hear your interior voice. You dream, you start reliving youthful adventures, adventures with women, you wonder what has happened to the people you used to know, what they are doing, where they are, you draw up a balance, asking how and why, you think of what could free you. Suddenly you become angry; you play the hero: if they should interrogate you, you will be firm, courageous, you will impress them . . . and then you wake up: you are here, shut up, and that is all there is to it.

"All the same, it's the bloody limit: here I am in Germany, and in a German prison!" I had escaped from Russian retribution that I thought would overtake me, knowing that their rule was to shoot any of the Waffen SS who fell into their hands. I had escaped execution on the battlefield. I had encountered men whom the euphoria of victory had transformed, and who had given me cause to hope that I would extricate myself from the huge collective drama, while, mentally, I was preparing myself for Siberia. And now that I had returned to the West, I found myself face to face with the moment of truth, which was going to prove a harder experience than any up to now.

At the end of a week, on a Sunday, I was summoned from my cell, about the hour of the religious services, and I thought I was being taken to Mass. When you are imprisoned you are asked your religion and whether you wish to attend services; and you say yes, because it is an outing. But now it was not a question of prayers; I was taken to the office, where a French non-commissioned officer and a private soldier, both in British uniforms, were waiting for me.

They had an order for my release. I got back my papers and other small belongings, matches, cigarettes, and signed my discharge sheet. I went out with my two military escorts, who told me to get into a front-wheel-drive car that had been camouflaged, the very same make in which I had originally driven into Germany, which struck me as quite funny. I sat in the back beside the noncommissioned officer and we set off without a word, without anything at all.

My companions treated me with indifference rather than curiosity. After about thirty kilometers we came to a prosperous-looking suburb of small, pretty houses flanked by gardens—the Germans have long had the secret of creating them. A flowering, gay, tidy place, just as if there had never been a war. Women walked about, children were playing. We stopped at a villa in front of which several cars were parked; it was a French headquarters situated in the British Zone.

I was taken to a cozily furnished room. I asked if I could smoke; I had developed the prisoner's mentality and asked permission for everything. I was told I could and I took out the cigarettes I had been given in Russia at our departure, which had been part of a consignment the Americans had sent to the French Embassy. They had been distributed, apparently, to give us a foretaste of the joys of homecoming.

After a short wait, the noncommissioned officer came for me, and I was taken to a living room that had been turned into an office with a desk. A captain, wearing the blue tabs of the cavalry, sat at it. He studied me carefully as I came in. "Sit down."

He had a look at the papers on his desk. "You're Christian de La Mazière?"

"Yes."

"Surprised to be here?"

I had to be careful and see how the land lay. "You know, nothing surprises me anymore. Though, in fact, I was surprised when a lieutenant called me out from among the ex-prisoners being repatriated, and quite stunned when I was taken to a prison. . . ."

"Didn't you declare that you belonged to the STO?"

"Yes."

"Which isn't true."

No point in being evasive. "Of course it isn't true. As you must know, if you say so."

"This is what happened: the lists of the convoys from Russia are sent directly to a center in Paris. The names are listed according to regiment. As it happened, yours was on a list of people to be investigated. We were notified by telegram and had you apprehended."

"I see, and now what's going to happen to me?"

The captain thought for a moment or two. "That depends; your case interests me, because your father was my commanding officer at the Saumur Cavalry School. It *was* your father, wasn't it?"

"Yes, that's right."

"A fine man."

"I think so too."

"I imagine that, as a soldier, he'd sooner see you dead than alive and on trial?"

"Possibly. I don't know. . . ."

"I'd like to hear your story; I won't take any notes because it doesn't concern me officially. My job here is merely to register you and then send you to France to be tried by a court of justice. You know of these courts?"

"Yes, I do. What's more, we heard on the radio that Brasillach was sentenced to death by one of them, and shot, Brasillach and many others. . . ."

"I think it'll be rather different in your case. I believe General de Gaulle, whom I know—I was in London with him—is a man who prefers those who fought to those who engaged in politics."

He then started questioning me about the Charlemagne. He seemed well informed and knew the names of fifteen higher-ranking officers such as Bassompierre and de Vauglas. We talked for some time, and then he said, "You can remain here a few days before you're transferred to France. I won't send you back to prison in Hannover. You'll sleep and eat here, but you must give me your word, as an officer, that you won't try to escape."

I gave it; as he was about to leave the room, he remarked, "It bothers me to see you in that uniform. I'll have another given to you."

I was taken to the kitchen, where I had lunch with the military personnel, polite and friendly fellows. They gave me cigarettes and cognac, my first in a long time. Then I was brought a number two British Red Cross package containing several pairs of socks, shirts, trousers with side pockets, battle-dress blouse, woolen tie, and a knapsack.

In three months I had worn three different uniforms. An SS one, which was the loser's; the Russian, which was still a prisoner's; and this one, which almost gave me the feeling of being a free man. I could wash under the shower and have a proper shave. I had been shaved in prison—it was a weekly ceremony—and my skin still smarted from it. We had gone out one at a time and in a corner of the corridor a barber, equipped with a big open razor, daubed us with soap and finished the job in no time at all. As we left with our mugs on fire, we were given a freezing styptic stone to stop the bleeding.

I could have gone out for walks, on parole, but I preferred to ask formally for permission, with all due deference. I saw children playing, I saw women—there were few men left—some of them young, and I trembled with desire, but I was breathing more freely. I've had a bit of luck, I told myself, and I think I'm going to scrape through.

Next morning I was up early. After making my bed, I talked with the two guys with whom I shared the room. With them I felt neither embarrassment nor that they despised me. They had fought, having gone to England and enlisted for the duration of the war. Their attitude had nothing in common with that of the Maquis who had operated inside France.

It was then that a new world in the process of bewildering

changes was revealed to me. I felt free to ask my companions endless questions, and I suddenly learned about the whole new situation: how the war had ended, how France had become one of the Big Four. With a ravenous hunger I devoured my first French newspapers, finding out what had been happening, what was being said, and about the proceedings being taken against the war criminals.

I heard of the concentration camps. There had already been some talk of them in Russia; their inmates, all in a state of acute weakness, had been the first to be repatriated. Many, I heard, had died through lack of food or of typhus, which had also been prevalent in German prisoner-of-war camps. But the Russians had not dwelt much on these subjects. Having lived with fear and wide-scale slaughter for almost four years, they wanted to enjoy their victory and the peace they had regained.

I admit my first reaction had been one of disbelief. For five years Germany had faced a large part of the rest of the world and I thought that it was natural enough that the victors would exaggerate the guilt of the vanquished. And, besides, one has to imagine the feelings of somebody like myself who had survived so much carnage. I had seen thousands of corpses belonging to all sides intimately mingled in death, I had seen women raped and children massacred. There had been so many horrors, and not committed by one side only, that for me the concentration camps became part of the general disgusting degradation. All this, it seemed to me, had happened outside the moral law; there was no more point in talking of the guilty and the innocent, the reality was the pitiless world of war where the law was that of the victors. I had emerged out of chaos and I was not made for that kind of world; I felt I was made to live, that life had a fantastic price, and that it had to be defended to the last, even at the expense of the lives of others. I was like an animal fleeing from the hounds, whose only impulse is to escape, to live, live. . . .

I was not able to accept the idea of collective guilt. With my comrades that I met again in prison later, I often discussed this question and all felt as I did. Our commitment had been a purely physical one founded on some high ideals. My own anti-Communism and my belief in the National Socialist revolution had been deeply and sincerely held. Besides, everything had happened so swiftly, too swiftly to have provided time, or the right conditions, for a reappraisal.

What could we have known of these camps? Near Neustettin, as I have said, I saw one being evacuated, and in Czechoslovakia I saw prisoners in their striped pajamas. But as long as I wore German uniform I knew nothing of the exterminations, the phenomenon of the concentration camp system and its monstrous developments; it was only later, imprisoned in France, that I became fully aware of these things. But it was in Hannover that I first heard the "final solution" mentioned, though without any precise details. And I did not understand why we of the Waffen SS were so hated, not knowing that public opinion identified us with those who had been in charge of the camps.

At Yanovitz, the anti-Semitism had been no more extreme than I had encountered in France as an adolescent. The emphasis was put on race, we were the superior and stronger one, as at athletics, but not to the special detriment of any other. And then, too, Germany was making her final stand, and indoctrination, as I have said, so important earlier, had been completely superseded by military training. Before all else, we were fighting troops, and slogans on walls were like out-of-date posters.

The young captain appeared to understand all this quite well. He was a follower of Maurras[1] and of an extreme nationalist outlook; for him, Germany was the enemy, de Gaulle and the Allies had given France back her sovereignty. Whereas our background was similar, he was not by any manner of means a revolutionary. Equally anti-Communist and anti-Nazi, he condemned my choice without, however, feeling the hostility toward me that would a member of the FTP.[2] Apart from that, I soon saw that as head of an information network he was more concerned with the Russians than the French. What interested him was to hear what I had noticed on my journey from Moscow to Hannover, the convoys, the war material, the Soviet forces. He thought, not without reason, that I had taken more note of these things than the average repatriated prisoner who had been out of circulation so long, and he kept asking me to make every effort to recall what I had noticed.

I had even been somewhat shocked. "The French Army," I thought, "has experienced defeat and victory; some rallied to de Gaulle right away, others joined up with the North African regi-

[1] A French royalist politician who edited the extreme right-wing paper *l'Action Française* before the war.
[2] Resistance group of Communist leanings.

ments, but in spite of all the chaotic events, the professional army forever remains Joan of Arc's army, with its automatic traditional patterns, and with Communism always seen as the real enemy."

"Isn't the Communist party sharing power with General de Gaulle," I objected, "and hasn't it some key governmental posts?"

I understood, however, that for this officer the presence of Communist ministers in the government was only a temporary expedient, constituting an internal political problem of secondary importance.

"Thanks to its initial reverses," he explained, "the Russian Army received such an enormous amount of American help in the way of military supplies that Germany, in spite of its fabulous secret weapon, was doomed to defeat. Germany was conquered by a combination of American war material and Russia's human potential. Now, looking at the imaginary frontiers defining the limits of the forward advances of the occupying powers, it could be said that half Europe has fallen into Stalin's hands. So is it not natural that our high command should try to gather as much information on the Russians as possible?"

I thus learned of the remarkable aerial and naval supply lines, thanks to which a badly mauled Russian Army was injected with new life by the relentless activity of American industry, which worked day and night to produce an endless stream of trucks, tanks, airplanes, and provisions. But I saw, at the same time, that, with the end of hostilities, the fixing of zones, the transfer of populations, Allied solidarity was going to crack, and nationalism would again rise up as in the good old days.

Well treated, well fed, allowed to stroll around, I found my new freedom intoxicating. Then one morning the captain summoned me. "You're going back to France, but I'm giving you a break. You'll travel by car with an officer and a driver with orders to take you to Paris. They'll let you get out there, give you a couple of hours' start, and then report your disappearance. The rest is up to you. . . ."

We drove through the British Zone, across northern Germany and Holland, and had lunch in Brussels. I conversed with my escort, a very polite lieutenant, and I never ceased admiring the troops we passed on the way; they were very different from those I had seen in Russia. These were the rich armies, the pampered ones of the war. As France came nearer, my heart started pounding. "Wonderful," I thought, "if they let me out at the place de la Concorde with two hours' start, I'll be able to phone my friends, and I'll manage to get myself out of this mess." We were passing frontiers without any formalities. The postwar period had not yet set in, uniforms were everywhere, and we were free of controls.

The French frontier, Lille! The lieutenant turned to me. "We're making a short stop here, I've some papers to deliver."

We drove to a building close to the town hall where the Military Police were installed. He said, "Get out and come with me."

I followed him and—do not ever speak to me again of the word of a French officer—he handed me over without batting an eyelid and departed.

We looked at each other, the security fellows and I; they did not know what to do with me. After a couple of hours' wait, a car came to take me to Loos. It was my first French prison.

I went through the entry formalities to the jibes of the guards and was led to a cell where three others were already shut up.

There was evidently much overcrowding, and I would have to learn to share a minimum of floor space. In the evening three mattresses were placed there; during the day they were piled on the bed that was allotted to the oldest of the prisoners. My companions gave me some lurid details of the purge that had swept France after September, 1944. Some arrested at that time had been in the prison ever since, awaiting trial, and were taken at regular intervals to be questioned by the examining magistrate.

The more notable of these was a very dignified gentleman, a graduate of the Paris Polytechnic and owner of a large industrial concern in the Lille-Roubaix district. He was accused of economic collaboration, that is, of having placed his factory at the disposition of the Germans. Every evening he knelt to say his prayers; a devout Catholic, father of a large family, he was the sort of man who would have been very much at home in the MRP.[3] His fellow prisoners were at his beck and call; he received generous food packages and, in short, it seemed he was a man of means.

As for the others, I was not sure what they had been charged

[3] Mouvement républicain populaire, the French Christian Democratic Party.

with. Anyway, in prison all are innocent and give their own account of their case. For my part, I had learned that it did not do to utter the words Waffen SS; even among the prisoners, it was the ultimate abomination.

We politicals were in a minority. The place was full of those charged under the common law, and one came on them everywhere: in the accounting department, in the office, in the kitchens. They occupied permanent positions as auxiliaries in the prison administration. Every prison is a small, enclosed town, with its own privileged class. At Loos, the common criminals made the laws and we were subject to them. We politicals were a collection of vulnerable individuals, suited for their kind of jungle; we were their inferiors and soon became their victims.

Insults rained down on us: traitors, bastards. These devoted patriots would teach us a lesson; to coexist with them we had to submit to their racketeering and blackmail. In order to have our soup properly served, or to ensure that our messtins were not accidentally upset when they had been filled and were being handed to us, to get a proper share, we had to pay in cigarettes or let them choose whatever they wanted from our packages.

This went on for nearly three weeks. I kept track of the time because, on entering, I had been notified that I would not be staying long. At that time, "collaborators" were served with two arrest warrants, one from the region where they came from, and the other from wherever they had been principally active.

I awaited my transfer with impatience. Nothing is more depressing than to idle away the time with three others in a cell meant for one person. If one wants to take a little exercise, one's cell mates have to remain motionless in a corner; one has to take everything in turns. And then there is the problem of the toilet. I held out for two days, but then it was high time that I went to the john and learned to use it in front of the others. The toilet was the type known as Turkish and had to be constantly cleaned with a brush and rag. The latter also served to stop the outflow when one wanted to wash. One pressed the flush lever and, on all fours, cleaned oneself in this makeshift basin. In short, we had sunk to the level of a herd of animals.

Shortly before I left, two of my cell mates were removed by the guards and replaced by one man who equaled both together, as he weighed at least 260 pounds. He was called Deleau and owned one of the biggest flour mills in France. He had asked to be put in the "economic collaborators" section of the prison, and with his arrival, abundance entered our cell. He received impressive-looking packages and must have bought half the guards. Our Polytechnician ceded him the bed that his own age and standing had previously entitled him to. I was amused by the tight-lipped expression with which the former regarded the fat Deleau, who belched, snored, and deafened us with his farts.

I was able to write a letter home, dealing mainly with the question of engaging a lawyer. My elder sister sent me a prompt reply. "We are doing what is necessary," she wrote. "From what we have been able to find out, you will be transferred and tried in Paris, which seems preferable to us; we are seeing to it that you won't be kept stagnating too long at Loos." I was told, at the same time, that money had come for me, so I could use the canteen, but there was not much to be had there.

Finally, with other prisoners, I was told to collect my belongings and go to the office, where the guards took me in charge. I was put in a patrol wagon, after being handcuffed, which is one of the most lugubrious sensations that I know of. But such is the regulation and it must be enforced. I have seen these chains clapped onto the wrists of cripples who, left free, could hardly take three steps. It was part of the systematic process of humiliation and intimidation. And I believe that the police need to hear the degrading iron grating of the handcuffs in order to confirm their sense of superiority. At the station at Loos everyone stared at us. Some, the women especially, appeared uncomfortable and threw us compassionate glances. Others made remarks; to them we were the defeated.

We were taken to a reserved compartment, but, as always in such cases, on a train for ordinary passengers; everything was well organized; there must be, obviously, an understanding between the SNCF[4] and the prisons, and a railway department specializing in the transport of prisoners. We occupied two compartments and constituted a free show for the other passengers, who went up and down the corridors to get a good look at us. As for the police, they had the impersonal faces of their tribe; they answered our questions openly and politely, otherwise they did not speak.

At the Gare du Nord we used a special freight exit. A police van was waiting and we were again scrutinized, but now with more indifference, by the station employees, who had grown

---

[4] The French state-owned railroads.

used to such sights. Evening was falling over Paris, and for a moment I drank in this familiar picture, then we were shut into the darkness of the patrol wagon.

We were taken to La Santé, which served as a transit prison from where the detainees were sent either to provincial prisons or to Fresnes. Other police vans arrived there at the same time as ours, from Brittany, I think; I saw a priest in his cassock emerge from one. It was late and the guards were in a bad temper, annoyed at having to go through the business of booking us. They made us stand in a courtyard with raised arms, forbidding us to move, in the beam of a searchlight mounted on the wall. And then they started insulting us.

It was the first time I had witnessed anything like this: guards collecting to insult their prisoners. At this time a patriotic flame, rekindled from the ashes, was burning in the hearts of Frenchmen, turning them into stern judges. So it was even with these screws who, like most of the police, had considered it their duty to revile the members of the Resistance during the Occupation. I want to state unequivocally that of all those people I have come across in my life, prison guards are the most miserable and contemptible. It is incredible to think that they are answerable to the Ministry of Justice for maintaining, in principle, the nation's moral equilibrium.

The manner of their recruitment already explains their mediocrity; to become a screw a school-leaving certificate is necessary, but as candidates for the job do not exactly apply in crowds, those without are also taken. And once enlisted, the system protects them; they never leave the prison. Within its precincts they earn their money and have their homes and their wives. It is also in the prison environment that their children are born and grow up, which is why the boys so often take the same employment, and son follows father as guard. These parasites are totally dependent on the penitentiary world and know no other. But they also live on the prisoners. If there were not all sorts of swindlers, if there were no unscrupulous lawyers, abortionists, cashiers caught with their hands in the till, bookkeepers who falsify the accounts, if it were not for such people to keep things running in all departments, from the office to the kitchens, the prisons would cease to function because they could not carry on on their own.

The prison administration has only one concern: to collect the prisoners who can keep it going. If they called a general strike, the prison would be paralyzed. For the screws alone are incapable of getting it functioning again.

Only common-law offenders were kept permanently in La Santé, including a number of short-term prisoners whose abilities in the offices and workshops were invaluable. Some of them joined with the guards in insulting us; especially singled out was the priest. They took advantage of the rare opportunity. . . . This went on for at least a couple of hours. Then a prison officer with a disapproving expression showed up—the performance must not have amused him—and told us to lower our raised arms. We were then locked up, without anything to eat.

Next day we were put through the everlasting ritual of being booked: fingerprints, measurements, can you read and write, etc. If anyone is unlucky enough to go through twenty-five prisons, then the same trifling formalities are fussed over twenty-five times: can you read and write? In one group those who can, in the other those who cannot: a method of selection that sums up the whole prison system. The politicals generally disclaimed any knowledge of either reading or writing.

We were then led back to our cells, and on the way I could appreciate the sinister perfection of the building. Like all the classic prisons, La Santé is constructed in the shape of a star; in the center is a rotunda with a splendid glass cage for the guards. From this they can overlook the whole complex: the cells in the radiating wings and the passages; and from this central lookout they can also see the rooms to which the prisoners are summoned for consultation with their lawyers, for visits, to receive their packages, and so on.

My cell was the largest I had yet seen. The screw opened the door and pushed me into it. It was already occupied by four common-law prisoners, who got up and approached me, with nasty expressions.

Luckily I am close to six feet tall and of solid build, and the degree of fitness I had reached at Yanovitz was not completely gone. Otherwise I would have been in for hell. Knowing I was a political, there was a flood of threats and abuse. It was essential to react quickly; I started shouting louder than they were: "Listen, you guys: the first one of you who makes too much trouble, I'll beat to a pulp. You may be four to one, but we'll all end up together in the hole and you'll know you've been hurt."

They immediately became wary. Convicts who are old hands, and return to prison again and again, like to play the big shot even if they have neither the physical nor the financial means for the part. They invariably try to intimidate the new-comers. God help the weak man who lets himself be overawed by their status or terrorized by men who are nothing but slow-witted brutes. They trample all over him and, inside a night, turn him into a physical wreck: all under the benevolent eyes of the screws. I had a narrow escape, thanks to being on my guard and the speed of my reactions.

I succeeded in gaining their respect. I picked out the boss and, without flattery, acknowledged his right of priority, which I would not challenge as long as he did not abuse it. He, for his part, took stock of the situation. He saw that I was young, strong, no fool, and that he had better take care. In any case, I would not be there for long, and as I was a political I might get some worthwhile packages. He showed me my corner and explained my chores. As the last arrival, I well knew that next day it would be my job to clean the cell and put away the mattresses.

A status quo was established inside the hour. Sitting in my corner, I talked with the fellows, gave them some chocolate, and was accepted. I spent the first day playing *belote* (a popular card game). Cards were, of course, forbidden but the prisoners cut them out from the wrappings around packages and drew the figures on them. The screws were well aware of this but shut their eyes to it for, if the need arose, it was an excellent means of extorting blackmail. And in prison, as I gradually came to realize, everything is at one and the same time prohibited and tolerated. It is only necessary to bribe constantly. By such deals and schemes some guards sometimes manage to make spectacular sums.

I remained at La Santé for five or six days. I had been told when I had been booked that I would be transferred to Fresnes as soon as I was informed by the examining magistrate of the charge against me. So far I had been held without an official charge, which meant that I had as yet no official existence in the eyes of the law and that, until such time as I had, I could never be welcome there. In these troubled times, though, the sacrosanct administration did not hesitate to flout its own rules, while at least it had the decency to inform you of them.

Finally I was charged. A clerk of the court brought me a copy of my arrest warrant. I was notified of the principal accusa-tions: endangering the internal and external security of the state, intelligence with the enemy.

"Intelligence with the enemy": strangely enough, this expression gave me some comfort, it sounded like a quality label. I was no longer an ordinary prisoner, and I suddenly understood the common criminal's hatred for politicals. "What does the phrase mean? What is hidden behind it?" These were the questions I read on the faces of my companions, all of whom were there for theft, embezzlement, break-ins, as they passed around and examined the small sheet of yellow paper that I showed them on my return.

Twenty-four hours later I was back in the office, being given back my tie and shoelaces and signing the discharge sheet. Then I left for a new world, the world of the political prison. I got into the prison van with the others, including the Breton priest. This time it was guards who escorted us. At the end of the afternoon we arrived at Fresnes, which, at that time, was the real palace among prisons.

VIII.
FRESNES,
PALACE OF MADNESS

In 1945 Fresnes was the most modern prison in France, and from the moment I arrived at the admitting office I was struck by the change of atmosphere. The screws were polite, the prisoners dressed as though they had just returned from a stroll downtown. It was the political penitentiary and had a kind of civilized air about it. For me, coming straight from a world of mediocrity and hatred, it was a real relief.

I was sent to the first division, among a kind of elite. A whole floor at the top was kept for those who were to come before the high court, that is, the former bigwigs, former ministers, generals, admirals, each of whom had a right to a private cell. On the other floors were journalists, businessmen, as well as the big-time operators who had been mixed up with the Gestapo. In the second division, which was less interesting, were Paris flunkeys who were there for the same reason as those in the third, kids who had hung around with the militia or the PPF, carrying on the traditions of their families. There were plenty of them; the state always likes to arrest minors.

I was lucky, the more so in that no intervention could yet have been made in my behalf; I had not seen my lawyer or had any real contact with my family. I was taken to cell 143, which was already occupied by two young men, though they had only just moved in. They had been transferred from the second division because they had been at Fresnes for some time. They were well thought of and were being done a favor.

These two boys had been friends since childhood and were inseparable. They had enlisted together in the Todt Organization, the pick-and-shovel army that had built, most notably, the Atlantic Wall. It had enlisted all kinds of civilian workers, both German and foreign; but it also consisted of armed groups for the protection of its projects, a kind of police force, in uniform. My cell mates had belonged to this section and that was why they were here.

One was a well-built, blazing redhead, and his mother worked as a concierge in the XVIIIe district, in the rue Ravignan. The other had brown hair and big blue eyes. I sensed an uneasy friendship between them. They kindly arranged my mattress for me and explained the machinery of the prison, of which they had by now considerable experience.

For the first time I became part of a well-organized prison world. My cell mates were visited weekly and knew the ins and outs of the mail. As long as one was awaiting trial, one could write as much as one wished, but it was wise to give the letters to one's lawyer since the prison authorities opened all incoming and outgoing letters. I learned about all these things, as well as the exercise times and the quality of the food. We shared our packages and also our canteen money.

A month went by. I had news of my father, who was being held in administrative custody. I met my lawyer, Maître Alain Ballot, an old friend who had been a liaison officer in London and who, at Maud's flat in 1944, had suggested my working for the Resistance.

Since he was still a soldier—he had been a liaison officer between the Americans and French HQ—he had no Paris office. But as soon as he heard I was in Fresnes, he had returned, made inquiries of the examining magistrate who was preparing my dossier, and had been given permission to visit me.

The lawyers' visiting room was on the ground floor of the first-division block. We were shut in a cell together, without a guard listening, and the time allotted was from fifteen minutes to an hour, according to the importance of the case. I was glad to see Alain again. He told me of my family's fears for me when they had no news of me and wondered if I had disappeared for good. Then he listened to my story and, after a thoughtful silence, said, "If you appear as a former member of the Waffen SS, you'll find yourself before a military tribunal, and that would be dangerous. I'll try to have you dealt with by a court of justice. We'll have to emphasize your journalistic activities, which shouldn't be too difficult. I don't suppose there is anything very serious in your dossier, and I'll be surprised if you don't come out of it all right."

He had brought a carton of American cigarettes with him. I did not much like them, but they were useful as a means of exchange. The meeting reassured me and my morale soared. I was no longer alone and forgotten; now I had a real line of communication with the outside world. I had spoken to him of my family: "Alain, there's something on which I set great store. I don't want my father to come and see me in prison, ever. I don't want visits from my family; you understand that?"

"I understand."

"On the other hand, do you still see Maud?"

"Yes, she has started playing small parts in films. Perhaps she'll become a star. . . ."

"Well, if she hasn't completely forgotten me, I'd like you to get her a visitor's pass. I want to see a lovely woman's face; for me, that's the best way of regaining links with the past."

"All right, I'll try."

"And you think I'll get out of this mess?"

"Listen, let's be quite clear about it. The way sentences are being handed out, you'll get at least ten or fifteen years, but we'll manage something. It's only the very obvious cases who'll get a life sentence or the death penalty."

Ten or fifteen years. . . . I told myself I had a wonderful hope; after all, it was not going to be twenty, thirty years, life imprisonment, or the firing squad. . . . Those sentenced to death were isolated on the ground floor and one never saw them. But when they went out for their twice-daily exercise, we heard the clank of their chains. They reminded us of the proximity of death, destroying the cocoon in which each of us was wrapped.

For in prison one very quickly becomes concerned only with one's own case and uses it as a defense. Even before being examined by the magistrate one invites opinions on one's case and hangs on every word. The three of us in our cell went over the charges against us without letup. We tried out on each other the arguments that we thought would convince our interrogators, decided what was best left out and what emphasized. We kept accounts of those on whom we were relying for help. "I was of service to so-and-so and no doubt he'll testify in my favor."

One was forever imagining how one's trial would go and, as I discovered afterward, nine times out of ten one's expectations were based on illusion. It turns out one is cleared of what one supposed were the gravest charges, and the actions one thought trivial are those that count most against one. In fact, there was little possibility of us evaluating our real situations.

We tried, all the same, to obtain as much information as possible about what was going on outside. But we were still subject to the same regulations as the criminal prisoners and were not allowed to see any newspapers. What pieces of news reached us came by way of our lawyers; we repeated and compared them. But when all was said and done, the world we fabricated from them was a quite unreal one, woven of puerile hopes and unfounded fears. What sort of government was it on which our fate depended? The Communists were in power, which was not encouraging as they were the most merciless; luckily, though, it was being said that they would not remain for long. In any case, the Minister for Justice belonged to the MRP and was a certain M. Teitgeu; what sort of man was he? Some said he was fairly easy-going, while others asserted he was particularly severe. In short, we lived in a closed camp where imagination ran riot and sometimes produced a strange delirium.

Fresnes, however, was also a kind of fortress protecting us. In the beginning there had been tortures, and summary executions. Then the army had intervened and the Minister for Justice had insisted on the observance of the law, after which a certain order was imposed in which people like us knew more or less where they were. The place had its customs and its history. We heard how M. Renault had died there, of Sacha Guitry's stay there, and how Tino Rossi had sung "The Divine Child Is Born" in the prison chapel at Christmas, 1944.

I had to learn to integrate myself into the life of the prison. I was still wearing my English uniform and was fed up with that soldier's outfit. I was always being asked questions, but I was suspicious of spies: in prison one must know exactly to whom one is talking. I had asked Alain to get some of my civilian clothes from my family. Then, looking less conspicuous, I could blend into this very special social universe, which was like a barracks and, at the same time, an adult boarding school. There was, for instance, a disciplinary committee made up of guards, the deputy warden, and the warden. If you were foolish enough to criticize the prison administration in a letter, stupidly complaining about thefts from a package while it was being examined, and so on, you risked being deprived of mail for a time, sent to the hole, or, in the case of a first-division prisoner, being transferred to the second.

It was true that the warden had let punitive measures fall into disuse. Not a particularly sophisticated type, he nevertheless showed some understanding, and his staff, in general, behaved correctly. As for the screws, they were of all sorts; some were Communists who sent communications to the Communist newspaper *L'Humanité* about the prison and the conditions in which we lived. Most of them, though, could be bribed. Shortages were still severe, and, as outside, a black market flourished in Fresnes. They grew rich on these constant dealings to the point where the administration had to turn a blind eye. Some used their accumulated savings to buy houses in the suburbs or the small bistros they had long dreamed of.

Thus the screws constituted a fairly tolerant group, more inclined to exploit than to bully us. Discipline was not strict and we prisoners had not much trouble communicating with each other. This we did during exercise and, especially, in the room where packages were distributed.

These packages involved quite a ceremony. They were brought on carts pushed by prisoners wearing a uniform made of drugget[1]—minor offenders whom the prison authorities kept in Fresnes for general jobs rather than sending them to local prisons. The packages were distributed in alphabetical order, the guards taking them in turn and, in the presence of the recipient, cutting the string, opening, and emptying out the cartons.

We waited patiently to be called in, chattering together like people outside the church after Sunday Mass, while the screws became quite excited at the sight of the packages. I think that so much abundance made them envious. The prisoners' families were obviously making great sacrifices, but the prisoners them-

[1] The word *droguet* ("drugget") comes from *drogue* [1554], "a thing of poor quality." It indicated a brown uniform specially made for French prisoners.

selves worked the system to their best possible advantage. Each of them had the right to one package per week of a maximum weight of six and a half pounds. Now in certain cells there might be a fellow who was well off and two who were not; the former would tell his wife, "Here are the names and addresses of my cell mates; go and see their families and give them a package to send." So the occupants of the cell received nineteen pounds, from which they all benefited, for it was rare that the packages were not shared in common. Thus, with the addition of the prison rations, we lacked nothing, except sufficient exercise to whet our appetites. At the opening of the packages the screws applied the regulation sadistically; in any case it was an utterly stupid one: it was necessary to verify that no secret message was hidden in the food, or more especially a file or any instrument that could be used in an attempt to escape. As if, on any of the floors, with the catwalks, peepholes and the constant inspections, one had the leisure to bore a hole in the wall with a spoon and disappear into thin air. . . .

But that is how it was. A packet of sugar? It was all emptied out. A tin of condensed milk? Opened and scraped through from top to bottom. A packet of chocolate powder? Split with one slice of a knife. A nice dry piece of sausage? The same knife, powdered with chocolate, cut it in three. Of course, suspicion grew if any article was at all unusual. One day I was beside Benoist-Méchin (a member of the Vichy government) when he received a package from his mother, whom he adored. The guard opened it and took out a tea strainer. Frowning, he asked, "What is this for, Minister?" (At Fresnes, everyone was addressed by his former rank.)

"To pass the time, my friend."[2]

The infirmary was a much-sought-after meeting place. Two doctors worked in it, one of whom now has a practice in the north of France; the other, Willy Corbel, has become my friend. He belonged to the FTP, fought with them, cared for their wounded, and later continued to work as an army doctor. He was a big, strapping fellow, just under six feet tall, and weighing nearly 220 pounds. One saw him swinging his big frame along the catwalks from time to time, on his way to look after sick

[2] A play on the French word *passer*, which means both "to strain" and "to pass."

prisoners in their cells. And for those who wished to report sick, he had the knack of diagnosing an unknown complaint. He acted the part of a benign providence easing the lot of the prisoners.

I never ceased marveling at the incredible diversity of this world. It was made up of all kinds of people, not just the upper-crust military and ministerial lot, but there were also "economists," factory owners, writers and journalists, businessmen, and crooks, as well as carpenters, street sweepers, and taxi drivers. In short, a complete society, with its class levels and its internal trading, an example of what is now called a satellite society. In the end it became a showplace among prisons.

In the morning, when coffee was served, one saw elegant dressing gowns and silk pajamas side by side with simple night-shirts. The men would move forward with the careless ease of those just awakened; the guards tried to speed things up, but in a tone of perfect urbanity.

"Come on, gentlemen, please; we don't want to spend an hour giving you your breakfast. . . ."

At the exercise hour, all the cells were opened, but many of their inmates were exempted, preferring to stay where they were. The guards strolled about, visiting these prisoners, chatting with some of them.

"Tell me, Mr. Guard, do you like the Americans?"

The screw sneaks a glance to right and left and then takes a packet from his pocket. "Would you like a cup of tea?"

"Why not?"

The prisoner takes a small tablet of solidified alcohol, a new American invention, and places it in a socket under a small bottle and lights it. Thus we could always make a cup of tea or Nescafé.

Certain individuals had their servants, recruited from among the prisoners. To pay them they had packages sent to them or transferred money to their accounts. These servants made their masters' beds and cleaned their cells. And those exempted from exercise liked to entertain one another and had arranged for a lackey to wait on their guests, prepare tea and wash the cups; then, having performed his services, he in turn sipped his tea while smoking a cigarette, in his own corner.

Thus in the first division a kind of social life was led by people who were well known outside and who kept up their old habits. One discussed the events of the day, compared cases, exchanged civilities.

"You haven't received your Nescafé yet? Unbelievable! My

dear fellow, I've still got a tin, please take it . . . between friends. . . ."

The screws naturally tried to oblige the important prisoners. Sometimes I heard my door unbolted, and a guard was framed in it. "La Mazière."

"Yes."

"Come along."

I thought I might be taken to see a visitor, but no, it was simply that a factory owner ten cells away needed a fourth for bridge. . . . In such a fluid state of affairs, it was not long before one got to know everybody and to hear everything.

The most civilized and opulent cell, where there were rare commodities like Scotch whiskey and champagne, was certainly Georges Prade's. He had been a municipal counselor in Paris during the Occupation. His position and personal prestige had enabled him to get a large number of people out of German prisons and during those difficult years he had managed to go on living his ostentatious prewar kind of life, dining regularly in the best restaurants. The malicious called him Topaze.[3] He knew important men and got what he wanted. I wondered why he was still in prison. He talked to the warden as an equal, and I do not recall the latter ever once contradicting him. He seemed to have as much influence outside as inside the prison and could easily arrange the most complicated matters. He liked to render these services both because he was generous and because it pleased him to test his power.

It was he who indubitably set the tone; he was like a ballet master to the first division. Some claim, these days, to have suffered in Fresnes, but this was only true in the first months. L'Humanité was not mistaken when, in 1945, it called the place "Fresnes-la-Folie," something quite out of this world.

One day, when the packages were being given out, I met Robert Combemale again. He had belonged to the newspaper syndicate and had been manager of *Paris-Soir* in the Occupied Zone, which was why he was in prison. Blue-eyed, with graying temples, he had the elegance of an accomplished tennis player, a man of the world with exquisite manners.

"Christian! What are you doing here?"

[3] A reference to the hero of Marcel Pagnol's play *Topaze*, who, corrupted by racketeers, ends up the wealthiest crook of all.

I told him in a few words. He thought for a bit. "I think I can help you. I'm in charge of the library for the high court prisoners and I need a helper. I'll ask the warden if I can have you. I don't want to raise your hopes, but I'd really be delighted to have you as assistant."

The high court detainees had a more comprehensive library than that for the other prisoners, who, besides, could only take out one book per month, while there were almost daily withdrawals from the high court library. So I would be in contact with all those who during the previous four years had dominated French politics as spokesmen for the Germans. After my adventures in the east, where I had gone through the mill, I found it fascinating to meet those responsible for things, all the big shots.

I thought of nothing else for three or four days. My two cell mates shared my good spirits inasmuch as their own affair seemed to be working out well. They were in touch with their examining magistrate—something I had not yet achieved—a man of goodwill and understanding, and devoid of prejudice, although a Jew. They had sworn that they had never left the offices of the Todt Organization, never carried a gun, and had only worn uniform because they had belonged to the administrative sector. They had kept passing the ball from one to the other.

"Besides, you can ask my friend," they told the magistrate, each in turn. These two slum kids were like two fingers of one hand; brought up together in the rue Ravignan, they had played together in the same schoolyard, and no doubt had the same girls.

I could pretty well imagine what the magistrate must have felt about them. To sit in the court of justice, to have big game within his sights, to compile important dossiers, that must be interesting. But to cast his line for carp and to catch only two wretched minnows who kept repeating the same phrases did not inspire him with a desire to insist. "That's all right," he must have said to himself, "they've been in jail long enough awaiting trial, I'll compile their dossiers accordingly."

This is what they both thought; their lawyer—they had the same one, of course—had assured them it was all in the bag. Thus the three of us went on dreaming in a shared state of euphoria.

Two weeks went by without anything happening and we began to worry. I managed to get a message to Combemale, and in answer I had a visit from a screw bringing me a book. He indicated discreetly that it contained a message: "My dear friend, you know all about administrative delays as well as I do. But you need have no fear that, if I am allowed to select somebody for this new job, it will be you; I have no one else in mind. You have all my sympathy." It really sounded like a ministerial communication: "There is no cause for anxiety; I have not yet seen the President, who is very busy, but the matter of the dossier is progressing satisfactorily. . . ."

Finally the holdup came to an end, first for my two cell mates. The judge decided to dispose of their case, while, at the same time, playing a trick on them. "These two fellows," he probably said to himself, "are always together and are expecting to get out together. Well, I'll see that there's a delay of forty-eight hours between their releases." He had perhaps liked one of them better. One fine morning a guard entered the cell and said to the redhead, "Come on, pack up, you're free."

"But . . . my friend?"

"Sorry, there's nothing about him."

Consternation; for two days the one that was left was a figure of utter misery. I kept trying to raise his spirits. Then his turn came. He was overwhelmed. "Look, old fellow, I won't forget you."

And it was true. For a long time he wrote to me every week; he even managed to get a pass to visit me. Suddenly I was alone in the cell; but not for long. A little later, Robert Combemale arrived, accompanied by a guard. "My dear Christian, get your things together; I'm glad to be able to have you with me."

There it was: I was "assistant librarian"; I closed my small suitcase and followed the other two to the stairway. I felt I was climbing Parnassus.

We came to two communicating cells; one, the library, was lined with books; we would live in the other, where a mattress had been brought for me. Enthusiastically I unpacked, while Combemale told me what to do with my belongings. "Put your things there, old fellow, you can have this shelf for your toilet articles. . . ."

In this part of the prison the cell doors were opened at seven in the morning and were not closed until ten or eleven at night. It was wonderful. This floor was full of life; people visited each other, conversed, compared cases. Each had his own cell and saw his lawyer daily. There was no one in solitary confinement—this fate awaited Laval, but he had not yet arrived.

I spent my first evening here alone with Robert. We cleared a table of books, spread a cloth, and laid out the food; seated on chairs, we ate a very civilized meal. While we dined, I heard the latest gossip about the high court, who the prisoners destined for it were, and how to address them. And very soon, I would become familiar with this little society.

From the forty or so persons who were its components, cliques had soon formed, representing the opposing factions that had been active in the Vichy regime. There were Pétainists, followers of Darlan or of Laval, those, like Benoist-Méchin, who had believed in a more active collaboration. They treated each other with politeness, but this did not mean very much. Their rivalries impelled each one of them to study his neighbor's case, looking for evidence by which others could be accused of the charges made against himself.

Their respective backgrounds played a large part in these groupings. There were a number of men from the services, admirals in particular; no doubt de Gaulle had decided that since the fleet had been scuttled, they were of no further use. The most attractive of them was Admiral de Laborde, the French Nelson, as the English called him. I often saw him, white-haired, in informal attire to which he had pinned his medal ribbons, striding up and down the gangways with his sailor's roll; he could still imagine himself on the bridge of his flagship. Imprisonment seemed to have given him the energy of a young cabinboy; every morning, on his knees, he holystoned the floor of his cell with a bit of glass from a broken bottle under the surprised glances of the "ministers" who passed by. It had become as clean as a monk's.

General Jacques Bridoux, War Minister at Vichy and cavalry officer, was also up early, anxious to stretch his legs. He was a friendly person, beaming and easygoing, with the sharp voice of the riding school.

I also came across a lot of former highly placed civil servants. One of the strangest was René Bousquet, ex–Secretary General of the Police, today one of the directors of the Bank of Indochina. The others were somewhat reserved toward him. As he had been deported by the Germans in 1944, they did not consider him as being in the same boat.

Besides, the Germans had never found him very pliant; many stories were told about him, which he did not deny because they amused him. At a time when he was one of the youngest prefects of police in France, it was said, for instance, a noncommissioned German officer had been killed in the occupied district for which he was responsible. Ten hostages were at once arrested and the Germans went to the Prefecture. "You've twenty-four hours in which to find those responsible; otherwise ten hostages will be shot."

Bousquet, very worried, discussed it with his staff, and suddenly he had an idea: "There's a mental clinic quite close. Have a predated notice sent to all police stations about an escape by one of the patients. Then get hold of one of the hospital inmates who can play the part right."

The orders were carried out. Police and clinic director were advised of the situation, a subject was found, and several hours before the deadline, Bousquet telephoned the Kommandantur: "We've solved the crime, and the culprit, escaped from the local asylum, has been arrested."

The Germans insisted on seeing him, tried to interrogate him, but of course the wretched creature appeared to understand nothing of what he was being asked. Finally they decided to shoot him. Then Bousquet stood up. "You can't arrest a madman, let alone try him, and to shoot him is completely out of the question. You would only discredit yourselves in the eyes of the French population."

This was in the early days of the Occupation, when the Germans were still very concerned about their image. They gave in, and once they were gone, it appeared that the madman came to Bousquet and told him, "You, at least, Monsieur Prefect, aren't a fool."

I was often visited by Jacques Benoist-Méchin, one of the library's most constant clients. He was equally at home reading works in German, English, or French and had a lot of books sent him, as he kept up his studies and writing. He was a highly cultured man and his advice was widely sought. I listened to him whenever I had the chance. I was deeply interested to hear of his first meeting with Hitler in the company of Admiral Darlan. He had, in fact, entered the world of politics by accident and had nothing of the professional politician about him as had the other ex-ministers in Fresnes.

The high court section of the first division on the fourth floor represented the top level of officialdom. But this whole division was of a high intellectual standard, as I discovered by taking advantage of the freedom I had there. For instance, there was the scientist Georges Claude in the basement. Very old and deaf as a post, he continued his work with rudimentary instruments that would have upset lesser research workers. He had also started experimenting with a miniature indoor tillage farm, using a small space allotted him, and had harvested three crops of corn.

On the third floor were the "economic" collaborators, whom one heard less about, those who had helped in the building of the Atlantic Wall or whose factories had made goods for export to Germany. There were also a number of crooks who had worked for the Gestapo. It was thanks to their financial abilities that these last were there: their organizations on the outside continued to prosper and they to profit from them. I found out about these gangster-novel types at the same time as Albert Simonin, who was a fellow prisoner of theirs, and who met in Fresnes models for some of his future characters.

The screws showed great consideration to these gangsters, who bribed them generously, and, what is more, had a deep admiration for them. The members of the first division, with the exception of a few, were the kind of people the guards were not used to, especially the intellectuals, whom they disliked instinctively and treated with scant politeness. As for the former generals and ministers, their impressive titles made them feel ill at ease. With the gangsters, on the other hand, there was a natural union, as of organisms living off each other.

I recall one of those fellows, called Gorari. He had a strong Corsican accent and wore the latest style in suits: a long, close-fitting jacket with narrow shoulders, double-breasted with two buttons, plenty of shirt cuffs showing, tight trousers ending well above thick-soled shoes, tightly-knotted polka-dotted tie, kept in place by a tiepin.

He spent the time playing poker. One day I passed his cell—he had got permission to keep it open like the high court people—and he had enlisted for his partner a young screw who had just entered the prison service. He generally played for money, but with this screw he wagered for the guy's mustache, a Clark Gable type of which the idiot seemed very proud. He said to the kid, "You'll see, kid, you'll lose every one of those hairs as we proceed."

The boy found this very funny and took up the challenge. After a couple of hours I came back to see how things were going. Gorari was busy keeping score; then he raised his head: "Well, kid, you've lost half your mustache."

The young screw laughed and got up. "All right, I'll go and shave myself."

Gorari stopped him. "I said, half your mustache."

The boy was startled. "What? That's impossible!"

Then Gorari stared at him and, raising his index finger, said in an ominously calm voice, "Go and shave off half your mustache. If you shave it all off, I'll tell my gang and the first time you set foot outside the prison, you'll be liquidated."

The screw grew pale. He went away and next day became a butt for ridicule with his half mustache. His pals were convulsed with laughter, but a sergeant appeared, took a look at him and asked, "What's this, you wanted to shave off your mustache and forgot half?"

"Well, yes, in fact . . ."

"Ridiculous. Somebody'll take your place while you go and finish the job."

"No, no. . . ."

He was in a terrible sweat. He could not admit that he had played cards with Gorari and confess to the stakes he had agreed to. On the other hand, he believed that if he reappeared completely clean-shaven he was as good as dead. The upshot was that he was forced to hand in his resignation.

In my library I received guests. The mornings were spent by Combemale and me collecting the requests for books; during the rest of the day we had visitors and kept a tea kettle permanently on the boil. Some got through a book a day, it did not matter what, merely to keep their minds occupied.

Fresnes itself had only a few books, collected some years previously for the use of the convicts. The Minister of Justice had no allocation of funds to purchase them and at that time there were no cheap paperback series. So the authorities had allowed books to be brought for the prisoners without these being counted as part of their package allowance. There was, however, one condition: the books became prison property. Thus Robert had managed to fill the cell in a short time and the happy faces multiplied.

The collection was quite a varied one—works on economy and history, and books by the new French writers who had come to the fore in the last months. But the classics predominated: Châteaubriand, Balzac, Proust. . . . Thanks to the collaborators, the Fresnes library today must be still one of the best in our penitentiary world. Of course, there were plenty of lacunae, as the censor kept a lookout for anything subversive. For instance, Plato's[4] dialogues had been confiscated, because there had been an Admiral Platon in the Vichy government.

Newspapers were strictly prohibited. But by means of the substantial sums paid over by the relatives of some prisoners, many guards brought them in on the sly, along with letters and cigarettes. Some also slipped in by way of the lawyers, and the separated pages circulated from cell to cell.

Certain detainees watched the political situation in the hope of a change favorable to them; most studied the articles that had a bearing on their own cases. What disturbed us were press campaigns such as those in *L'Humanité* that constantly developed the theme of the "corruption at Fresnes." What should be done with these people? And the gist of the argument was, why, instead of these people being tried, were they able to lead lives of debauchery? Those whose trials were approaching feared these outbursts; they did not want public opinion and, consequently, juries, to be thus incensed against them.

Truth and gross distortion alternated in these papers. I read, for instance, that to obtain such a job as mine, one had to pay an incredible sum, equal to a million old francs. I happened to be in a position to evaluate this statement for what it was worth.

On the other hand, I would not deny that I lived a pleasant life, almost as if free: the job was interesting and easy, the system under which we lived was flexible, the food healthy—I do not speak, of course, of the prison diet, which was mediocre in the extreme, but of what we could buy in the canteen, receive in packages, or procure with the help of the prison functionaries. Thus in the morning the baker appeared, his small cap on his head, and brought us fresh rolls hidden under his smock. In exchange we gave him cigarettes or had money transferred to his account outside. And if we did not want anything disagreeable to happen, such as the shock of transfer to another division, we had to keep our promises.

Time passed uneventfully, but meals, reading, small duties such as I performed were not sufficient to fill it; there remained

[4] Plato is Platon in French.

talking and dreaming. On the fourth floor especially, since the doors remained open, there was an enormous expenditure of words.

The pre-trial investigations naturally headed the list of subjects discussed. The lawyers gave their clients a copy of their file. I saw high court prisoners carrying theirs, as big as those of a minister actually in office, in their arms, and was full of admiration. All had only one idea: to delay, to drag out the time. They told themselves that new institutions were going to replace the present setup and that in the new republic they would have a better chance of getting off lightly. Brasillach's execution obsessed them; he had been the victim of speedy justice and nothing could have saved him, not even a petition signed by the most illustrious artists and writers. He had not been allowed more than two or three examination sessions, while now even those with the less serious charges against them were summoned to at least fifteen interrogations.

The economic collaborators were less concerned, knowing that they did not risk execution, that the worst that could happen to them was to be forced to repay millions and millions of francs. But during the war many of them had amassed incredible sums while living sumptuously, and they could afford these fines.

All the same, waiting for the trial to start caused each prisoner an insidious anxiety, and in order to exorcise it we would often think up imaginary menus. I never knew food to play so important a part as it does in prison. Those who formerly made a business of being gourmets or simply liked good food evoked, in the idleness of their cells, the memory of what their mother had cooked for them, what their wife had prepared, that marvelous, slowly simmered dish to which, before the war, women had time to devote themselves. And I have seen guys recall with a haunting precision recipes that they had heard absentmindedly, rediscovering, as they talked, a traditional Auvergne stew, without forgetting the smallest ingredient, and, in addition, reincarnate its smell and how it tasted. Out of all the recipes that the prisoners recollected, one could have compiled fantastic cook books.

And then there were women. They were our chief lack and therefore our main torment, faced with which even the most self-controlled betrayed themselves.

Some prisoners, who were sure of themselves, of their love, or simply unconcerned, never doubted a wife's fidelity, expecting her to wait for them like a sailor's wife, no matter how long. Others, less self-assured, tried to persuade themselves. And there were the tormented, the sufferers who spent whole nights on their beds asking themselves, "But what can she do? Pretty as she is, she can't be expected to remain alone. . . ." Then when she came to see him, the entire visit would be squandered in quarreling because, instead of sleeping, he had been ruminating over old jealousies.

I was often visited in my library by guys from other floors who only came to pour out their hearts to me. Many knew of their misfortune; some, who had grown rich on the Germans, heard that their wives had gone off with the loot. To evade taxes, orders of restraint or fines—at this period the state was making every effort to refeather its nest—they had, by means of predated documents, transferred the greater part of their assets to their wives. And the wives, once the deed was signed and sealed, made it known that they were seeking a divorce. So the poor fellows suddenly found themselves once more without a sou; and there was a certain justice in their having no possibility of help from the law.

On the other hand, there were cases of remarkable faithfulness. Edouard Bonnefous, for instance, a former minister in the Vichy government, had Gaby Morlay as his beloved. She wrote to him daily, never missed a visit or forgot to send a package. If she was acting on tour, she sent somebody in her place, and when Bonnefous was freed they married.

Whether faithful or not, however, a woman no longer seemed like a real person in this society of men, closed in on itself, nor for that matter did most of the people in our lives. Absence induces the memory to oversimplify, and some people become absolutely extraordinary; others, devoid of qualities, still others, bastards to be done away with on the spot.

And, in the same way, those faces of women that prisoners pin to the walls of their cells do not represent anything but a kind of myth. The ugliest are adorned with all the virtues, the most stupid with every subtlety. They are the last refuge, protectresses from pain and sorrow, those on whom one sets one's hope, much more than on one's family. For it is natural to count on one's relatives, but a woman's love is fragile and miraculous: it seems something that one can count on and be in awe of at the same time. Even the cynics who imagine a thousand betrayals and like to describe them are in reality only seeking to exorcise the fear within them.

Thus, at eight of an evening, when all the lights were put out, Fresnes was transformed into a huge dream factory. This hour of nightfall, when nothing shines but the beams from the nightlights of the screws through the peepholes to check that the prisoner is on his mattress—the aperture opens, there is a knock on the door, from under the covers one must give a sign to show that one is there. Before sinking into the first sleep is the time of greatest vulnerability, when all the love and sorrow that a man has in him is released.

Combemale and I were allowed to keep the light on until eleven o'clock. We read when we wanted to; but often, after drinking our coffee, we launched into long conversations, bringing events from the past back to life.

I often think of our low-voiced dialogue, in the dim light of our cell and surrounded by the great prison silence. The guards' footsteps and the jingles of keys were smothered in it. At regular intervals the nightlight shone gently through the aperture and glided over the opposite wall.

It was through women that we had entered into each other's lives. There was nothing common or vulgar, nor, I hope, any smugness in our attitude. We needed to evoke these women and girls, as children who have no mother and as men whose desire cannot be stilled in another body. I talked of the girls I had known, idealizing them so much that when I saw them again I could no longer understand how I could have felt about them as I had in telling of them.

Robert talked about his wife, Hélène, and it was as if she was there with us. There were two photos of her in the cell. In one she was playing tennis, bare-legged in a short, pleated skirt; she seemed real and alive. I met her later, and she was altogether as charming as Robert had told me. For once, absence had not added anything that was not already there. And if, since then, I have always felt a deep tenderness for her it is because she resembles the creatures of my dreams more closely than those who instigated them.

For me, moreover, through the magic that was created when Robert evoked her, she ended by eclipsing the women I had known; and I only found some attraction in those in whom I saw some resemblance to her. Hélène shared our life, embodied our friendship, became our constant source of reference. She set a standard to which we deferred in everything we did, read, even ate: "Would Hélène like this?" I would ask Robert. "Have you written to Hélène and told her about . . . ?" I'd mention some incident in our daily lives. "No, I didn't think of it, but I shall in my next letter." She came to us as in the André Gide novel *Les Nourritures Terrestres,* "at that hour of the night when one has opened and then closed one book after another."

I do not think I shall ever forget those great prison moments, that intensity of feeling born of a kind of complicity between us, of our secret life together. Of all the favors granted us by the administration, this perhaps was the most unusual: "always three, never two, bad luck to the solitary one." Such is the prison precept, as it is in Jesuit colleges, which Rebatet rendered in a notebook that I still keep: "With the same stones go the same habits."

Among all these people waiting to appear before the high court I found myself in a very different sort of world from that I had come from. It was one that surprised me, and I frequently asked myself what had become of the people I had known. I was also anxious to meet again those whose destiny seemed to have some similarity to mine.

Shortly after my arrival, during one of the package distributions, I heard that Bassompierre had escaped from the Russians. He had actually managed to cross occupied Germany, get to Italy, and hide in a monastery there. He had been on the point of going to Argentina, when he got himself captured in the stupidest possible fashion. It happened in Naples, as the ship was about to leave. He stepped onto the gangway, his bundle on his shoulder. But to two men from the military police who were watching there seemed something unusual about him. Somewhat at random, one of them shouted, "Hi there, Bassompierre!"

Instinctively, he turned around. The men made a sign to him. Bassompierre thought that it was someone in the same fix as himself, who was also using this escape route. He turned back and was nabbed.

Not long after I had settled in on the fourth floor I received a note from Roger Pingeault, who had just been imprisoned in the second division. I immediately arranged to go and see him.

It was he all right, with his thick glasses, his shock of hair, his withered ear.

"Don't say you're here too! But seriously, I thought you'd managed things all right."

And it was true that he had at first cleared himself, having succeeded, in August, 1944, in rejoining the FTP, and with that, the Communist party. As he had journalistic abilities, the Party had given him a job on one of their rags, where he had gone from collaboration over to the extreme Left without the slightest intellectual scruple: "O.K.," he told himself, "Fascism is finished, and in order to demolish the capitalist system, there's nothing left but Communism." He was like a fish in water in his new job.

One day, however, a ridiculous arrest warrant had ruined everything: indications of his associations with *Le Pays Libre* had been dug up and the cops came to his apartment for him. It was a nasty shock, but even more so for the Party, who discovered at one and the same time that the fiery militant had been both a defrocked clerical student and a former "collabo," as they were then called.

He took his misfortunes in his customary philosophic fashion. He was glad to see me again, and I gave him a brief account of my own story. I asked him about Maud, about Paris after I had left it. And we had the feeling of having told each other almost everything.

I offered to give evidence in his favor. He agreed, and I was taken twice to appear before the magistrate dealing with his case. I swore that I had asked him to join *Le Pays Libre,* whose attitudes were not his, that he had become a temporary journalist through my influence, that I had practically forced him to follow me to Normandy. My dossier was already fuller than his and any new liabilities that I shouldered would not greatly add to it.

I saw him from time to time. Then one day I received a letter in his small, incisive handwriting. It came from outside; he had got his case dropped. The Party had also dropped him from its lists, and he was looking for a job.

It was then discovered that his lungs were completely eaten away; he was sent to the mountains at Assy, where he remained till his death. Having wanted to experience a series of great intellectual adventures, he died in this banal fashion, in a ward with others, among his books.

I also came across some guys who, like me, had been in the Waffen SS. Bernard Laignoux from the South, was one. He had had close contacts with Noël de Tissot, had taken part in the terrible battles the Storm Brigade had fought, but had never joined the Charlemagne. Also the brothers B——, one of whom is now prominent in film circles. They had been in the Charlemagne but had not seen combat, having remained at the base at Greifenberg. They looked amazingly youthful and I think this had been a help to them. The examining magistrate, though well known at the time for his severity, must have thought that in the dock these two members of the SS would look like a couple of kids, which would be ridiculous. He had preferred to drop the case, and the brothers heard no more of it.

The high court prison library proved a veritable listening post. I should mention that the first division was an anteroom to the other two, where all the important people were first booked, even if later they were sent elsewhere. Thus it was that we witnessed the arrival of our first member of the Resistance, the hero of *The Battle of the Railroads*, René Hardy, a man whose appearance suggested strength of character and dignity. I only saw him two or three times, in fact. Among us, he felt in an alien world and kept himself apart. As for the "collabos," they had nothing to teach him.

His peers accused him of having betrayed his Resistance network to the Germans, a charge that was never proved, and his presence in Fresnes gave rise to all kinds of discussions about torture and its effect. This was an ever-present subject to us. It must not be forgotten that the French police used torture, if only casually rather than methodically; or that at the Liberation, the FFI[5] and FTP indulged in it to their hearts' content. The places where torture and summary executions had taken place were engraved in all our minds and, taken together, constituted a legend that in some respects equaled that of the Gestapo in the domain of horror.

Some among us had given information without even being tortured, others had remained silent in spite of the pain. Had we, in the name of these last, the right to condemn the former? I often discussed this with Benoist-Méchin and we agreed that there was no final answer.

The most extraordinary person, however, that I ever met is one whose name I cannot now recall. One day our medico Willy Corbel told me, "I've a remarkable case that you should come and see."

I followed him to the infirmary, where a strange-looking

[5] Forces Françaises de l'Intérieur: Resistance Forces inside France.

individual, strong and fairly tall, was sitting. His skin was tanned and I sensed that his face had been transformed. His eyes were dull and the lids so heavy that only the narrowest look came through; his slitlike eyes increased his resemblance to a Mongolian. "Take a good look at him," said Corbel. "I asked him if I could take some photos; it's an astonishing case of physical mimesis."

This fellow had fought in the Storm Brigade. Before that, he told us in awkward French, he had worked in a Paris bakery. During the fighting in July, 1944, he had been taken prisoner by the Russians. He was lucky not to have been shot and, instead, had been sent to a camp in Siberia with German prisoners.

After spending some weeks there, he had taken advantage of the good weather to escape. He had wandered through forests as large as continents, managing somehow or other to orientate himself.

"I'm not going to return to the West," he told himself, "above all, I mustn't get lost in the far north; let's go east, or, better, southeast."

He walked for months and months, sleeping in the forest, pilfering food from the outskirts of villages, running away when he was seen. His power of speech became atrophied, and he almost turned into an animal. Without being aware of the fact, he reached Outer Mongolia. One evening, venturing out to look for food, he ran into some passing nomads who seized him. It was impossible to communicate with them; he spoke only French and a little German, but he was treated with great kindness. They gave him clothing and kept him with them.

They turned out to be a tribe that lived in a state of semi-rebellion, attacking Soviet convoys, pillaging and killing. So, in their company, he continued his war against the "Ivans." Like the others, he had his little horse and began to learn their language. Every day he grew more like these Mongolians; only his greater height distinguished him from them.

He lived through the long Siberian winter clothed in animal skins. He married a woman who came from an important Mongolian family. A feast was held to celebrate the occasion and he was given a tent of his own, where his wife waited on him and did the cooking.

Then came spring and the end of the war. The "Ivans" decided to clean up these intractable tribes. The Mongolians ran into an important motorized Red Army unit on its way to China;

it was the time when the Russians were preparing to join in the war against Japan.

An ambush had been laid for them and they fell into it, but they fought like lions. Our friend was wounded and taken prisoner. He was interrogated and, of course, the Russians did not believe that he was French. Then, in their own leisurely way, they found his name on a list from the camp from which he had escaped. He had been repatriated to France with some Alsatian prisoners, the famous *Malgré Nous*[6] brigade. That was how he came to Fresnes, preceded by a long account of his story from the Russians.

He had indeed fascinated us. I know that Fresnes was then an incredible caldron in which the most diverse people, with the most varied outlooks and the most fantastic backgrounds, were mingled. But in this case the unusual went even beyond the wide spectrum of political prisoners. Very soon the guy returned to his baking, but I doubt, after what he had been through, if he was content to remain at the kneading trough. He was the type more likely to enlist for Indochina in order to return, even if in different latitude, to the Asia for which he was homesick.

His examination was quickly dispatched and he was acquitted by the Military Tribunal. I told myself that my own adventures were not sufficiently exotic for my case to be settled so satisfactorily. I had to begin thinking of myself now, and very seriously.

[6] "Against-our-wills," an expression that came to signify those French forced into German service.

IX.
THE HOUR OF
TRUTH

It was not long after being appointed as librarian that I was summoned for the first time to appear before the examining magistrate. Up to then all I had had was a copy of my commitment order and a preliminary report that Alain Ballot typed for me. Now the fateful hour had arrived.

The prisoners were still asleep, it was dawn. An interim release order was made out and my departure entered in the book. In order to make myself presentable, my tie and some other accessories were given back to me. Then, with a few other prisoners, I got into a police van. We arrived at the Palais de Justice on the stroke of nine and then the waiting started.

I sat on a wooden bench, handcuffs on my wrists, guarded by a policeman whose duty was to lead me through the maze of corridors and staircases. The time dragged; sometimes one was kept cooling one's heels for three hours. I watched the lawyers moving about in their robes in a kind of ballet, or motionless as they stood talking to each other. Witnesses passed on their way to and from the courts. The animated scene was like a tiny breath of freedom.

Finally I was taken to the judge's gloomy, old-fashioned office whose windows looked as if they had never been cleaned. A lot of dossiers roughly tied up were piled in disorder on law books. The place reeked of parsimony: no proper files in which to keep the loose sheets, the only typewriter an ancient Remington with a bell that clanged and a carriage that rasped, and, behind it, a decrepit clerk of the court.

The judge, in a magnanimous gesture, gave the order: "Gendarme, remove the handcuffs."

He was soberly and impeccably dressed, and he made me sit in an armchair opposite him. Beside it but slightly farther back was another for counsel, in which Alain Ballot sat. They knew each other already, having met twice. I answered questions as to my identity, which is the prelude to all examinations.

The judge then turned immediately to the subject of the charge: my articles in *Le Pays Libre,* a collaborationist activity, but not a particularly precise one. He asked, "But what did you really do in Germany?" This was naturally a question I had discussed at length with Alain, who had advised me to stick to what I had told the Russians: that I was a reporter with the Charlemagne, attached to the Propaganda Kommandos. I therefore answered on these lines and the judge made a note. "Very well. I shall have to make a thorough inquiry, for which I am getting a report from the Soviet authorities. You'll be brought here every week as your case proceeds."

The whole interview took place in an atmosphere of politeness and ease. I met this judge on about fifteen occasions, in all for a total of nearly thirty hours, and during that time he showed an increasing understanding of my situation. Alain, who was still in service and stationed outside Paris, could not always be present. He had wanted on these occasions to send a colleague from Isorni's office[1] as a substitute, but the judge had quickly told him, "This is going very well. There's no need to have somebody else as a replacement. If any particular problems arise, I shall let you know."

In any case, the lawyer has very little to do at these examinations (unless he happens to be a famous counsel who knows the

[1] Isorni was a famous French lawyer of the time, who specialized in defending former Vichy and collaborationist people.

judge well) except to reorientate the interview with a word here and there and keep his client to the point when he is going off on a tangent. It was quite a new little game that I was learning with some amusement.

In his corner the clerk of the court, a regular typing-machine, dozed over his Remington, only rousing himself when addressed by the judge, to continue making five copies of what I said: one for the examining judge, one for counsel, one for the prosecution, and one for the president of the court of justice. . . . Then I signed my name at the end and initialed the bottom of each page when there were several. The judge told me, "Take your time; read it through and make any necessary changes."

He himself sometimes tightened up phrases that could be wrongly interpreted to my disadvantage. "I don't think this exactly expresses what you want to say. Surely this would be better. . . ."

He ended by getting to know me quite well, and a certain friendliness was established between us. Not that mine was one of the important cases of his life; on the contrary, I felt that he was overwhelmed by a mass of more serious ones. But mine interested him and he honestly tried to clarify it. As was his duty, he made inquiries in my native province as to my moral standing there, and the police sent him favorable reports. He was impressed by this and did not really attempt to look for witnesses for the prosecution.

The examination need not have taken long, but he was obviously prolonging it. Sometimes he made me go back over some statement in one of my editorials, which, read by three thousand people at most, had not made a very serious contribution to the fight against de Gaulle. But he obviously wished to get everything clear. Finally, we began to exchange general ideas, while discussing books we had read.

Thus I spent some surprising hours with him. Then one fine day he completed my dossier.

"My job is done, and I'm rather sorry because I don't suppose we shall meet again. I'm glad to have come across you, and now I'm going to make a summary of the case. I can tell you it won't be unfavorable. And good luck!"

And suddenly the anxiety that these hours with the examining magistrate had almost dissipated returned. However, now I had to wait until the government prosecutor took up the case and the president of the Chamber fixed a date for the hearing. Once more, I was alone. My case might not seem all that serious, but the court would be approaching it from a different angle. How would it react?

Alain, as I have said, had arranged for me to be brought before the court of justice, thus avoiding the military tribunal to which my activity in the Waffen SS would normally have brought me and which, of the two courts, was the one we feared more. To us it was a court that never compromised, whose judgments were based on the military sense of honor, tradition, patriotism— all of which were strictly interpreted—and that could send one directly to the firing squad. The courts of justice, we supposed, were primarily concerned with the big fish, while the smaller fry had a good chance of getting off lightly.

Ironically enough, this piece of what seemed shrewd reasoning might have cost me a great deal, for it was totally wrong. I later saw that it was the military tribunals that had handed out the lightest sentences of any of the special courts of the period. Those who had worn the German uniform appeared before officers whose background enabled them to understand the attitude of these accused because they shared their anti-Communist feelings. There were comrades of mine in the Waffen SS who were quite simply acquitted or whose sentences were equivalent to the time they had already spent in custody awaiting trial, which counted as double, as had the time spent in Russian camps during the war.

I think my examining magistrate had guessed my true story but had prepared my dossier to substantiate the one I wished to have accepted.

To begin with, in going back over my past, he had emphasized the fact that in 1939, when I was a student pilot, I had volunteered to go and fight on the side of the Finns. There was a tendency to forget this war that Marshal Mannerheim had conducted against the Russians while the latter were about to divide up Poland with their German allies. Finland, at that time, was very popular in France and there had been a considerable number of recruits to fight for her, particularly in the air force. In spite of my not having completed a sufficient number of flying hours, I would undoubtedly have been accepted. I had told myself at the time that I could complete my training over there and become an accomplished fighter-pilot. Then the defeat had crushed those hopes, whose only souvenir was a letter of thanks from the Finnish government and a proposal to give me a decoration.

The judge had adroitly allied these facts to the general continuity of my political thinking, which, after being formed under the influence of Maurras in the Young Royalist Movement, had led me, at the time of the Spanish Civil War, into the circle of Jacques Doriot, at that time mayor of the working-class Paris suburb of Saint-Denis. Doriot had come from the Communist party, from which he had made a spectacular break, snatching the Saint-Denis district out of its grip. But he was distinguished from the traditional right-wing supporters by his revolutionary ideology and unreserved hostility to capitalism, which was what especially impressed me. Many workers had followed him, as well as a number with right-wing affiliations. He managed to win over intellectuals, including some prominent persons at the Sorbonne, better than did the Communists, whose main catch was Malraux. My need for action, which impelled me to fight for my ideas, and which, as far as the cause of Finland was concerned, weighed in my favor, was part of my logical development, which my examining judge deemed proper to consider objectively.

Finally, alongside my work on *Le Pays Libre,* he underlined the liaison role I had played in 1944 between, on the one hand, the civil population made homeless by the Allied landings and, on the other, the Ministry of the Interior and President Laval. I had worked with the prefects and the bishop of Rouen, Mgr. Petit de Julleville. It was essential to provide help for those in distress or who had already been turned out on the roads. It was necessary to ensure that they managed to live with the least suffering possible, that they were fed and given instructions about what to do. The paper that I was assigned to start, when I went to Normandy with Pingeault and Bauer, was part of this effort and had had no political slant. I had been nothing more than a kind of state agent, a fact confirmed by witnesses during the examination.

Naturally, at the time, I did not know about this interpretation of my case, but I did realize that for the first time since I was back in France a real dialogue with the world of the judiciary had been established, the other system to which, sooner or later, an accounting had to be rendered. This was for me something even more important than the contact with my lawyer, so I sank back into a rather melancholy frame of mind when, at the close of my examination, I was back in my cell.

Combemale, with his customary sensitivity, did his best to dissipate my anxiety. I also had Maud, whom I had found again. This was something I owed to my judge, who alone had the power to issue permits for visits and who had acceded to Alain's request in my name, although normally only visits from close relatives were authorized. The ordinary prisoners had no difficulty in getting permission for visits from their mistresses, a relationship that is almost institutional in their world. But in the eyes of the prison administration the politicals practiced a stricter morality.

As I have mentioned, I insisted on not being visited by my family. Alain Ballot told them of my feelings in this respect, and in my letters home I tried to explain my position. With his deep emotional intelligence, my father fully understood that I wished to spare him the humiliation of seeing me behind bars. And since he too had not been spared a similar indignity, he knew how I would feel about it.

He had, in fact, been under house arrest for a year, and at the Liberation the FFI had even made an attempt on his life because of his Pétainism. For a very short period he had held a military post in the Marshal's cabinet. He had then returned to his native Touraine, where he became regional head of the Legion, an association of veterans devoted to Pétain. Besides their cult of the Victor of Verdun and their activities, which were similar to church leagues and the Boy Scouts—holding ceremonies at monuments to the dead, keeping contacts with prisoners of war in Germany—they kept alive a traditional nationalism.

This kind of ancient chivalry ideally suited my father's temperament. He had fought stubbornly in 1940, resisting to the last at the head of his battalion. The Germans had finally taken him and his men prisoner three days after the signing of the Armistice; but he had been freed and allowed to return to the Unoccupied Zone with his weapons and equipment after being accorded military honors. That fact had a profound psychological effect on him; no wonder he had subscribed to the policy of Montoire, which included a belief in the possibility of holding a dialogue with the enemy while remaining completely loyal to France.

Besides which, in 1940 almost the entire army had rallied to the Vichy government behind Generals Weygand and Huntziger —Father knew the latter—as well as General de la Laurencie, one of the negotiators of the Armistice whom Father had known as a young man and whose adjutant he had been at Saumur. For the soldiers in the old tradition, de Gaulle was only a general with a provisional rank given him because of his membership in Reynaud's government, in other words, for political reasons.

With the establishment of the Pétain regime, these traditionalists returned to their old dream of a professional army. The Germans had authorized an army of a hundred and fifty thousand men, a very great advance on the number permitted by the Allies to Germany in 1918. And the French militarists wanted to do precisely what Germany had done after the First World War: take advantage of the terms of the Armistice to rebuild the army and its morale so that it would be capable of taking the country in hand. As well as this force, there was a superb navy still intact, and also a number of aircraft, and although the time they could spend in the air was strictly limited, nevertheless they were well maintained. The soldiers, who had all volunteered for three years' service, could at last be treated seriously, subjected to an iron discipline without any fear of a deputy making a fuss because of the voters who were their parents.

Thus Vichy had reanimated that traditional waltz in which well-polished leather puttees and the latest Saumur riding boots gamboled. In its first years the regime had danced to this tune, carrying along most of the French people who were inspired by its dictums, such as, "I hate the lies that have done us so much harm," etc.

My father, however, ended up by removing himself from these military circles and withdrawing into himself to examine his illusions. For my part, I was also taking stock of mine, and we still needed, before meeting, a little more silence. So I had not yet seen him.

Despite my formal request, my sister, on the other hand, did not act on it. I did not yet know that she had put herself to great trouble on my behalf with that natural impetuosity of hers that had made her take the destinies of the family in hand and caused us to call her "the baroness." Her husband was a surgeon who had been captured by the Germans while attached to a Senegalese regiment. Sent to Le Cateau-Cambrésis, where no sanitary corps remained, he had practiced his profession with wholehearted devotion. He had later been set free in recognition of his services and had gone to live in the Unoccupied Zone.

Attracted for a time to the Vichy regime, he had fairly

quickly turned toward the Resistance, with which he had preserved friendly links. In addition, one of his high school friends had become director general of prisons and he was thus in a position to help me. My sister was relying on him as well as on a Paris attorney who was a friend of the family.

The "baroness's" idea, which she wanted to impose on me, was to present me as deranged. In contrast to my examining magistrate, she considered the fact that I had enlisted in the air force, had wanted to become a pilot, and had volunteered to fight in Finland proved that I was absolutely cracked. She was making inquiries along these lines and had been told that because of my brother-in-law's influence, I could undergo a medical examination that would reveal a brain injury or, at the very least, an unfortunate mental condition, due to all I had been through. Without further ado my case would be dropped—a madman cannot be tried—and I would thus escape a shameful sentence. I would be put in a mental clinic from which I would quietly emerge after some months; that at least was what she was told.

She had asked for permission to visit me to tell me of her plan, and one fine day I was called to the visiting room. Delighted, I expected to see Maud, but instead was confronted with my sister. When the door of the tiny room was opened and I saw her through the grille I was petrified.

"I asked you not to come!" Then, with much affection, she tried to explain why she was there. Poor woman, she was not prepared for my reaction. I was humiliated and furious. I would have preferred a dozen bullets in my hide to the thought that, later, I would be pointed to with the words "There's the madman." Infinitely better: "There's the criminal!" It was as if she wanted to be sure of killing me.

To top everything, she added, "But, you know, according to my information, it's going to be bad for you; you'll get the death sentence. Isn't it better to spend a couple of years in a psychiatric institution and then be free?"

The upshot was it ended badly, with my knocking on the door for the screw to come and open it for me—the stupid fellow was walking back and forth outside, trying to listen to what was being said and seeing that nothing changed hands—and I had myself led away before the end of the time, leaving my sister really furious.

Both Combemale and Alain had laughed heartily when I told them what kind of stupid farce I was to have figured in as hero. The days passed and I forgot the incident, continuing my quiet routine as prison librarian.

And then one morning I was called to the office. I went down and was handed a piece of paper. My hand trembled slightly as I took it. I was summoned for May 7 and 8, 1946, to appear in court 12 of the court of justice, in which the presiding judge would be Didier. Next day Alain confirmed the date.

"In my opinion, you know, we've been lucky. Right now they are rather harsh in dealing out sentences and I could try to get the case deferred by delaying tactics. But May 8, when the speech for the prosecution will be made, as well as mine for the defense, is the anniversary of the ending of hostilities, a coincidence I'll make the most of. It's in your interest to appear at that time." So I was coming up for trial on May 7 and 8; only two weeks remained before I stepped onto the stage.

The wait seemed interminable. Over were the evening reveries about girls, old times, good meals. I experienced a new kind of tension, like when one is preparing for an exam. And it was indeed an important exam that was in question, where one defended not an academic treatise or dissertation but one's own personal memoir and dignity. And I asked myself anxiously how I would conduct myself, because the ordeal was also a kind of spectacle to which people would come to watch me.

I had followed a number of trials in the newspapers. I knew how the accused could be grilled between the president of the court and the prosecuting attorney, how what he presents as a justification is often manipulated in quite a different sense and how variously the witnesses' statements can be interpreted. And then the sentence falls rudely, practically without possibility of appeal. I do not recall any proceedings in the court of justice having been attacked for procedural errors or a sentence having been reversed. Judgment was final. If one was sentenced to death, nothing remained but a pardon from the head of the provisional government.

May 7 arrived, and I was taken from my cell at eight in the morning. I was wearing a navy-blue suit, with a white shirt and blue tie. My shoes shone; it was essential to make a good impression.

I was taken at once to the Palais de Justice. As my session started at two o'clock sharp, I had plenty of time to stew while waiting for the jurors and magistrates to finish lunch. Then, at one, police came and conducted me by a kind of trapdoor to the antechamber of the courtroom, which was rather like a sacristy.

I sat on a wooden bench. Maître Ballot, his robe over his arm, had just arrived with two assistants and some colleagues. They came and went, helping to keep up my morale. Alain told me that the president of the court had authorized him to appear in his military uniform; he would say some words in it and then put on his counsel's robe.

The atmosphere was oppressive, recalling the minutes that precede a bullfight; all that was missing was a little chapel in which to meditate. One awaited a killing, but it was on oneself that the attempt would be made. I prepared myself inwardly, forcing my mind to concentrate. When I raised my head and looked about me, I saw the guards with their masks of indifference. But they were only doing their job and even with a certain kindness; if you wanted a light, they gave it to you; if you offered them a cigarette, they took it. Every day they escorted the accused here, whether criminals or politicals, it was all the same; in their eyes you hardly existed.

Then, little by little, while I kept thinking and occasionally exchanging a few words with Alain, I began to relax. I had learned over the years to keep my nerves under control. Unexpectedly, I had the feeling of another Christian, not my real self, who would be in the dock.

Suddenly a bell rang; the hour had come. A small door opened, I climbed some steps and was in the dock, which was large enough to hold, if need be, several prisoners side by side. I sat down and took a look around the courtroom: on my left, the judge's bench, an imposing structure with its ancient wooden carvings, the scales of justice, the symbolic arms. At one end, almost opposite me, was the prosecutor's seat; it was he who would accuse me of all my sins. In front of the president's tribune and the jury box were tables for the court clerks.

Counsels' bench was at right angles to my enclosure. The main part of the courtroom, to my right, was almost full; I could sense the tremor of excitement in the crowd. Smaller than an assize court, it held, all the same, a lot of people. At the far end, through a double door—one could have been in church—the public entered, showing their papers to the guards beside it.

Everyone was staring at me, some whispering together, asking each other about the accused while watching him. As for me, I tried to see if I knew any of them; I had told my family I did not want them there. I saw some old friends come in, then the journalists, notebooks in hand. The majority came out of curiosity, women, mostly, who were not so young. Some were calm and self-possessed, but many looked like firebrands. These were habitués of the Palais de Justice, who from half-past twelve crowd around the bulletin boards and choose the trials they wish to attend. When the doors are opened, they are the first through in order to get good seats. For the past year or so they could indulge themselves to their hearts' content in this permanent and free film show.

"Ladies and gentlemen, the court." A handbell tinkled; my heartbeat quickened. In red cape trimmed with white ermine, the Legion of Honor ribbon round his neck, white-haired President Didier made his entrance. It was he who had presided over all the trials in connection with the collaborationist press: *La Gerbe, Je suis partout, Le Petit Parisien*. It was said of him that he was strict but just. He was, I believe, the only judge who had refused to take the oath to Pétain in 1940. The others had reconciled themselves to working under the Vichy regime, sometimes even taking part in the trials of members of the Resistance. Now, like the police, they continued in their posts; governments change but institutions remain unaltered.

President Didier made up for the others; he had taken serious personal risks. His attitude and outspokenness had landed him in the camp at Châteaubriand,[2] and he might easily have been among the hostages that were shot by the Germans. He had nothing to reproach himself with, and this fact allowed him to exercise a real liberty of spirit. My lawyers considered it a piece of luck that the case was being tried by him; and they had prepared a short, well-phrased speech for me to deliver at the start of proceedings, in which I would express my satisfaction at coming up before a man whose reputation guaranteed impartiality.

Accompanying the president was the government prosecutor —a black-plumaged bird, sober, dignified—then came the four jurors and two substitutes, among them three women, two of whom were wearing the deportees' badge. My counsel rose at once and turned to the president:

"I am Maître Alain Ballot, representing the accused."

[2] An internment camp in Brittany to which militant left-wing personalities had been sent after the Armistice.

"Yes, Maître."

"I am wearing this uniform because I want you to know that I am still a member of the armed forces. I obtained special authorization to come here to plead this case; in any event, my presence here is as much as a witness as a lawyer."

"I shall not forget that, Maître."

Alain slipped on his robe and returned to his bench. While the bailiffs were arranging the dossiers and everyone was getting settled, he came over to me. "What would you like me to do? Object to the two former deportees?"

"That won't make any difference, it will only make everyone uneasy."

"All right, we'll leave them. But three women among four jurors, it's not a good start. . . ."

"That's too bad. We'll soon see."

Now all is ready; the president speaks: "Accused, stand up."

I rose like a robot. Unexpectedly there was a weight on my shoulders.

"Proof of your identity will now be established."

A bailiff asked me if I was in fact Christian de La Mazière.

"Read out the charges against the accused."

There commenced the reading of the bill of indictment, drawn up by the prosecutor. This was no longer the atmosphere of the examining magistrate's office; the bare facts sounded terribly bad. I made a great effort to remain attentive but, little by little, I began only to hear isolated words, bits of sentences. I was in fact thinking of the little speech I was going to address to the president and was afraid I would not find the right expressions. I kept telling myself, "Come on, come on, remember exactly what you're supposed to say." Alain attached importance to this preliminary. He had told me, "I don't think anyone has given Didier due credit for his past. He was certainly one of the oustanding members of the French Resistance, and this should please him. We must play this card."

The clerk went on speaking in a monotonous tone. I saw the public pay attention, already beginning to try to estimate the outcome: "Will this involve the death sentence?" I heard extracts from my articles read aloud and presented as appeals for repressive measures against resistance to the Germans. I was anxious, knowing that there was no sympathy for journalistic collaborators. All the same, mine had not been an outstanding name in the press.

I did not know that a bill of indictment is something of a formality that is forgotten as soon as the trial proper starts, and that the President directs the proceedings according to the opinion he has formed from a study of the dossier. Above all, I did not know that the prosecutor was an old schoolmate of my brother-in-law's and that he had told him that the case was not all that serious, and that, in his opinion, I would get off with ten years. I tried to make myself angry at this funereal-looking individual in order to revive my energy. I took a good look at him: young, thin, not bad-looking. He was my enemy and I must face up to him with as much force as he would put into crushing me. I had to hate him.

At last the clerk concluded his reading. I asked, and was granted, permission to speak. Suddenly my voice was almost breaking, paralyzed by emotion. Though one may well be twenty-five, in certain circumstances one is no more than a kid. Then I got some control of myself, told the president what I knew about him, the trust I placed in his independent spirit as a guarantee that he would understand my reasons for acting as I had. From his slight smile I saw that my statement had touched him. But at my right were these two women who were watching me fixedly with expressionless faces. "If they're akin to those women who sat knitting under the guillotine during the Revolution, I'm in for ankle chains and the scaffold," I thought to myself.

The trial pleadings started. The president questioned me about my intellectual and political development. I told him about my adolescence, my attraction toward l'Action Française before the war. As Alain had advised me, I always tried to keep my answers short. Then quickly we passed on to my activities as a member of the staff of Le Pays Libre. It was on these that the principal charge against me rested. The more violent of my articles were referred to, and then we came to my leaving to join the Charlemagne.

"According to the dossier compiled at your examination, you joined as a journalist."

"Yes, Monsieur le Président."

"Why?"

"Because a war correspondent's job is quite exciting. . . ."

"But France, at that time, was completely liberated! I see also that, according to witnesses testifying at your examination, you could have joined the Resistance."

"That's right. But I was curious to see the Frenchmen who were fighting in the east."

The president shook his head. To him this seemed inconceivable, and at the same moment he said to me with a pained air, "You must admit that was quite mad. You had the possibility of becoming a member of the Resistance. Your previous record wasn't so bad as to have prevented you from joining the Second Armored Division as it advanced through Normandy if you were absolutely determined to get a first-hand experience of war. But no, you went off to the east, to face the Russians and see how they handled things! Don't you see that this isn't the act of someone with a well-balanced mind?"

All this was uttered, moreover, not unkindly. As for the prosecutor, a slight smile never left his face. He occasionally intervened with an incisive remark, and I answered him sharply several times. I had taken a great dislike to him and this kept me going.

The main problem, the one at the heart of the proceedings, was that of journalistic responsibility; because of people like us some Frenchmen had become collaborators and been active against the Resistance; we had made ourselves into agents of the Germans, propagandists of the Nazi doctrine. And the interventions of the president and the prosecutor generally reverted to this theme: "Even if the scope of your responsibility was limited by the small number of your readers, you can recognize now, I think, the extent to which it existed. . . ."

And, in fact, I could not forget the young worker who enlisted in the Waffen SS because he had read my articles. But my journalistic activity dated from a period when the press was not credited with having very much influence on public opinion. It is only now that we know how greatly the mass media can condition a social group. And, after all, *Le Pays Libre* was neither *La Gerbe* nor *Je suis partout*, a fact to which I kept returning.

The prosecutor had in particular drawn attention to an article about the Voiron crime. It may be recalled that in 1944 the deputy chief of the militia in Voiron had been executed by high school students at the instigation of the Maquis. These kids had killed him with a burst of submachine-gun fire at the door of his house. His wife and his mother, an old lady of seventy-five, had rushed out and had also been shot. The schoolboys then killed the three children, including the baby in its crib.

I do not know if this massacre had any political justification.

Many crimes have been laid at the door of the German occupying forces and the militia, but to my way of thinking, this was something unique. It had, moreover, embarrassed the London radio and Philippe Henroit[3] had made it the subject of several of his editorials. It led to a series of cruelties. The high school pupils concerned were court-martialed and condemned to death and shot in front of their teachers, some of whom had a determinant influence in creating the frenzy that had led to the crime.

I was on the spot to do a story for my paper and had attended the funeral of the militiaman and his family. My article was, naturally, very violent. I demanded merciless measures against those who instigated such killings and concluded, "If this terrorism calls itself Resistance, then Resistance is itself terrorism."

The clerk had read the text of the article in its entirety and I had sharply defended it. From time to time I looked at the two women deportees. It struck me that they were both the farthest from me and, at the same time, the closest to me. I wanted, if not to convince them, at least to make them understand. At intervals they wrote questions on slips of paper—in a court of justice jurors cannot intervene directly. They wanted to know if I had known what had gone on in the concentration camps. I had replied that I knew people were arrested, but that the purpose of these camps was to carry out "the final solution" was something I had not known until after the end of the war. They also wanted to hear what I thought of the hostage system and summary executions.

I had to establish and stick to my position, which was not that easy in face of the pressures I was under. There were moments when the line of least resistance tempted me to repudiate my past and to make an implicit appeal: "You must surely see that I was only a poor jerk; please don't crush me completely." But I did not want to deny what I had been. What I wanted was that the others should, for a moment, put themselves in my place. "Try and understand how it was," I felt like saying, "I held certain beliefs and it followed that I could not help associating myself with certain actions." I decided to take a risk, not out of pride, but simply because it was only by a certain frankness that I could keep my self-respect.

In my cell I had thought over the question of hostages and

[3] Vichy minister of propaganda in Paris who denounced the Allies on radio.

partisans, and had made some notes, prepared some arguments, foreseeing that this would play a central part in the trial.

To begin with, I brought up the rules of war as defined by the International Court at the Hague, noting that these only protected soldiers who wore uniforms. Even in occupied territory, somebody who bore arms without belonging to a recognized army, though motivated by a pure patriotism, put himself outside these conventions. In engaging in an underground campaign, the resistants accepted all the risks of guerrilla or partisan warfare, with the inexorable results.

Now, in the milieu in which I had been brought up, the international rules of war had been held in respect. My father had told me that during the two years he had been in the Rhineland after the First World War, the French occupying forces had had trouble with snipers, former members, no doubt, of the disbanded German Army. He had presided at military tribunals where these resistants had been condemned to death or given life sentences. From the moment that they are accepted, these rules of war are valid for everyone; and they were still valid, it seemed, since the leaders of the defeated army were being tried for having violated them.

This was a somewhat theoretical argument, suggested by the circumstances. In actuality, rather than it having been a question or principle, my reaction at the time of the Voiron affair had been a feeling of horror and indignation: I am one of those always horrified by the massacre of innocents. But I see more clearly now that in advocating repressive measures, I was associating myself, more or less consciously, with something quite other than the maintenance of law and order. What had deeply disturbed me since the Spanish Civil War was the realization that the old, more chivalrous world, of which the Hague Convention had been one emanation, was on its way out. In 1944 classic and revolutionary war were inextricably mingled; and in choosing Fascism I, too, had opted for revolutionary warfare. I had opposed the resistants but I had shared their kind of world and their logic. That was why the summary executions had not shocked me, even if the unnecessary shedding of blood revolted me, and still does.

Death is part of revolutionary action, which itself is an act of love to which one is totally committed, and not one where one calculates the consequences. Consequently, what rules are relevant? Personally, I do not believe in the final value of national or international laws. There is man, and that is all; there are those I like and those I do not. It is the merit of revolutionary combat that it has done away with illusionary distinctions; there are not national wars on the one hand and civil wars on the other; a friend is a friend, an enemy an enemy, even if he is from the same country as yourself.

In 1944 I considered myself a revolutionary and questioner of the establishment. Now, with the perspective of time I realized that I was only that in the abstract. I had got into a position that contradicted what I was educated to believe, the small amount of culture that I had absorbed, and my own deepest nature that put friendship above all else and hated death, no matter whose face it had. But the ambiguities of National Socialism had helped me to overlook those of my own position. By means of its ideology I too had dreamed ot the pure revolutionary act. I recalled this attraction of mine, at this moment in the prisoner's dock, and, at the same time, I was conscious of that duality that is part of my nature: a lover of liberty and full of the joy of life, thinking of all I would try to do to get them back, wanting, at the same time, to accept all the consequences of the choice I had made, even at the price of a death sentence, which, it seemed to me, could be a logical conclusion.

There were no witnesses for the prosecution, an important point. My concierge, for instance, might have been called upon to testify, but she had nothing to accuse me of, for which I was thankful. Concierges put cooperating with the police even before their duties as caretakers; they also were agents for undertakers. These are immediately informed when there is a death on the block and a well-dressed gentleman arrives at the widow's before the corpse is cold. With exquisite courtesy he arranges for a funeral adapted to her means. A little later his assistants come to bundle up the deceased and the concierge is handed an envelope.

She is both the confessor and the moral arbiter of the building. Hers is an institution and, as such, it cooperates in keeping public order. The mail is in her hands, and after ten at night, so is the electric device that, at the press of a button, opens the front door. For her the night is a large-scale accounting for the visits received by the tenants. Now, while one is entitled to have one's pleasures, it is not necessary that they become public knowledge. From the moment in court proceedings that a private life is investigated, the concierge becomes all-powerful. People previously held in esteem have been destroyed in a flash. And a concierge with the gift of gab can get you four or five years extra, particularly if the jury has working-class sympathies.

On the other hand, I had witnesses for the defense. And above all I too had my Jew. His name was Grundstein and he was a tailor. One day in 1943 a friend came to see me about him. He had his clothes made by him on credit and ran up debts; but, in return, sent the tailor customers. Grundstein had, rather ambitiously, put up the sign: "Sport Taylor." He made suits to order and also ready-made ones; at that time if ten similar fashionable garments were turned out, they ranked as ready-made clothes. This friend said to me, "An awful thing has happened; Grundstein has been forced to close his business. Some of his family have been arrested, and he is at my place, his yellow star in his pocket. We ought to do something for him, find him some safe place."

I set to work and secured ration cards and identity papers, which was not so very difficult in the Paris of 1943. There was no need to belong to an underground network; everything was arranged with a typically French casualness.

"Ah, yes, you'd like an identity card? Quite simple, just wait while I telephone. . . . You want a piece of pork, ten packs of cigarettes, documents to get you to the Maquis on the Mille-vaches hill? No problem!"

In short, everything could be come by, for everything was on sale, though the business often ended badly.

So I bought an identity card with a common French name on it, found Grundstein, and got him over the demarcation line and into Touraine. There I got him a room at the hotel in my village.

He was the typical little Jew from the rue du Sentier, bent, spindle-legged, pot-bellied, dressed like the perpetual fugitive. His nose met his chin; his hair was sparse, and a dull yellow color. The needle had ruined nicotine-discolored fingers; they were virtual pincushions. His nails, dirty and hard as horn, were striated with tobacco-stained furrows.

In short, no need to be a physiognomist to have picked him out. Luckily there were no Germans in the district; they only passed through, and as they used the major highways one never saw them, to the great disappointment of the resistants, who had nobody to pull a trigger on. So in those parts they had had only two wounded, one from a grenade exploding in his hand and the other shot accidentally by one of his comrades.

And in order to live Grundstein continued his tailoring. But it was in vain that he called himself "Sport Taylor," he was as much cut out for that particular profession as I for a religious writer. And I think that the fear and anxiety he had felt when he was hiding out in my friend's maid's room had increased his clumsiness. His hands trembled, and he completely botched the suit that my father had ordered. My father was also contributing to his support, and this had irritated him so much that his old atavistic anti-Semitism flared up. "Really, that awful little Polish Jew. . . . I knew them in Poland, they don't even know how to work properly. But I did see some wonderful craftsmen in the Warsaw ghetto."

In his mouth, the word *craftsman* was indeed a title of nobility and had nothing to do with worker. There was the artisan and then the peasant. For him a good tailor should have had the heraldic arms of his guild: open scissors and a spool of thread on a field of lilies.

I think Grundstein dressed everyone in the village with any money, but I would not swear to it that they wore the clothes. They fitted badly and stubbornly followed the zoot-suit fashion, making the local landowners, shopkeepers, and aristocrats who had ordered them furious. But everyone protected him, though he was not popular. Occasionally my father would run into the innkeeper and ask, "Well, how's your tailor doing?"

"Oh, Monsieur de La Mazière, what is this Jew that your son brought us?"

In that small hotel in the Indre-et-Loire department, where there was butter on the table and where meat was not rationed, where there were plenty of vegetables and wine flowed like water, Grundstein recovered a zest for life; and, though he depended on public charity, he bullied his clients, people firmly rooted in their native soil and habits, who happened to represent all the things he hated. He became impossible.

He was summoned to my examination and it would have been only right and proper if he had not spoken badly of me. But he never stopped reproaching me for my ideas and kept bringing up my guilt. Finally, the judge had given him the scolding of his life: "But, good God! That's not the point. You're alive. Who saved you? It's very important that you tell me that."

Grundstein had a basic core of decency and he explained what had happened, and the judge recorded his statement without the comments.

And now there he was in the witness box. I was a little ashamed at having him testify for me: I had not saved him because he was a Jew and I wanted to save all Jews, or because he was my friend or my tailor; I had saved him because a friend had asked me to.

He was just the same as ever: bent, badly dressed, and in the courtroom his Moldavian-Polish accent stood out in strange contrast. In some preliminary words, he explained that he had reopened his shop but that he had had to hire other workers as his own former ones had not returned. This was not a very hopeful start.

The president, who had Grundstein's testimony at my examination before him, interrupted these opening remarks. "Let us come to the facts, M. Grundstein. Tell us what happened, or if you prefer, I will summarize it and you can confirm it as we go along. M. de La Mazière, the accused, here present, went to look for you, gave you the necessary papers, and took you to his hometown. And you were able to continue your work there?"

"Yes . . . but they didn't like the clothes I made. . . ."

He had let out what was bothering him. Poor Grundstein! A little later he was to die of cancer and I dare say he died cursing Touraine.

His intervention was both comic and moving. Feeling that the atmosphere was somewhat more relaxed, I got to my feet and explained that it was quite normal for Grundstein to feel he had been humiliated because he had wanted above all to make trousers that clung to the legs, and jackets to the knees with wide skirts.

The President smiled and then asked a question that gave me a chance of explaining myself. "But think back for a moment. You performed a good deed for the witness, but why did you not go the whole way and join the Resistance?"

I gave what seemed to me the only possible answer, though, no doubt, a too facile one: "If I hadn't been among the collaborators, perhaps it wouldn't have been so easy to shelter Grundstein. And if every French person had saved a Jew, how many would have been left for the concentration camps?"

My second witness was Louis Ancelin, an admirable person. We had been at the same school in Saumur and been inspired by the same ideals. We had both followed the Spanish Civil War, in which two revolutions confronted each other, watched by out-dated capitalist powers, with intense concern.

His father, badly wounded in the 1914–18 conflict, had been a public prosecutor: one of those old-fashioned attorneys, of whom there were many before the war, especially in the prov-inces, a man of severity and integrity. As for Louis, he was an intelligent young man, irrepressible and with a mercurial tem-perament. A devout Catholic—Joan of Arc was his favorite heroine—he had held the opinions expounded by Maurras and had never since questioned them. He still held to the precept: France, nothing but France, a sentiment that, little by little, I ceased to be able to feel. He had dreamed of entering Saint-Cyr, for which he prepared himself. But it was a wish he had had to renounce, as he was not tall enough. It was the disappointment of his life.

He was consumed by military ardor. Saumur, at that time, had had a life that throbbed with the rhythm and magic of its cavalry school, which with its exercise grounds, huge riding school, and endless stables, took up nearly two-thirds of the town, stretching from the bank of the Loire to the walls of the first large residential areas.

A large part of the town's commerce depended on the mili-tary school. Everyone had their riding boots made in Saumur—it was out of the question to have ordered them in London or anywhere else. The school bootmaker was a fabulous craftsman, as my father would have said, one of those who molded the leather with subtlety, between thumb and index finger. He shaped his boots on wooden models that had the proportions of his customers' legs. Thus he kept models of my father's calf, instep, foot, and heel, all jointed together, which seemed to me wonderful. One had only to phone him and he quickly made whatever boots were required: black or mahogany-colored, for riding or hunting.

Then there was also the extraordinary "Plazanet" shop where the Saumur riding breeches were made, whose cut allowed the material to slide lightly over the kneecap so that the knee itself had complete freedom of movement inside, breeches that did not sag anywhere and that, while fitting close, were sufficiently mobile to allow a good trip on the saddle and control of the horse with a free movement of the boots. Of course there were other kinds of breeches, Italian or Austrian, and jodhpurs originating in India and worn by fashionable young Englishmen, but there was no authentic horseman anywhere in the world who did not have his pair of Saumur breeches.

The town awakened to the trumpet and echoed all day long with the sound of horses' hoofs, which, company by company, clattered on the cobbles of the rue des Récollets or the rue Jeanne d'Arc. On its outskirts, one heard the sounds from the riding schools and the gallops, and of the words of command. The town was an immense military university filled with the life of the cavalry school, the comings and goings of students and teachers. All the young second lieutenants from Saint-Cyr, who had chosen the cavalry, came there for a year to learn both the art of horsemanship and the technicalities of motorized units.

For Louis and me, as for all the boys, our school year ran parallel to the cycle of the cavalry school. Even more important than the distribution of prizes in our school was the military festival that was held at the end of term. Standards streamed in the wind, horses neighed, officers of the "Cadre Noir" on their prancing and cavorting mounts brought back past times, and the motorized machine guns rumbled past in whirls of dust; we did not know that these were obsolete, and to our ears the name Hotchkiss echoed like a fusillade. It was the great military entertainment. I watched my father at the head of his Algerian troops, cloak blowing in the wind, wearing a light-blue kepi, with drawn sword, as he saluted the general commanding the cavalry at Saumur. At that time an instructor, he later became the general's adjutant, and I then saw him seated in the reviewing stand.

The Algerians kept Ramadan strictly and its ending was made the occasion for further feasts. All the town notables were invited to the great barbecue and each had to tear the roast mutton to pieces with his fingers.

All that was during the years between my ninth and seventeenth birthdays. And, like my comrades, I dreamed of becoming a perfect horseman. Thursday mornings I went for my equitation lessons; and at the end we galloped off in a group and the last got a soaking in the drinking trough that was lukewarm or icy according to the season.

Louis shared in the general enthusiasm, more perhaps than I did because he wanted an army career, and was therefore bitterly disappointed at not being able to enter Saint-Cyr. But the defeat—he had not taken part in the 1939–40 war—had helped him to get over it. He had vainly tried to reach London and then had gone to Paris. His father had joined the Resistance, been arrested by the Germans, and did not return, and Louis, in turn, had joined the Maquis and become an officer.

That was early in 1944. He wanted me to follow him into the Resistance, and there had been a clash—both of us were impulsive and had, in fact, somewhat the same personality, but we were very fond of each other. Since he needed permits to get about, I provided him with travel permits signed by the Germans.

At the time he was living in the rue Lauriston, near the Etoile, and only a few steps from Gestapo headquarters. Yves Le Gall, another of my childhood friends, lived with him. The latter was a young man of astonishing intelligence. His father, a civilian veterinary surgeon at Saumur, had, like Louis's father, been arrested by the Germans. He had been sent to the camp at Drancy and I had tried to do something for him, but without success.

I remember the long discussion the three of us had had together, at the end of which Ancelin had left us to go underground. That was the day when our destinies diverged. Louis had gone off, my mind was made up as to my own path, and as for Yves, he did not want to commit himself, although his leanings were toward the Resistance. He was a person who lived on abstract ideas, he listened to the London broadcasts and made his calculations. He had tried to prove to me that I was making a mistake. He had explained that the Americans turned out so many ships an hour, put together a bomber in a matter of minutes, and "no ideology can withstand this rate of production," he concluded. "Mathematically, Germany is beaten."

He had continued his studies. Since his father had been arrested and he was afraid of what might happen to himself, he had managed with false papers and under a false name to register at the HEC.[4] He did brilliantly there and, at the Liberation, received a diploma in his own name, something that, in that school, certainly was without precedent.

As for Ancelin, with the help of the Maquis, he had become an officer in the Foreign Legion, being officially given the rank of lieutenant, and awarded the medal of the Legion of Honor as

[4] Graduate School of Business Administration.

well as the Croix de Guerre with numerous citations. And one day, when on leave, he heard that I had survived and telephoned my sister.

"I hear that Christian has some problems. I'd like to testify for him."

My sister was glad to put him in touch with my lawyer and he had duly been called to appear as a witness.

He wanted to show up in uniform, which would not have been without its effect, but—the military authorities are strange —he had not been given the necessary authorization. And I must say that in civilian attire he lost some stature. I can still see the president leaning, with an instinctive movement, toward this small young man buttoned into his suit as into a uniform. It was tight, not really a good fit, but spotless, impeccable. His medal ribbons introduced a lively note, looking as if he had forgotten to wear them and had sewn them on only at the last minute.

He stepped resolutely forward when his name was called and, standing before the small handrail reserved for witnesses, did not lose an inch of his height. Looking at him, I had the impression he was standing on his toes.

In that moment I garnered a harvest of memories. There passed before me those eight years of childhood and adolescence. I saw the two of us playing bicycle polo—we had started the craze in Saumur—plotting together, selling *l'Action Française* at church doors, learning to use the latest weapons while many of our schoolmates only thought of masturbating. We were activists at a very early age, quickly and passionately. . . . I listened to what he was saying, and it warmed my heart to see him again with all his honesty, so true to himself.

He told of circumstances in which I had come to his help, mentioned our youth together. He spoke with passion, but as if making a military report, drily and with precision. He was so convincing that at one point the president interrupted him and addressed me, "It's really incredible; I see you'd every possibility of becoming a hero, and yet you're here!"

I rose and replied once more, "Monsieur le Président, if I'd followed the path that Louis Ancelin did, perhaps he wouldn't be here now to tell you what I did for him. What help I gave him was made possible by my own position."

The President made a gesture that caused a movement of his ermine-trimmed robes, as though to say, "Get the hell out of here, you stupid prick!"

And for me, that was the climax of the trial: I believe I must have looked like the king of pricks. But how to explain that the magic of certain ideas is stronger than anything else?

Ancelin continued his testimony. He began to argue that in no case could I have been a traitor. That was for him the main problem. Now he was on his own ground, an officer, and the honor of the cavalry school still rested on his frail shoulders. His tone of voice took on strength, and he ended on a high note of exaltation: "Monsieur le Président, even if you sentence him to death, you can be sure that Christian, because it is his deepest nature, will face execution with the cry: 'Vive la France.' "

I shrank in my box. For once, and in this place and circumstance, it was the very thing not to say! He, my boyhood friend, my school comrade, my accomplice in all my early adventures—he could see me, hands tied behind my back, walking, with firm glance straight ahead, along the raised platform of Fort Montrouge and saying, "No, don't tie or blindfold me," and then crying, "Vive la France!" While my one desire was to spit on the whole lot of them, country and all. . . .

My eyes met those of Alain Ballot, who I saw was dumbfounded. But I am not sure that when all was taken into account this outburst harmed me, because Louis's forceful personality had struck the president, and his decorations—especially the Legion of Honor that Didier also wore—had impressed him.

I have never had an opportunity to meet Ancelin since, and I am sorry. All I know is that he continued for a time to live the kind of life that was marked out for him. Then he married and had a number of children, left the army, to which he had devoted his whole being, disappointed, no doubt, by the contradictions and inconsistencies that were its undoing. I think his nationalism was too intransigent. He is now a geography teacher in Angers, on pension from the army. One of the things that I would like to do before I am too old is to be present at one of his classes, because, if he, who must have burned with enthusiasm to keep Algeria French, has debates in them, it must be amusing.

I would also like to see him at home. I heard that every morning when the whistle is blown his children take up their toothbrushes, squeeze out the paste, and rub energetically for five minutes. Then, all in a row, boys and girls file off to the shower, wash themselves, dress, and depart for school.

I heard these details from Le Gall, who has got on well in the world. He married the daughter of a big contractor who had some trouble at the time of the Liberation. But Yves's father having been shot by the Germans, he had the necessary martyr in the family and was able to get the firm out of its difficulties. He took over its management and is now one of the most successful businessmen in central France.

I often think of our three different destinies. One of us enlisted in a lost cause; another saw the kind of civilization for which he fought collapse even though victorious; the third, more clear-headed, knew how not to involve himself too deeply. I think that in this short epitome is contained the fate of the bourgeoisie of that whole epoch.

The court session had ended about seven in the evening, after the proceedings had lasted five hours. It seemed to me, at the close of the day, that things were not going too badly. By then we knew each other better, the action was calmer, we had grasped one another's use of words.

I was brought back to the anteroom and the police van returned me to Fresnes. In the office they took away the same belongings that had been restored to me in the morning, and I found that Robert Combemale had prepared a good little dinner. I told him how the day had gone and he was optimistic. "Don't worry; my feeling is that it's not going to turn out badly." Not that this reassured me much; my own impression was that I would be lucky to get away with ten years, and that I probably risked twenty. But, in any event, this was the first round, we had to await the second.

Once again I was taken at dawn to the Palais de Justice, and at one o'clock I was back in the anteroom, where my lawyers had come to be with me. They seemed not dissatisfied, and again Alain told me he had telephoned my family to reassure them. Then he sank into thought; this would be the first time he pleaded in an important case and he wanted to prepare himself with as much care as possible.

At the ring of the bell I went back to the dock, between my two escorts from the Garde Mobile,[5] impassive and indifferent on their stools. The place now seemed familiar to me, and the edge of the dock had a warmth that made me feel quite at home. By now it was as if my gestures came to me naturally: I was calm, with folded hands, trying to look like a sensible young

[5] Militarized, mounted, or motorcycle police.

man. Then when one is questioned, one automatically stands erect, in the position of an orator, grasping the parapet whose wood has been polished by all sorts of hands and has taken the shape of a pick handle. It has retained the stains of all the moist and anxious palms that have shaped it.

The court enters. I watch the president, this man whom I sense is approachable, with something paternal about him. He has a helpful smile, the necessary humor, an encouraging curiosity. Behind him is the government prosecutor, always with his detached and slightly ironic smile. Then the jurors, including those two women, who both interest me and make me uneasy.

The proceedings recommence. For the first twenty minutes the president summarizes the pleas and statements of the previous day with intelligence and understanding, drawing attention in particular to my twenty-five years. At that time, when only minor responsibility was given the young, they amounted to very little. And now, when I am old enough to be "important," youth is everything and I am only good for retirement. . . . I was certainly born too late or too early, I often tell myself.

There were some further questions; then the president turned to the prosecutor to ask if he wished to interrogate me, and the latter said he did not. Then the defense was asked if it had anything else to add, any further witnesses to call. The answer was again in the negative. The president then addressed the black crow of a prosecutor again: "Prosecutor, you may now address the court."

And this individual whom I hated—whom I wanted to hate—began, in a severe voice, to expound on the responsibility that rested on me both because of the articles I had written and the attitude I had adopted. He constantly referred to the testimony of the texts themselves. Time dragged on and weighed me down; I felt as if today I had started off on the wrong foot. Then his exposition took a different direction and his tone changed, and all I was aware of was that my enemy was bringing up my age and my background. He referred to the evidence of my witnesses and his speech took on some aspects of one for the defense: "I know and I see," he said, looking at the jury, "that there are among you some whose bodies and whose freedom have suffered, but, in regard to the case that concerns us now, it is necessary to assess carefully how much complicity in this can be apportioned; for my part, I do not believe that we can impute responsibility to the accused for the horrors that we have recently been made familiar with. . . ."

He ended by saying that he was not relying on Article 75, which punished acts against the exterior security of the state and whose penalties included the death sentence, but was basing his plea on Article 83, which dealt with offenses against internal security. In other words—and this was what was vital—my crime did not rank among those that formed a collective European guilt, but on the purely national level.

When I heard this, my heart leaped. "But that's fantastic," I thought to myself, "then the worst I can get is ten years' hard labor!"

The speech for the prosecution ended; it had taken forty minutes. It was now the turn of Maître Alain Ballot. He rose and repeated the phrase with which he had first introduced himself: "I am here as more than a lawyer; I am a witness." He began by expanding all the themes in my favor touched on by the prosecutor, during whose speech he had constantly taken notes. Thus he gave a detailed description of my family background, and the longer he spoke the more stunned I was. My father became a militant sedition-monger and a querulous despot who stressed his wishes with strokes of his whip against his riding boots. With my mother's death, I had been deprived, at an early age, of all affection and had pursued my studies in a harsh isolation with this tyrannical father and unsympathetic sisters. Being shut into an arrogant and self-sufficient social circle had been for me a traumatic experience. . . . I suppose Alain imagined that this vitriolic picture would appeal to the jurors whose origins were, on the whole, modest and who probably had Communist leanings.

But for me, this web of untruths filled me with shame, and I felt deeply humiliated: my sister had already tried to have me sent to a mental clinic and now, with equal craziness, they were making me out an unconscious victim.

Alain continued, his sleeves flapping as his rhetoric took wing. He recalled the statements of the witnesses for the defense, Ancelin's in particular. Then he announced, with, all the same, a quite astonishing audacity in a court of justice: "I ask for an absolute acquittal. The positive acts of my client, saving one person, enabling another to join the Resistance, helping the war victims in Normandy, should be sufficient to allow him to regain his freedom this very evening." He ended by stressing the date: May 8, 1946. "Now the days of wrath are over, except for punishing the real criminals. But let us give back their liberty to those others whose only crime was to believe in an ideology whose criminal and pernicious nature could not then have been fully evident to them."

He sat down and gathered together his notes, which one felt he knew by heart. I saw that he was excited and pleased with himself; it was indeed his first big fight.

The president asked me if I wanted to add anything. I rose to my feet and said:

"Monsieur le Président, I simply want to say that it is neither my family nor my friends nor bad influences that are responsible for my being here. I was sincerely defending certain ideas in which I believed. My anti-Communism doesn't date from yesterday, it goes back to the time of the Spanish Civil War. What I did, I did in all honesty, and now it is for you to judge me in all equanimity. But I would like to say this to you: since it has been shown during the trial that I was not a criminal, I have no repudiation to make."

I sat down. Some surprised glances were directed at me; perhaps I had ruined everything. The court rose.

In the anteroom Alain was not too happy. He told me I was a fool and that I should have kept my big mouth shut, adding, "Yes, I know, you wanted to shoulder your responsibilities! Well, you'll see, they'll slap a ten-year sentence on you without blinking an eyelash!"

We waited a half hour: They must have been arguing back and forth. Then the bell rang for the third and last act, for me the most frightening one. We filed in again. Everyone stood up while the president pronounced judgment. The blood beat in my temples as each "whereas" and "considering that" followed one another and I tried to grasp what was being said above this noise in my head that was making me dizzy. I only heard that Article 83 had been retained and that it had been unanimously agreed that there were extenuating circumstances, because of the people I had helped, both here in Paris and in Normandy. Therefore, I was sentenced to five years in prison and ten years' loss of civil rights.

It was all over. I was overwhelmed, and for a couple of minutes I stayed where I was in my box, relishing my good fortune. Five years! With the time I had already done, which counted double, a good bit was already taken off. . . . And after a year and a half, I could, perhaps, apply for parole. I already felt free.

In the anteroom everyone was embracing. Alain was beaming; it was a triumph for him. Up to the last, he told me, he had expected ten years for me, which, at that time in a court of justice, constituted a fairly light sentence. Five years, with all the possibilities of appeal that went with it, was almost an acquittal.

My anxiety had completely vanished. In the police van I kept telling myself, "Only five years, five years!" By the time I was back at Fresnes, night had fallen, and the prisoners were in their cells, but on my floor the doors were still open. They were all waiting for me, and the news flew from mouth to mouth. The others who came back in the van with me had received fifteen or twenty years, and even life sentences—but I had only got five, and this gave them some hope. "Well, there you are, they said that things were changing." Some must have said to themselves, "In that case, I should get off!" And even those whose cases were very serious felt reason to regain a little confidence.

Naturally, I made a tour of the floor. I went to see Benoist-Méchin to tell him the news. He looked at me with his honest glance from behind his glasses. He believed that he himself, taking into account the position of responsibility he had occupied, was destined to be executed. He had to face the high court, composed of newly elected deputies who would give no quarter and who nonchalantly sent away the condemned with chains on their ankles. For him, the problem was how to stay as long as possible in Fresnes.

I slept and woke up in a very happy frame of mind. I now knew my fate. My immediate object, however, was to stay here and keep my job. But this position was greatly sought after and there were constantly new arrivals. Many guys who had been in hiding were being arrested. And that upright French public who, for four years, had made denunciations to the Germans through the mails, had not given up so good a game. In short, in 1946, the fruits of collaboration still flourished in the streets of Paris and the prison had to be cleared for all the newcomers.

Thus, after some weeks, I was notified that the Ministry of Justice had issued an order that as few convicted prisoners as possible were to be kept at Fresnes and that my name was on the transfer list. But I did not worry, I would not be sent to one of the central prisons.

These central prisons were what we feared most. In principle, they were for the convicts sentenced to solitary confinement and hard labor. But the courts of justice had sent not a few

of the former members of the militia there with the object of
further stigmatizing them. In these prisons there was an iron
discipline, such as none of the politicals who found themselves
there could have imagined. It was total degradation, a plain
penal colony without the exotic touches, worse than Devil's
Island, where the tropical climate allowed some relaxation.

Behind those high walls, under the rule of perpetual silence
and the forced labor, the prisoners were buried alive. They were
allowed only one letter a month, with the perpetual threat of
even this right being withdrawn, a letter of not more than ten
lines on prison paper imprinted with the motto "Liberty, Equal-
ity, Fraternity," for the motto of the republic is always in
evidence where there is no liberty, where the inequality is
ferocious, and where there is no use for fraternity. These letters
or cards, being stamped by the penitentiary administration, could
not be delivered without the mailmen and concierges knowing
where they came from. For the prisoners it constituted a threat to
their families and many preferred not to write at all.

Luckily, with my five years, I would be sent to one of the
new prisons for those with short sentences, which I had already
heard spoken of by the guards and lawyers. Those who wanted
to earn something could work in them. These places were being
built in all kinds of areas, wherever there was a need for labor.

So I prepared to leave. Combemale and I were both rather
sad. Then, one day, I was summoned before the governor.
"You're leaving tomorrow with a convoy of young convicts for a
camp near Epinal, made up of unused barracks that have been
converted. I think you'll be all right there. So I'll say good-bye,
and may I add that I have been very satisfied with your work
here."

Once again I put together my belongings: writing paper, ink,
pen (fountain pens were not allowed, as were no valuable ob-
jects), food supplies, shirts, and other personal articles that I
would need, because in that camp one did not wear prison uniform. In short, quite a pack, just like in the army.

Then, after eating my last dinner in Fresnes, I went round
saying good-bye, and taking farewell of all my distinguished
clients to whom I had distributed books. Now new tasks awaited
me: "At Epinal," I had been told, "you'll be chopping wood." So,
after the library, some fresh air. As I fell asleep I tried to imagine
that I was going to a vacation resort.

X.
THE CLOISTERS OF CLAIRVAUX

I went through the prison office, with the others of our small group, as day dawned. This ceremony was by now just a routine for me; we were like workers who have their cards punched by the electric clock when they go to work.

The screws were all smiles, like hotel managers when one pays the bill. One was not very welcome when one arrived, but later when they knew that one's sentence was not very stiff and that one would soon be leaving, they became quite polite and even displayed a certain solicitude and concern for one's future. "Well, good luck! You won't be badly off, down there. You'll soon learn new dodges."

Then we were handcuffed by twos, a left arm to a right arm. I was furious. Now that we were sentenced, resigned to our fate, I had thought we would be left in peace. According to what I had heard, I thought it was only the Germans who treated prisoners like this.

We were shoved into the patrol wagon, we heaped our suitcases and packs in the narrow aisle and were squeezed two by two into the cells on each side meant for only one prisoner. My companion sat obliquely with his legs under the small bench while I stood with one arm hanging straight down because the chain was short, my nose pressed against the partition so that I had a glimpse of the streets.

At the Gare de l'Est the screws handed us over to the gendarmes. Prisoners must always, in fact, be accompanied by armed guards, and the screws were not authorized to carry weapons outside the prison except if there was a breakout or an attempted breakout. Confronted with a mutiny inside the prison, they were obliged to ask for help from the CRS. But we would find them waiting for us again at the other end—nothing had changed in the penitentiary system.

A train was waiting for us and, as usual, among the crowd we were confronted by hostile, curious, or pitying looks. And we were a wretched sight, we Siamese-twin convicts, one with his suitcase in his left hand, and the other in his right. "Don't feel sorry for yourselves," the cops told us, "normally you ought to have had your feet chained together too." Indeed, that had been done with previous convoys of prisoners; nothing had changed since the days of the early-nineteenth-century police detective Vidocq.

It was much worse when we ran into some railroad employees. They gathered together to insult us, and the gendarmes had to make them clear off. And this notwithstanding the fact that during the war the stationmasters had not been recruited from the German railroads, the locomotives had not been driven by Germans, and yet the convoys had continued to be moved smoothly, including convoys of deported prisoners. . . . Today I can still hear these shouts of abuse and travel by train as seldom as possible.

We got out at Epinal, where we were put into army trucks. This was a pleasant change. Sitting on a bench, I looked out the back window at the countryside sweltering in the heat and felt like a draftee again.

The camp was just a collection of one-story buildings that had formerly served as barracks. Some were in ruins and the outer walls of others were somewhat rotted and had plenty of cracks. But, wonder of wonders, I saw no barbed wire; only the watchtowers and searchlights suggested a prison atmosphere.

We soon came to the administrative office. We were the second convoy to have arrived there. Any object of value,

watches, jewelry, wedding rings, medals, etc., were listed opposite the name of their owners; they had been brought along in
separate envelopes by the gendarmes. Then we were packed into
our respective dormitories, each a long hut with barred windows.
In a corner was a metal pail containing some stale water and
scum in the bottom that smelt of disinfectant. Two rows of bunk
beds faced each other along either wall with a mattress and two
blankets on each; the army world, in short.

We chose our beds; I got rid of the mattress and replaced it
with my sleeping bag; all of a sudden I had a strange feeling of
freedom.

The screws appeared, and one of them addressed us, "It's
like this: We're not yet quite sure what to do with you; we're
waiting for orders. For the present, you'll be staying here. You'll
exercise two by two for a quarter of an hour every day. You'll
have your coffee and your ration of bread every morning, lunch,
and dinner, and you can write home right away."

He turned round to show us a big notice pinned to the door:
"This is the address you must give."

They went away, after bolting us in. We were about twenty
in the hut. Some put their things away and lay down; others
began to talk about the change. In the middle of the room there
were a table and two benches. Guys joked and whistled—it was
real relaxation.

A month passed pleasantly enough in idleness. The administration was not adapted to deal with this place, which was outside its usual experience, and for this reason the rules governing
our existence were liberal. We received letters from home, packages, and even playing cards. Sometimes we lay daydreaming for
hours on end on our cots. Or we started writing long letters that
filled a whole morning. One guy organized a bridge tournament.
I remember he wore a GI uniform because he had been an
interpreter at an American HQ when arrested. He was a reserved
individual and I never found out why he, like me, had got five
years. Now he is a translator for the *Série Noire* crime novels.

The food, on the other hand, was frightful: stale bread and
thick potato and carrot soup. We soon got diarrhea and there was
an impatient jostling to get one's turn at the bucket. Except for
the fifteen minutes of exercise we lived with a constant smell of
shit; but one gets used to anything.

The dormitory contained all sorts of people. One that caught
the eye was a dress designer called R——, an elegant homosexual

and well supplied with food parcels. We had given over a double-level bed for his sole use; he lived on the top cot and stored his boxes and food supplies on the bottom one. He kept permanent open house, looking after five or six of the boys who had no families and no supplies of their own. In the morning he strolled up and down the room in an embroidered dressing gown, calculated to seduce a young "collabo" with big eyes and well-curved leg. He created a bachelor's apartment in miniature for himself and in our midst quietly indulged his tastes.

It was owing to the patriotic vigilance of his colleagues, I believe, that he found himself there. In spite of his wealth, he was not one of the influential group of high fashion who had prospered under the Occupation, living as if there were no war and maintaining in Paris a luxurious existence untrammeled by the restrictions. And in this milieu with its fierce jealousies he had not been overlooked. He had been accused of having put part of his workshop at the disposal of the Germans and of having made sheepskin jackets for the soldiers on the eastern front who, during the first Russian winter, had almost died of cold in their lightweight overcoats. At the same time he had got hold of a quantity of raw material from the Wehrmacht, which he had made into coats to be sold on the French black market. In spite of his imprisonment, his business was being carried on. His sister had taken it over and he himself expected to be pardoned shortly.

As for me, I had met again some veterans of the Waffen SS, and we soon formed a little group together. We told the stories of our adventures, we argued and exchanged opinions. Once again I saw how different we were, how dissimilar our concepts had been all along.

There was Arnaut, my companion from Körlin. I had seen him getting into the patrol wagon at Fresnes in front of me, and that had been a big surprise. He had come up before a military tribunal and, like me, had got only five years. I should mention that his father, who had been a leading member of the Resistance, had been deported, and had barely escaped with his life, had stood loyally behind him. When Papa had appeared in the witness box, this had had a great effect. In his rough, outspoken way, he had told them all some home truths.

Then there was André Imbert, a fine big fellow with a whimsical turn of mind. His father was a writer of verse plays, of mystery plays in particular, which were a draw when performed in front of Notre Dame Cathedral during Holy Week. While he was writing his morality plays and his wife was busy with her ceramics, the children ran wild. Everyone adored them but nobody bothered about them and they simply turned up every evening at the kitchen table with its plentiful but unvarying dishes. In a word: wealthy bohemia.

Imbert had been in Körlin as liaison officer, but I had not come across him there. His job had entitled him to a bicycle and it appeared he had never let go of it. When we had broken out at night, he had done so on his bike, pedaling through the Russian lines. Unfortunately he was literally frozen crossing the Persante. The Russians captured him, although he was nothing but a block of ice; they took him and beat him to a jelly, and the story ended with him practically losing the sight of his right eye.

They then sent him to the notorious Tambor prison camp. He was one of the rare ones who ever returned from it, arriving half-dead at Fresnes on a stretcher. At the infirmary, Corbel had restored him to health but made sure that when he appeared before the tribunal he was still on a stretcher.

The Russians had an enormous number of German prisoners at Tambor, among them many Alsatian members of the SS who had never ceased declaring that they were French. So, to keep them company, the "Ivans" had sent prisoners from the Charlemagne there. Thus it was that Imbert had met them, and he had not many happy memories of them. Playing the victims, these phony "malgré-nous" had made life hard for him. They were simply trying to get themselves out of a nasty fix, for, as everyone now knows, only volunteers were enlisted in the Waffen SS.

According to Imbert, the "Ivans" treated him well, even sharing their *maorka* (tobacco) with him. But food was almost nonexistent, as was sanitation. And typhus had speedily broken out and made serious ravages in the camp. Of about fifteen thousand prisoners, hardly any had escaped it. The Russians, hampered as always by administrative inefficiency, had no vaccines; and though the Germans had already been immunized, after all the privation they had endured, they were in no state to withstand the epidemic; hundreds died every day.

For two weeks Imbert had pushed a cart full of corpses to a huge ditch dug by a bulldozer into which they were thrown. He had to walk through snow and mud in almost bare feet, his captors having taken his boots, and had improvised some footwear by fastening small boards under the "Russian socks." On his journeys back and forth he had to defend himself against the survivors, who stole whatever the corpses had on them: clothes, tobacco, a crust of stale bread.

This experience left its effect on him, and, moreover, his eye did not get better, and he had to have horribly painful injections, even in the pupil itself. From time to time, he was seized with bouts of manic happiness; he was nice to everyone, laughed, danced, and sang after lights out, and kept up a series of extraordinary comic acts and jokes. One evening, for instance, he took his blanket, spread it in the middle of the room, and lay down on it. When the guards looked in they tried to make him go back to his bed. "No, no," he shouted, "I'm not worthy of sleeping on such a soft, comfortable mattress." The screws shrugged and left him where he was.

Besides Arnaut and the unlucky poet, there were Croquignol and Petit-Louis. The former was a young guy with long hair and an even longer nose, who looked like Filochard's[1] accomplice. From a worker's family, he had been brought up in a Communist milieu. His whole family, a large one, stood behind him, keeping him well supplied with packages.

As for Petit-Louis, he was a boy from the back streets, a regular Paris urchin, gay, agile, and sharp; I do not know how he managed it, but in no time he had found where the kitchens were. We took him partially under our wing because he never received anything from outside. Orphaned at an early age, he had led the shadowy existence of street gangs, living by robbery, shoplifting, and petty burglaries. Then one day he decided that in order to ensure that he eat properly, he might as well join the militia, and he had ended up at Wildflecken.

He got on well enough at first in the Charlemagne and became an officer's orderly. But when that ended badly, he went over to the "Ivans" and managed later to reach the interior of Germany, where he passed himself off as a foreign worker. But he had his telltale tattoo. At the first check point he was made to raise his arms, and our little worker had been nabbed and, without further ado, locked up. The military tribunal, however, let him off lightly; he had to get something on principle because he had a record, but it was only three years.

Time passed; we lived like lords in idleness, each of us

[1] Croquignol and Filochard were members of a gang in a French comic strip in the 1930's.

concerned with our own ideas and discussing them with our companions. But one day the noncommissioned officer responsible for us arrived at our mansion. He was a lance sergeant and exercised a provisional authority pending the arrival of higher authorities.

"I've good news for you. Starting tomorrow, you'll be able to work."

He belonged to the older order and he must have thought he was doing us a favor. But it was one I could have done without. I went up to him. "Those who want to can work, but not me."

"Yes, yes, it will be obligatory. The camp has to be fenced in and you'll drive in the stakes and hang the rows of barbed wire."

Afterward, a discussion broke out. The guys seemed for the most part quite happy about it. "That's fine, we'll get a bit of air." The screw went out, bolting the door. I turned to my companions. "You're nuts! Let them do their own dirty work. The moment we're caged in behind barbed wire, our whole situation will change. You'll see, we'll be treated like real convicts, while, up to now, it's been more like waiting to be demobilized. We can't leave the camp, but that's all."

This was followed by a confused discussion, in which most of the others expressed disagreement.

"O.K. Those who agree with me, stand here beside me."

I gathered around me a small number made up, essentially, of my group of personal friends. We were determined not to give in. Next day we laughed, watching the jerks go out to build a cage for themselves while we remained comfortably in the suddenly quiet room. We were not let out for exercise anymore as a punishment.

This went on for several days. The camp authorities were worried, wondering if we were an organized group who might be plotting other acts of insubordination. And in fact we did have a plan: we had heard of a wonderful camp in the south. Thanks to a courageous young screw, who brought us in cigarettes, Arnaut had been able to write to his father asking him to use his influence to have us transferred there. We intended to play troublemaker until the administration had had enough and got rid of us. It was then, as though by a happy coincidence, that the intervention from outside would have taken place that would speed us to a more clement climate.

The plan was good but needed a little time. Unfortunately, we were informed on by one of the guys who had joined my side,

237 | THE CLOISTERS OF CLAIRVAUX

and one evening the screws burst in just as Imbert was doing one of his comic turns in his underwear. But this time they were not amused; they took him just as he was, then they grabbed Arnaut, also in his shorts. Although the camp was badly run down, the individual cells, as though by chance, had remained intact. They were thrown into these where they remained a whole week, without food, in extreme cold.

To keep warm, Imbert sang, resting an hour and bawling away for the next one. It was eerie. From the dormitory, we heard him day and night; the screws never succeeded in keeping him silent. He had a whole repertoire: hymns, Scouting songs, Russian songs, and the songs of the Waffen SS, all came equally to him.

Then one morning when the others were at work and we were dying of boredom, the "chief" appeared:

"Come on, pack up. You're going to be disciplined."

We got back Imbert and Arnaut. Both were in an extremely weak state; Arnaut, in particular, looked thin, with a shriveled face. We were given a thick soup and then chained together. Truck, train, gendarmes: the same old rituals that accompany all such journeys.

We arrived at night at the station of Bar-sur-Aube. We got out, all of us who had refused to work, all except the one who had given us away, and that is how I got to know who it was. There are betrayals that pay, and this must have been such a one for him. I heard afterward that he was given a position of responsibility in the camp at Epinal, that he collected some recommendations for parole, was pardoned, and has a good job now. I hope he is happy and that he does not think too often of this business; and if he does think about it, he is right, because without him, I would never have come to the logical end of my journey, I would not have experienced Clairvaux.

We got into a police van divided into cells. I sat on the small bench in one of them, and Imbert, chained to me, was gazing through the slits in the wall of the patrol wagon. All he saw were woods shrouded in darkness. Suddenly the van stopped.

"What can you see now?"

"A wall, a huge wall. And a door being opened in it."

We moved on again for what seemed a long time, then stopped once more.

"And now?"

"A wall."

A door scraped on the ground. We moved on again, but this time very soon came another halt.

"A wall again."

Shouts: we were to get out. The guards stood waiting for us, flashlights in their hands. They opened huge grilles, disclosing a great shadowy corridor in which we were swallowed up. Then up a large, majestic stone staircase. Every twenty meters, a barred door opened and closed behind us. The noise of locks and the grating of hinges echoed under the vaulted ceilings and ended by blending into a continuous rumble. I had the feeling of embarking on a journey of initiation into the absolute center of incarceration, where there is no longer an outside beyond the bars.

"You'll be taken care of tomorrow." We were in a vaulted cell without a window, but only a deep, barred opening that emphasized the thickness of the walls. On the ground were five mattresses. I was finally living out my old nightmare that Hannover had briefly re-echoed. I was in the Citadel of Silence.

Clairvaux: an ancient Cistercian abbey. Long ago, Abelard had come here to weep for the one he had lost. It was only a step from Colombey, the future national shrine. There was no lack of symbols here.

When they selected a retreat, the monks were seldom wrong. The site, a hollow surrounded by wooded hills, had a serene and slightly austere beauty. As times and governments had changed, however, the place had undergone a whole series of transformations. The monastery had become a barracks, then a prison: a downgrading that betrayed a certain logic. It was in the time of Louis XV, I think, that the light cavalry had succeeded the monks. Clairvaux had a strategic importance then, on the eastern frontier. The monastic buildings had been adapted to the needs of troops and large stables were built. Even today, the older part preserves its former grandeur, but with the establishment of the Third Republic the penitentiary imagination had seized on the place and in reconstructing the buildings, had disfigured them. Watchtowers were erected, walls rose up, and new structures were added, spoiling the architectural harmony.

Thus Clairvaux had become a closed system, without links to the outside. The immediate neighborhood was practically devoid of life. The village consisted of only a few small houses and, principally, the hotel that prospered on the patronage of the prisoners' relatives.

The center of the prison was formed by the quadrangle of the former cloisters. In the middle was the courtyard, on which the dormitories opened, and, also on the ground floor, four halls given over to unemployed prisoners known as the "inos" (*inoccupés*). These were all those who did no work, because they did not have the minimum professional qualifications or the physical strength. Among them were a number of cripples, as well as the elderly, many who were over sixty. There was even one prisoner of eighty-two, a record only to be surpassed later when Maurras was imprisoned. These old men were assigned to a special hall, "Ino 4," a regular old folks' home.

The quadrangle made up a closed, self-contained block. Through its iron gates one came to the workshops, many of which were part of the original structure that retained its ancient aspect. This was the active part of the prison. There was a factory that made army boots, a clothing factory specializing in prison clothes out of drugget, as much a distinguishing mark as convict's stripes. The pride of the place was the carpenter's and cabinetmaker's shop, which occasionally turned out truly remarkable pieces of furniture. It was this workshop that supplied, and, I imagine, still supplies, those big furniture merchants whose 50 percent reductions are so striking during their famous sales weeks, for prison craftsmen are paid starvation wages, half of which, furthermore, is kept by the administration for room and board.

Like the central compound, the workshops were closed in, and behind this second enclosure were the newer buildings: the infirmary, administrative offices, and adjoining the workshops, the guards' living quarters. This little complex was encircled by a third wall, from which stretched an open space as far as the wall that encompassed the entire prison territory. In it was the cemetery; a school for the screws' children; some plots where the prisoners grew cabbage and leeks, the main part of their diet; a post office; and a chapel which the villagers could also attend— they were known by sight and the gate was opened for them.

Thus the central prison constituted an autonomous universe. Standing over the silent countryside, animated by the searchlights that dug through the dark and swept over its walls, it looked like a great ship, a ship that had an immense slave-galley.

We had lain down on our mattresses without undressing. The screws had brought us a sanitary bucket and a pot filled with some sort of mash. Then they locked us in. Imbert, who had had an empty stomach for a week, threw himself on the food and emptied a couple of messtins without taking a breath. My own appetite was poor. I was looking at the vaults: getting out of this cellar seemed hopeless.

We all realized that a new kind of life was beginning. Perhaps Arnaut's father had got his letter and we would be rescued. . . . We did not really believe it. We began to miss Epinal and to decide we had been fools.

Stretched out, arms behind our heads, we were engulfed in a deep silence, hearing only, from time to time, a clock striking: midnight, one o'clock, two. . . . I thought about the monks of long ago; I, too, was going to have the hours measured out for me by the clock. Finally I fell asleep.

We awoke with a start at seven in the morning; the vaulted ceiling resounded with an infernal din, the sound of thousands of wooden shoes whose clatter was punctuated by commands: "Left, right, left, right." It came from everywhere, from all the staircase, piercing the walls and invading the cell, diminishing at one moment, then increasing and diminishing once more. We followed the sound. Now the prisoners were in the courtyard. We looked at each other, not wanting to express our thoughts: "My God, this is the real thing!" We had congratulated ourselves on having escaped the central prison, and here it was!

We remained where we were without speaking. Then there was the loud noise of a key in the lock, the door opened, and a screw entered, preceded by a prisoner bringing us coffee. We had only our messtins and it was poured into the cleanest; in turn we drank the blackish brew that had grains floating on it. At least it was hot and revived us somewhat.

We were taken to the reception office, where we saw how different everything here was from Fresnes. All the detainees wore coarse prison clothes and their heads were shaved. We each stepped forward when our name was called and then reformed a group. A sergeant came over to us, a big fellow with an alcoholic's face, with red and yellow blotches, in which two small bright eyes were almost hidden.

"This is the last time I'll call you by name. Here you're nothing and nobody. What you'll be taught here will be of use to you. Perhaps you think that when you leave you'll never come back, but I can tell you that almost all my clients return sooner or later. We'll be seeing quite a lot of each other."

That was the kind of talk considered suitable for ordinary convicts. At that time there were over twelve hundred prisoners in Clairvaux of whom not even two hundred were politicals, and it was a farce to lump us all together.

"Oh, you're smiling, are you? I forbid any smiling. Each of you will get a number, which must be sewn on the left sleeve, and you had better know it by heart because you won't be hearing your names anymore. No names, nothing but numbers: get that into your skulls, for a start. Just a number, right? And now, strip."

We had had plenty of practice and were undressed in a few seconds. Our clothes were taken, rolled up, and had labels attached to them, which we signed; then each man had his anus probed.

"Now for the physical measurements!"

"But we had that done before."

"Silence! Here we have a special anthropometric system, and what was done elsewhere doesn't count here. And understand this: you are convicts, and so you don't ask questions. Answer when addressed, otherwise keep your mouths shut. Say a word and you go to the hole. In any case, you'd best have a look at what it's like when we're finished here."

Somebody arrived with a pair of compasses and slide rule; jawbone, chin, and nose were measured. The color of our eyes was noted down, as were any scars. When I left Clairvaux I would have liked to have got hold of these details to keep among my personal papers.

After that, we went to the fingerprint section. We were made to press our fingers first on a black, then a white surface, like piano exercises. Still naked, we had our photos taken from all angles, and finally some prisoners brought our drugget uniforms consisting of trousers and collarless shirt. Now that's a fashionable attire, but it was introduced at Clairvaux long ago. We had kept our socks and were given wooden clogs, which we had to learn how to walk in. It was now the barber's turn. In an adjoining room a prisoner was waiting for us, clippers in hand. At that time, I wore my hair rather short, in army style; I had always worn it that way except for a few months when I had let it grow, to the annoyance of my father, who had remarked that the young were taking to bad ways.

"Come on, sit down!"

It was then that I said to myself, You don't yet know what the hole is like; too bad, for you're going to find out. I stood right in front of the lance sergeant:

"I refuse. I have been sentenced to five years' imprisonment, and I have the right to wear my hair between an inch and a quarter and two inches long. It's the prison rule."

I had found this out at Fresnes. "I warn you that if my head is shaved, you'll have to take the consequences. That's all I've got to say. If you still want to shave my hair, you'll have to use force."

The "chief" did not lose his head. "O.K., that is the regulation. In general, guys who come here have been sentenced to hard labor or solitary confinement, in any case, to more than five years. All right, what's your number? 83–11. Very good, 83–11, with a five-year sentence, measure his hair." My hair, which had just been cut to an inch and a half, was measured. Because of my protest, no attempt was made on my companions' heads, and the sergeant was already looking at me a little differently.

"And now you can have a look at the hole."

Stumbling along in our clogs, we followed the sergeant like tourists behind a guide. We passed through endless corridors, barred at regular intervals by huge grilled doors, each of which opened with a different key, which the screw selected from his bunch: this was indeed a prison in the purest classical tradition. We crossed a couple of small courtyards and came to an isolated building.

There we saw what the punishment block at Clairvaux was like: a tomb. The cells, or rather dungeons, practically unfurnished, without blankets, never heated, were deathly cold. Prisoners often only emerged from them when they were carried out; at best, with tuberculosis, when they were sent to the prison sanatorium. The hole was in the hands of a common convict, who, it was said, was a double or triple murderer, and who terrorized those undergoing punishment by blackmail and base acts of violence.

A sight of this place obviously gave the convicts a good deal to think about. Clairvaux could well display above its entrance: "Supervised Training Institution." It was the kind of training that produced brutes, killers, and cowards. And the sergeant was right: they usually came back. Of the twelve hundred detainees, nearly four hundred were here for the second or third time. So the best training was to be given the jitters from the start.

I will never forget the sense of inner panic produced by this spectacle, and I must say that our knees were rather weak when we were led out. We were taken back to the large courtyard to be inspected by the warden, a medium-sized, rather stout individual who struck me as quite a good sort. His mania, and it was an obsessive one, was to want to put everybody to work, and the politicals had nicknamed him "Sauckel."[2] However, he had no real authority, nor had the deputy warden. Power was shared among the screws, the sergeants, and the lance sergeant. The latter was absolute master of the place; the decisions he took and the punishments he meted out were never called in question, even when they infringed the regulations.

The warden had a look at our papers and questioned us briefly. After this ceremony, I was called, or rather 83–11 was called, and I followed a screw to "Inos 3."

I had, in fact, become one of the unemployed, having stated in the office that I knew no manual craft. The sergeant had bellowed, "Oh, you can't do anything? O.K., we'll have to teach you."

Therefore it really surprised me that I was taken here. Not that they could, in any case, make me work. And since I was not a pauper, I did not give a damn for the seventy-five centimes an hour I would have been paid. My more nervous comrades had pretended to know how to chop wood or cut cloth, which had made me smile to myself. They had been particularly fascinated by a workshop that made coat hangers, which they thought ought to be a wonderful sinecure, not taking into account that even to make such stupid things one had to use a hand saw where one could easily leave a finger or two.

I packed up my things and left them a little sadly, knowing that we would have no occasion to meet again either in the dormitories or during the day. And like a boy kept in school for punishment, I reached the "Inos 3" hall. When I entered, the guys lifted their heads and looked at me with gloomy expressions while the guard who had brought me spoke to the screw on duty there.

---

[2] Gauleiter Sauckel's job in Nazi Germany had been to direct foreign labor into the factories of the Reich.

I was in a huge room whose stone floor had been polished by many feet over a long period, with a ceiling of large, majestic-looking arches. It had been set up on the public school principle: with rows of benches, firmly bolted to the floor, on each of which five men could sit, facing five small desks, a stove that burned sawdust from the carpenter's shop, and the chair where the guard, whose sole duty was to enforce the rule of silence, was sitting.

Some of the "inos" were reading, others writing—but for that, a whole lot of authorizations were needed. Most were drowsing with vacant eyes. I was allotted a bench and desk and I might again have been at school with my small satchel. Inside it was some leftover food, soap, towel, and toothbrush, but no paper or pen, these having been confiscated. And no cigarettes, as smoking was forbidden. I had to put on my number, which had been written in India ink on a yellow tab: yellow indicated ordinary imprisonment, from five years to a life sentence; green, solitary confinement; white, hard labor. But I had nothing with which to sew, and how to get what I needed when I was not allowed to speak? Finally, the screw summoned a prisoner:

"77–12, a needle and thread!"

He took them and handed them to me. I took off my shirt, after putting my pack behind me. My neighbor—he had not stopped eying me—nudged me with his elbow. "Your pack!"

He made me understand by a gesture that the fellows behind me were getting ready to filch my provisions, so I replaced the knapsack on the bench. In spite of this, I had to keep a constant eye on it.

When I had finished my sewing, I crossed my arms and took a look around. Some of the others made signs to me; there were types of every imaginable kind. From time to time the screw shouted, "Silence!" and hit the desk with a metal rule, the same rule that he used to check the bars. On one occasion he made an "ino" stand in a corner, just like in a classroom; it was quite incredible.

At last the clock struck. We ate where we were, using the small desks. I was given messtin and spoon and started on the food, which was neither very plentiful nor good, in fact, nothing to write home about. I supplemented it with stuff from my pack. Then came a blast on a whistle: "Get ready for exercise."

I closed my knapsack, kept hold of messtin and spoon, and followed the general movement, which took me to the middle of the yard facing some kind of trestles. Four barrels, cut in half, were wedged into them, and that was where we washed ourselves in the morning and scoured our belongings. I dipped my eating things in the greasy water and let them drain. Then it was "left, right, left, right," on the way out to exercise. We walked around and around the quad and I had a chance to observe another group of prisoners who were exercising in a circle that skirted the buildings. There were not many of them and they were talking to each other. They were holding small pieces of wood in their hands and dropped one each time they completed a circuit.

The track they were covering was a curious one; there were a succession of different surfaces: a bit of plowed ground, followed by tarred and paved sections, then a bit covered with gravel, another of sand. It was cut across by short paths leading to the entrances to the "inos" halls.

What on earth were they doing, I wondered. While walking around I practiced speaking through my teeth without moving my lips. Little by little I learned that they were testing out footwear, and in their unvarying circuits trying out the boots made in the workshop for the army.

Suddenly I caught a sign from one of the prisoners, a small fellow with broad shoulders, a ridged chest like a chicken's breastbone, and thick hair on a knobby-looking head. He had small, muscular hands. He wore his number on a white patch, showing he was doing hard labor. He completed a circuit, deposited his piece of wood, and with another sign he indicated a place where one could urinate between the four wooden tubs. I had not noticed it but had seen some of the men silently raise a finger and heard the screw say, "Go ahead," keeping an eye on them as they left the ranks.

I lifted my finger and went over to the latrine; the other guy did the same and we met there.

"I'm Guissenhofer; remember me?"

"Oh, yes. We met at Radio-Paris."

"There aren't many of us politicals and we have to stick together. I'll have a word with Vitout from *Le Petit Parisien*, who's a prisoner here. Don't worry, I'll try to keep in touch; but be careful, keep a sharp lookout; a lot of the ordinary convicts hate us and are in with the administration. I test out footwear. It's badly paid, but gives one the right to a little extra bread and a small ration of fat. We manage to smoke and I'll bring you a butt tomorrow, if you like. You go to the latrines; I'll light it, take two or three puffs and leave it behind me when I go out, and when you come you'll find it there lit. You can have a few puffs, put it back, and someone else will come and finish it."

A real pal! Suddenly things seemed a bit brighter and the rest of the day passed more quickly. The afternoon I spent doing nothing in "Inos 3"; we had dinner, and then we climbed the immense staircases, whose stones were hollowed and polished by centuries of feet, mostly wearing clogs. We went down long corridors and reached a large, vaulted room: our dormitory, furnished with about fifty chicken coops.

That apt term was a reminder of the precision of the prisoners' language, for each bed was completely enclosed by a cage, about six feet square, with a wooden frame covered in wire netting, in which there was a door, part boarded and part wire, between two wooden uprights. The cages were side by side but allowed no contact between the occupants.

We were given five minutes to get to bed, and we had been warned: "Don't forget your number and don't start looking for your bed, otherwise it's the hole." The hole . . . a word that could make the crippled run. I hurried to my cage, which was almost entirely filled by the bed and sanitary pail. I got out my sleeping bag, spread the blankets, and put my clogs outside the door.

Then I was locked in. The door of the dormitory itself was locked. The screws, on their night rounds along the corridors, unlocked the room doors and made a tour of the cages. When there was a trusted kapo they were satisfied by asking him if everything was all right.

These "kapos" were the prisoners responsible for the dormitories. As in the concentration camps they served as intermediaries between the detainees and the prison authorities. They were allowed certain privileges, being permitted to smoke on the sly, and received more generous rations. They were also the only ones to have the doors of their cages always open.

When I was in bed I was visited by mine.

"You're the new one? Keep cool and perhaps things can be made easier for you, but we'll have to see what sort you are. You know nobody is allowed to smoke, so be careful that the screws don't smell it. If you happen to come by any cigarettes you must let me know. You'll need my help and, in any case, you'll have to go shares."

He went away and I was alone again in the dense, humid

darkness. I was overwhelmed by a sense of pain that was choking me. I had caught a glimpse of a friend but could not talk to him, and of a "kapo" whose only thought was how to fleece me. And as for my family, they did not even know where I was, and there would be only one letter a month to say I was still alive. I counted the days that I had still to do here, it was an eternity.

I felt I was doomed. And for what I think was the first time, I wanted to cry.

Finally I fell asleep like a log. It was a harsh reveille: strip the bed, fold the blankets, get into prison clothes and clogs, empty the slop pail into an enormous communal bucket that was later emptied by the maintenance unit. All this quickly and in silence.

Then we formed rows and, knapsack on back, it was "left, right, left, right," and downstairs; a good walk to give us an appetite, a not unnecessary precaution because the breakfast was wretched. After that we congregated in the middle of the courtyard around the four tubs to wash ourselves. I stripped to the waist but a guard quickly made me put on my shirt again; it was forbidden, apparently, to wash in "Nazi" style.

I had a right, true, to a monthly shower. The apparatus discharged tepid water over six hundred prisoners, after which it was quite cold, and the drying took place automatically, in the drafts of the long freezing corridors.

I went back to my "ino" and small bench—places could not be changed. Passing the interminable time was like trying to empty the ocean with a teaspoon. I was learning to speak like a ventriloquist while remaining motionless, at the same time taking care not to glance instinctively at the guard, an act that would have given me away, for he would see that I was trying to communicate with a neighbor and would start shouting at me.

After a moment, I saw a man with smooth hair and a rather fine face come in. He went over to the guard and made some request, then, dragging his clogs, he came over to me.

"Pierre Vitout, formerly of *Le Petit Parisien*."

"Oh, yes, how are you?"

"We've just five minutes. Guissenhofer told me about you, and I'll try to have you taken from this 'inos' lot. You could become a lecturer, like me, without too much difficulty. There's a lecture every week to each 'inos' section so that makes four times. I'll ask for an interview with the warden and I believe he'll agree to nominate you. Then we can sit at the same table to prepare our talks and can speak to each other as long as we don't raise our voices, and read and write. You'd also have the use of the library. . . ."

"Wonderful . . . that's really very good of you."

"Not at all; we must stick together. The ordinary convicts are in a majority, which is bad enough. Now this is a kind of work that they can't do. The warden told me that they are going gradually to be sent to other central prisons and that Clairvaux will soon be kept entirely for politicals. But it's not so far."

The day had until then been as monotonous as the previous one, but now my morale rose like an arrow. "Marvelous," I told myself. "I'm as lucky here as I was at Fresnes. Although this guy doesn't know me, he comes to me. I'm not alone anymore."

A few days later I was called before the warden.

"I've been told that you'd like to become one of our lecturers. I've just had a look into your file and there's nothing there against it. As you probably know, you can only talk on historical or literary matters, all political views are strictly prohibited."

"Of course, sir. Thank you, sir." And there, all of a sudden, number 83–11 was promoted to the teacher's rostrum, allowed to move about, to speak, to write. I felt as if I was regaining possession of myself, bit by bit, even if, in doing so, I had ceaselessly to ask all sorts of permissions.

Vitout introduced me to the librarian, a former country schoolteacher, nicknamed "Jelly," who had been too fond of his pupils. In order to attract them, he had smeared his sexual organ with the stuff and let them suck it off. This soubriquet had been given him in the office where his file had come into the hands of detainees who worked there. Our good "Jelly" had copped twenty years hard labor: at that time the question of moral habits was not to be taken lightly.

Since he was the only intellectual among the common convicts he had been made—learning, like nobility, has its obligations—head of the library, and allowed to live, and install his cot, there. So he reigned there, in cozy tranquillity, over a collection of old books that nobody ever asked for. Because there, too, the name: "Supervised Training Institution" caused a smile: for purposes of further education, all "Jelly" had to offer was insipid and old-fashioned novels.

His place, however, was at least a haven of peace. One could smoke there if one took the precaution of dispersing the smoke with one's hand. It was enough for a screw making an unexpected appearance, in a bad mood, and smelling tobacco, for everyone to be sent to the hole. "Jelly" handed me cigarettes with all sorts of warnings. His wife, also a teacher, managed to send them to him and, from the backwoods to which she had been transferred, to send him packages regularly. She had always refused to believe in his guilt, a fact which he used to protest his innocence.

He, too, gave lectures, talking about women and introducing all the courtesans of the eighteenth century. As for me, I searched the shelves in vain for something with which to inspire me and finally decided to concentrate on old French legends; with all I had heard during the evenings of my childhood, it would be funny if I could not make a go of it. And so I started to weave idyllic tales for a completely bored audience. They could not have cared less, nor did I. I was delighted to have got out of the prison rut, while they only thought of food. In that period prison was totally repressive and nothing mattered but the struggle to stay alive another day.

As far as that was concerned, my situation was brighter. I had written home, weighing my words carefully, for each letter was scrutinized minutely, informing them of my position, and packages, sent on from Epinal, began to reach me. A new phase was starting in which I could breathe a little more easily. I had gained much more freedom and instead of stagnating in my "ino," and occasionally raising a finger to ask to go to the latrine, I had the right, in addition to the library sessions, to walk in the courtyard in order to better reflect on my talks and to stimulate my thoughts. . . .

I took advantage of this to accompany Guissenhofer on several circuits of the track—he was popularly known as Guissen—as he applied himself assiduously to his job; by the end of each month he would have an impressive number of kilometers to his account. We talked and compared experiences.

He too, came from *l'Action Française* group. At the time he was taking his M.A. degree, he was spending his evenings at the newspaper's composing room. Of an inquiring turn of mind, and wanting to be everywhere and study everything, he had been shaped in the pattern of Maurras. Brasillach and Rebatet had been his friends.

Demobilized in 1940, he was soon involved in the political struggle and was one of the first to join Radio-Paris. Because of his knowledge of German—he was an Alsatian from Haguenau—he could form a link between the station and the occupation authorities who controlled it. When the Allied landings took place he was very anxious to report from the front, and without much ado he had departed for Normandy with a sound-recording assistant. Unluckily they both got caught in the British offensive and were arrested immediately before they had seen anything.

Guissen was the first big game that the Gaullists had bagged after landing in France, so his trial had not been protracted. He had had only two examinations before a magistrate and had appeared in Normandy before one of the very first courts of justice, which had sentenced him to hard labor for life. And he could still consider himself lucky.

With France finally liberated, he had been sent to Clairvaux, as the first political to have arrived there. And if he survived those early days there, it can only have been because he had nine lives. He was subjected to all sorts of pressure, the victim of endless hostility and brutality in complete isolation, for he had no means of communication with the outside world. He was so conscientious for others that he did not want his aged mother in Alsace to know what had happened to him. He had never written to her so that she might suppose he was lying low somewhere or other.

Overnight, this man who was still comparatively young turned gray like an old man. But he gritted his teeth and endured; and as soon as he could, he seized on the job of boot-testing. It allowed him some respite from the jungle.

He witnessed some extraordinary settling of scores; the convicts showed a diabolical ingenuity. In central prisons there were no knives, it is true, but prisoners from the shoe factory managed to get hold of some of the thin steel strips used to stiffen the legs of boots. The screws kept a close check on anything taken from the shop, but there remained some broken ones that were thrown into the trash bin. The inmates later recovered them, choosing the longest pieces.

The men in the clothes-hanger workshop were making a handle on the sly, after which all that remained was to pierce a hole in the blade, fix it to the shaft with a nail, and bind both tightly together. At night they sharpened their device on the flagstone inside their chicken coop. This required a certain perseverance, but there is no one so obstinate as a prisoner, and one fine day they had a particularly sharp instrument.

The settling of accounts generally had homosexual origins. There were powerful "queens" who had boyfriends they visited after lights out. The kapo, who was afraid of them, opened the doors of the cages with a tool known as a duck's beak. Then he kept watch while the fellows were occupied with their boyfriends.

When one of these queens believed himself injured or deceived there was often a fierce and swift retribution. One morning, Guissen told me, the prisoners went down to the yard as usual, silently and keeping step. Suddenly one of them grabbed the man in front by the hair and with one sharp thrust severed his throat arteries.

Naturally, those who got packages were subject to extortion. The prisoner chiefs took the guy in question aside and told him: "O.K., this week you'll give me the canned stuff, as well as so much sugar." And to resist one had to have plenty of muscle.

I myself had been subjected to various harassments and had always sent the extortionists about their business. But I had to be constantly on the alert and to see that I was not next to one of them when we walked in file.

The general situation, however, tended to improve. From Paris, from Fresnes, as well as from every part of France, the politicals began arriving to replace the ordinary convicts, who were transferred elsewhere in batches of fifty. Soon the only remaining veterans of Clairvaux would be the small core of those sentenced by military tribunals.

These were essentially the North Africans who had fought with extraordinary determination for France, in the battle of Cassino and in the retaking of Alsace. By the time they reached the German frontier they were pretty exhausted, and to raise their spirits they were given to understand that the country they were entering was theirs for the taking, that is: for looting and all the rest.

Some were innocent enough to take this literally. On Christmas Eve they wandered through the ruins of Stuttgart, with nothing to do and no girls. And on the stroke of one o'clock they found themselves in front of the cathedral at the moment when the crowd was emerging from midnight Mass, in a flood of light and incense, a crowd in which they only saw women and girls;

the men were far away, in prison camps. And it seemed to them a gift from heaven!

There was no question of singling out one or two, they fell on the women en masse and raped them there on the square. The German bishops issued a vigorous protest that had repercussions in French ecclesiastical circles as well as echoing among Italian ecclesiastics. And de Gaulle, who never dilly-dallied when it came to matters of religion, promptly had these riflemen brought up before a military tribunal, forgetting that, pulled out of their own country to liberate France, they had only acted, after all, as all other armies have been acting for ages. They were sentenced without delay, getting years of hard labor. "I swear to you, my captain, that having won the Military Medal, the Croix de Guerre, I don't know what was wrong in thinking that those *fatmas* were for me." Nothing to be done; France recompenses them by sending them to Clairvaux.

Prison being but a reflection of the world outside, at Clairvaux everybody was against them. The ordinary convicts harassed them even more than they did us because we knew better how to defend ourselves. They constantly insulted them and called them filthy Arabs. The politicals also regarded them with distaste: "So much for the Army of Liberation, we're sick of hearing about it!"

Of course they were given all the dirty work, distributing the food, emptying the slop pails. Every society has people to use as forced labor at will; and it is always the same ones who get the brooms and pails thrust into their hands.

Until, that is, the day when the army authorities remembered them again at the outbreak of the Indochina war. Since only volunteers were being sent out, the army was short of manpower, so the North Africans were contacted again. I can imagine the dialogue:

"Well, Ahmed, you raped the *fatmas* in Stuttgart?"

"That's right, my captain, but I didn't know. . . ."

"You love France, don't you, Ahmed, you look on her as your mother?"

"Oh yes, my captain, France is my mother, she has always been my mother."

"Do you know how you can make up for what you did, Ahmed? How you can get yourself out of prison? You know that the army is your family and won't let you down?"

"Ah, is that really true, my captain?"

"Yes; you've only got to sign on, Ahmed, and you'll be sent to Indochina. You'll like that, won't you? You'll have nothing to worry you, over there; it's far from France and there'll be no talk about the past. Not bad, eh, Ahmed?"

And Ahmed put a cross at the bottom of his enlistment paper, exchanged his prison garb for a uniform, was sent direct to Marseilles, and instead of carting shit at Clairvaux finds himself immersed in the shit of the rice paddies. At the time he did not yet grasp what was happening; much later, when he did, it cost France dearly.

Some weeks after they had been approached, we in our turn were given the chance to listen to the song of the sirens in uniform. One morning the order came from the warden: "Everyone into the yard!" We rushed down with a loud noise of clogs, and there we were in three ranks. Warden, deputy warden, and lance sergeant enter, accompanied by an officer with four rows of decorations, a magnificent Foreign Legion warrior, flanked by a couple of noncommissioned officers. Well, well . . .

The officer walked past us as if inspecting his regiment, chin out, looking us in the eye, and along the ranks I saw a ripple of smiles.

Then he stood in front of a group of prisoners in their coarse drugget, a fine-looking lot! Mostly older men, though some younger ones, about forty in all, principally survivors of the Charlemagne.

"Gentlemen, if I'm here today it's because I admire many among you."

Ah, not a bad start!

"You made a mistake, admittedly, you chose the wrong path. How sorry I am for all those of you who fought in the Charlemagne! How I would have liked to have had you with me in Libya, Tunisia, at Monte Cassino, in Alsace: we would have shared these victories together."

At that moment I caught a voice from the ranks: "And now we'd probably be in the Cassino war cemetery."

"But no, no. Come, you are men and it is only human to have been mistaken. France needs you, and, whatever else, you are and always have been French; the tricolor still moves you."

We listened and saw what was coming.

"Well, France is a great nation once more and has regained her colonial empire. You were wrong to believe only in Europe, and a Nazi Europe at that; that was not the solution. That is now all over, but out there in Indochina France is facing very real difficulties. Therefore it is now or never for you to redeem yourselves. Come to us, we'll receive you with open arms. Those who were officers or noncommissioned officers need have no fear; after a short training they will get their ranks back. We know that you have been at one of the best combat schools that exist anywhere, and that you've proved yourselves exceptional soldiers. So, come with us. You already know our motto; it's not so very different from the Waffen SS's. Besides, I may as well tell you that we enlisted some former German members of the SS, after being assured, of course, that they weren't war criminals. They are going to help us defend the French flag in Indochina, help us keep that wonderful province for France."

I said to myself, "It can't be true!" A movement went through the ranks as a crazy desire to laugh was partially suppressed.

"So let any volunteers step forward and come over here. We will then go to the warden's office, where they can sign their declaration to enlist, and, within twenty-four hours, I give you my word as a legionnaire, the Legion will have taken charge of them. The past will be wiped out, and you won't be dragging along here for ten years, twenty, or all your lives. So join us! In defending the honor of France you will be reestablishing your own."

No one made a move. The officer was obviously astonished and directed an aggrieved look at us. He was offering adventure and rehabilitation to us disreputable individuals, rejected by the motherland that we had betrayed, and his words raised nothing but their own echo! We were more deeply corrupted than he had imagined.

"Give me an answer at least. Is there not one of you to say something?"

Then a guy stepped forward, a sort of street-kid type: "Captain, just think a minute. We've been through experiences where, hundreds of times, we never expected to escape with our skin. I got ten years. You know how it is with politicals, I'll be granted a parole after five years at the very most. And then I couldn't give a shit who points a finger at me because if they point at me it means I'm alive. What do you want me to do in the Indochina rice fields, defend who and what? The military tribunal handed me ten years and you're asking me to enlist in the service of the same French militarists. Never. I'd sooner stay where I am, where I'm left alone. I've nothing I want to defend anymore, not my honor or anything else; and at least nobody here is going to shoot me."

Deeply dismayed, the officer raised his arms to heaven.

"This is really unbelievable! I can't get over it. The Legion is a family with an inspiring environment. Foreigners come to us to find again . . . to find again . . ."

To find again precisely what? Everyone was talking and making fun of him. The older prisoners, those who in any case had no chance of being taken by the Legion, made sarcastic comments. There was utter confusion.

"Listen, listen! I'm remaining here another couple of hours. If any of you should change your mind, you can tell a guard and he'll bring you to me."

The warden had his minions restore order.

"So I'm giving you two hours to think it over. Any who want to enlist should present themselves during that time."

And the captain withdrew to the shouts of "Long live our glorious army!" "You'd make a good road show!" "To hell with France!" The noncoms who were with him were enjoying it, but as for the captain, there was not a smile out of him. He had grasped nothing of what had happened. His reasoning might have worked with Germans who did not know any French, or with ignorant Montenegrins, and all sorts of people who did not fit in anywhere. And if there were, later, some veterans of the Charlemagne who took the road to Marseilles, that was after they were freed and because they could not readjust to civilian life. But not a single man in Clairvaux volunteered, and I doubt if it was ever tried again in any other central prison.

Our bold warrior, in short, was out of touch with the general mood. He could not imagine the impression made on men who had been through the courts of justice and the military tribunals, after which a central prison, however miserable, represented peace and shelter.

It is true that, in one sense, a prisoner's whole thinking is focused on the outside world. At Clairvaux we were only allowed one letter a month and visits were rare; many families could not afford the journey and had to choose between sending packages or the price of a train ticket. We had only a sketchy idea of happenings outside, and all we could do was to dream constantly about the little that did reach us.

Gradually life took on an utter strangeness. I am thinking of

Guissen, who had been there since 1945 and who now knew only those walls and corridors, and hardly recalled what a leaf, a flower, or a bird was like, for birds do not come where there are no trees.

This confinement, however, gave us a wonderful sense of protection, and we were as snug as the tortoise inside its shell. As prisoners we were untouchable and storm waves from outside died down at the foot of the walls. We waited, we were told that the unusual events that had landed us here were returning to normal and that one fine day it would be all over . . . as if one could come out and leave one's memories behind. . . . We were outside all the activity that forms history, like convalescents, and, for the moment, we were not moving out.

With the departure of the Algerian soldiers, there remained only political prisoners in Clairvaux. Each found a niche for himself somehow or other; the earlier arrivals were given the more important jobs, but, by sticking together, we managed to find some for the newcomers. I continued to give talks and hatch out my folk tales. My audience had changed, but these pious legends still left them uninterested.

At this point a talented batch of prisoners arrived, consisting of the *Je suis partout* staff of Rebatet, Cousteau, Algarron, and Jeantet, in particular. The court of justice, presided over by Didier, had sentenced them to death and they had been sent to Fresnes, in leg irons. But their sentences had been commuted and they had been transferred to Clairvaux.

It could be said they had barely escaped death. At the time of the verdict, Léon Blum was premier and all kinds of pressure had been exerted on him to have them executed without delay, while, at the same time, he had received numerous petitions asking for a show of clemency. There had been great solidarity on the part of artists and journalists. Almost all the outstanding ones had signed with the exception of Picasso and Sartre, the two whose records as resistants, it seemed, were indisputable. . . . A curious fact, however, was that during the Occupation I recall they could often be seen about. I was at a performance of *Les Mouches,* and the theater was full of German uniforms. . . .

Léon Blum had been in an embarrassing position: there is no doubt that during the war *Je suis partout* had shown a virulent anti-Semitism whose consequences had not been negligible. In the end he had made a remarkable decision, which is not well enough remembered: "I am head of a provisional government," was the gist of what he had said. "There are going to be elections for a permanent one and, after that, for a President of the Republic. The death sentence is not provisionary, it is very serious and, once carried out, irreversible. So I leave to whoever becomes head of state to decide whether to confirm or commute it. As for myself, I am leaving these people where they are and will make no decision one way or the other."

That, I believe, is what saved their lives. Vincent Auriol was elected President of the Republic and commuted their sentence. These two Socialists certainly did not compromise with the revolution, but they applied their ideology to human beings rather than in a vacuum. They were dedicated to their principles and sought, as far as possible, to put them into practice. I do not know if Cousteau, now dead, Rebatet, Algarron, or Jeantet have ever recounted this or will do so, but I believe that they must sometimes have a thought in memory of Léon Blum. Under someone else, they would never have been seen again.

These former members of the staff of *Je suis partout* were the advance guard of some notable arrivals. Following them came Admiral de Laborde, Jacques Benoist-Méchin, and Maurras, who was immediately moved to the infirmary. And, from then on, the prison climate, despite the regulations, started to change.

"Jelly" had been transferred, and in the library Pierre Antoine Cousteau, known as "Pac"—brother of the naval officer— had taken his place. Before that he had been in charge of clothing materials and, taking advantage of the position, had had himself made two prison suits to measure, so that he could always have one cleaned and pressed. He became the dandy of Clairvaux and was much admired when he visited us in "Inos 3."

He was a kind of great gentleman from Bordeaux, consumed with pride and his own talent, giving himself, by means of an ornate way of speaking, a somewhat haughty air. During his trial he had shown a great deal of courage, even trying to provoke, it was said, a death sentence. One felt that he regretted not having been shot like Brasillach, who had been a rival of his and whose departure from the paper he had instigated, and that he would have liked a heroic end. In short, a rather difficult person to understand but not lacking in character.

Rebatet was drafted into the boot-testing section and I saw him trudging around the courtyard deep in conversation with Guissen. He looked somewhat like a tramp and lived in constant fear of his wife, Véronique. Since he was not popular with the other prisoners, we often had to intervene as heated arguments broke out that ended in fireworks. Many of the prisoners, in fact, reproached those who had important intellectual responsibilities and who had admitted them all too quickly in the court of justice; and they were also the butt of guys who claimed to have gotten involved because of them.

I watched all this with interest, but in the end I was overcome by boredom and my lectures were becoming a burden. I longed for the open air and asked for a job outside the prison; these were reserved for those who had not been sentenced to more than five years.

In the state forest surrounding the prison there were road works and a timber yard. Some prisoners worked in a quarry, extracting and crushing the stone, and then, with only pick and shovel, constructing a road through the forest. Others cleared a path, cutting down trees, which were sold later at a good price.

I was sent to work at the road. There were ten of us, watched by a screw with loaded rifle. I was delighted. Stone-breaking perhaps evokes the typical image of convict life, but nonetheless it is excellent exercise and, in cold weather, has a wonderfully warming effect. And after months of wasting away in a vacuum, one is suddenly glad to be engaged in real work, though, it is true, I had once had illusions about this. A long time after my release I went back to have a look at my road. It started from the village but, after a kilometer and a half, petered out in the forest. It went nowhere, the quarry had been abandoned, and the Department of Bridges and Highways had paid the prison administration for nothing. . . .

However I looked at it, this new kind of life was full of advantages. We brought our food with us, and the screw had his own, but he did not refuse to share ours; we were on friendly terms with him, which made things easier all around. On the way through the village we bought all kinds of things, especially potatoes, which we peeled and cooked with our meal. Of course, we had no money, so we had to buy on credit. Relatives who came to see us either wiped the slate clean of what we owed or deposited a sum for us to draw against.

Being in the open gave us the opportunity to smoke. Once in my new job, I sent word to Maud; the permit she had been given at Fresnes was still valid and she and my lawyer were the only persons to come and visit me. In the visiting room I had surreptiously explained to her that she could meet me during the week in the woods, that if she asked at the hotel someone would show her the way, and that she should bring a good supply of cigarettes. Furthermore, she should get hold of a large box, say a biscuit tin, and put the cigarette packets inside, well wrapped up, and I would bury it under a tree.

Thus I had a reserve supply under a mossy corner, and, in the evenings, I could offer the guys a smoke. We were only superficially searched on our return and could hide a pack inside our underwear. The screw who accompanied us never squealed —we had given him his share. Should we have any trouble, he was supposed to have seen nothing, which went without saying. On one or two occasions some guys were found out, but they never turned him in. They knew very well that the other prisoners would have taken it out on them and that the staircases at Clairvaux were very dangerous.

In my biscuit tin I also kept matches, I left them there at night because inside the prison we had lighters of an absolutely new type: everything posed a problem there, but the prisoners patiently reinvented the tools of everyday living. One took a greasy rag, squeezed it into a tin of boot polish and, after closing it tight, put it on top of the stove. The rag caught fire and burned away, leaving a residue like tinder or touchwood. Then we managed to get hold of a lighter flint, which we fixed in a small piece of wood. Finally, with a nail from the carpenter's shop, all we had to do was rub the flint down the nail toward the tin so that a spark ignited the burned rag.

I had soon become as strong as a professional hammer-thrower, with muscles that developed day by day. My body tone was improving and all the more because, twice a month, I could indulge in some fun with Maud in the woods.

The complicity of the guards—there were two who relieved each other—was not too difficult to obtain: a note slipped to them, a drink bought by Maud at the hotel bar. At the time arranged, I asked the guard for permission to go and take down my trousers. He knew I would be away for an hour, and when that had elapsed some blasts of his whistle announced that the merrymaking was over.

As for Maud, she seemed to me more lovely than ever. I had dreamed of her so much. Until now I had seen her only behind bars without being able to touch her so that my desire for her had grown even greater. Naturally, we could only make love rather awkwardly, it was not very comfortable in the woods, but the soft grass, the birds, the minutes stolen from the prison all lent an air of poetry to our frolics.

Then came the return to the midst of those immured in abstinence. With the departure of the ordinary convicts, homosexuality had almost disappeared; and it was not as if we were in a Latin American country where prisoners can visit a brothel. So the prison was full of repressed and excited senses, and some guys went half-crazy, undermined by enforced continence or else by masturbation, that great purveyor of ever-deceptive dreams.

At first I wanted to keep my amorous escapades a secret. But soon everyone got to know of them and a kind of legend began to be woven around them. It was known that Maud had begun a career in films and that she drove to Clairvaux in her car. In my pack I had two crumpled photos of her, a portrait by Harcourt and a snapshot in a bathing suit. They all wanted to have a look, and everyone got to know her. So when I came back I had to pay for my good fortune. Even when I was not meeting Maud, I could detect envy on the faces of the others and at times a kind of hatred. Of fifteen hundred prisoners, there were only twenty of us on outside work: ten on the road construction, ten at the tree felling. I sat down to our five o'clock meal, bronzed, invigorated, with the good smell of the outdoors on me, beside my gray and dejected comrades. And I was conscious of an injustice: I had got five years, others, for having done no more than I, were doing ten long years.

I handed around cigarettes and I had to tell them about Maud. On the days she had been there, they all wanted to know the details. Rebatet asked, "You saw her? How did it go?" He wanted to hear it all, and so it was in the evening from chicken coop to chicken coop.

"She was there, eh? And then?"

And, of course, there were the men's-room remarks. I would have liked to have been left to myself to go over the afternoon in my thoughts, but it was not possible. Everyone was too keyed up, Clairvaux was a world where frustration was unending, and not just the sexual kind.

Our spirits, too, became restless; we wanted to talk, smoke, correspond with our relatives and friends; live, in short. Requests accumulated on the warden's desk, appeals for a relaxation of the rules, suggested improvements. But Sauckel did not want to hear anything. He had no wish to change the status quo and dug himself in behind the regulations.

It reached such a point that an idea began to circulate that nothing would change our situation short of a revolt. How this arose nobody will ever know, what was certain was it did not originate in the circle of intellectuals. And an idea of this sort in the conditions of prison life rapidly ferments. Some days elapsed and then the word passed from one to another: "Tomorrow, when the chicken coops are opened, we are to grab the guards and hold them as hostages while we occupy the prison."

And nobody expressed a doubt about it. The screws were quietly overcome, the cages remained open, we took possession of the "inos," then of the kitchens, where the food was thrown on the floor—a stupid act, for in the case of a siege there would be nothing to eat. And—an extraordinary fact—from Poissy to the south of France, four central prisons for politicals, all across France, mutinied at the same time, under the same conditions and for the same reasons. Clairvaux was immediately surrounded by Gardes Mobiles, while inside the prison there were nothing but shouts, meetings, and demonstrations. A committee was formed to go to the warden and tell him what was behind the revolt, which the prisoners wished to conduct without violence but were firmly decided to go through with. With all the noise it was causing, with the attention it would receive from press and radio, the Minister of Justice would certainly have to intervene.

Sauckel, however, realized it would be a very serious step to call in the army to crush it. He got in touch with the director general of prisons and reported the situation, which was the same in all four central institutions. And the latter replied that he would come down in three days, would have discussions with us, and would see what could be done, with the approval, naturally, of the minister and the government. No sanctions would be taken, but the hostages must be released and order reestablished.

This was done. Sauckel gave his word that these promises would be kept, and we waited. The Gardes Mobiles withdrew. I remained with my comrades, because all outside work had been suspended.

Three days later the director general of prisons, a young, active man, arrived. He had a lengthy discussion with the administrators and then questioned the guards. Finally he toured the "inos," beginning with number 3 because that was where Rebatet was. He also had my name, given him by my brother-in-law, who had been at high school with him.

He came over to me and I told him about the conditions of our life and what we were asking for: to be able to read the newspapers, not the politically slanted ones, but at least the illustrated and literary weeklies. To have the right to smoke and buy cigarettes. To be allowed to write to our families once a week instead of monthly; personally, I had gained, God knows why, two good-conduct stripes, which permitted me to send a weekly letter home, but this was a very rare favor, and unjust. To be able to organize sports, or even theatrical performances, to be allowed to talk at least among our own immediate group—in short, to live like political prisoners. I also asked him if he had had a look at the hole or if he had counted, in the cemetery, the number of those who had died in it. He listened and made notes. Then I told him that there should be no reprisal taken for our action, and there he interrupted. "You know the four people responsible for the revolt. They won't be punished, but they'll be removed, and you should not raise any objection. This will help the central prison system to maintain a measure of discipline. But nobody will be sent to the hole."

So be it; we were in no shape to argue, we were not in a position of strength. The director general of prisons went away. But in the following week the reform was instituted: and Clairvaux became a civilized prison.

This was, I recall, at the beginning of 1948. Everything changed very quickly at Clairvaux, as if a new era had suddenly set in. Prisons are like sensitive photographic plates on which the attitudes and inconsistencies of an epoch are imprinted with great clarity.

The hole, which stood for the old tradition, was done away with, and the ruddy-faced chief sergeant disappeared at the same time. Anyhow, he was approaching retirement and applied for it with all his efforts, for he knew he no longer belonged. Not that he was the worst, all things considered, but he had identified himself with the system that had made the prison part of the Third Republic, Vichy, and the Occupation.

Discipline had become good-natured. We were still nothing but numbers, but the screws were now polite. We could move around as we liked in the courtyard and in the "inos," and could talk, as long as we did not kick up a row, could write and receive a letter once a week. We could also get magazines and books and, perhaps the principal gain, smoke, except in the dormitories, though the guards shut their eyes even there. In short: a barracks, no longer a jail.

The prisoners themselves had suddenly ceased to be a uniform mass. Ideas were exchanged, those with common affinities came together, and groups were formed. I gave up my job as road-worker to be with my comrades, and to have time for reflection, to make some personal notes, and read. And it was perhaps at that period that a whole youthful phase, which events had unduly prolonged, ended for me.

Suddenly I had a staggering perspective on the experience I had lived through. What I had undergone began to fall into place, to acquire lights and shadows. I read with excitement and astonishment David Rousset's *Les Jours de Notre Mort*.[3] I got to know myself better through all the books, selected somewhat at random, that went through my hands. At the same time I got together an anthology of poetry, helped by Rebatet, who wrote the preface for it.

Incarceration certainly weighed on us, and for some, condemned to long terms, much more heavily than on me. By now I had reached the halfway mark in my sentence and had been told to sign two documents, one asking for a pardon, the other for a parole, and I had begun to think I had not much more to go through. But even men who had been given the heaviest sentences appeared to have acquired an inner tranquillity. Behind these walls we were the masters of the society we formed; and the running of the prison service was in our hands.

The workshops, of course, functioned as usual, but now it was not necessary to make useless things. And a lot of prisoners kept working there, all those who did not receive money or packages and needed some cash, however meager the pay.

The one unsolved problem was the lack of women; continence was as torturous as ever. Some could boast of quick encounters in the infirmary, and those in the furniture factory had been in luck for two weeks.

In their workshop they had a large tool chest, which the guards kept a close eye on in case some of the instruments should be taken to use as weapons. But what they had not noticed was

[3] *The Days of Our Death*. A book about the concentration camps.

that behind the chest was a door that led to the apartment of one of the screws. And in this apartment was a woman, the screw's wife, who could not get enough of it. She was a petulant type from the south, not badly made. She must have been fed up with her shit of a husband, who strolled about with his cap over his eyes, making trouble for the men who only thought about girls. The prisoners dreamed about her but it was she who found how to get out. And it must be agreed that spending one's life in the precincts of a prison is not very amusing for a woman.

She, too, had noticed the door. A few signs to the prisoners and each did his part: she found the key, they moved the chest, and everyone was happy. One by one, the guys left the workshop; if anybody asked, they were in the latrine.

She was well acquainted with her husband's schedule. When he left the apartment, she took down the key and hurried to the door. The prisoners presented themselves one by one and she gave each a fine tumble. What is more, she bought them cigarettes and did many little favors for her transient lovers.

Even the best things have an end, however. The story began to get around, and everyone was laughing behind the screw's back, who had been cuckolded on such a grand scale. Until the day that someone—there is always a stool pigeon—threw the facts in his face. The door was sealed up at once and the wretched fellow, who had never experienced such a misfortune, was called before the warden and given a telling off. Finally, with his wife, he was transferred to another central prison and was seen off by many smiling faces.

The lesson, all the same, was not lost on the authorities. Whenever a prisoner had a job to do in the screws' quarters, whether he was a plumber, electrician, or carpenter—all the craft guilds are represented among the prisoners, who constitute a free labor supply—the head of the workshop also went along and did not turn his back even for a moment. Because of the long abstinence that tormented the prisoners, the screws' wives did indeed run serious risks, although, with the exception of the one from the south, they did what they could to discourage them.

But now we had athletic and cultural activities with which to divert our energy. A sports field was allocated and we began to get teams together. Then the administration decided to form an amateur theatrical company from among those serving shorter sentences, which betrayed the fact that certain injustices persisted.

"That suits me fine," I said to myself, "I'll have a hand in this." There were plenty of candidates, and their names were listed and sent to the warden's office. And the warden made the selection, without even asking whether the guys had any acting experience.

One fine day the names of the troupe were posted. I was put in charge. A building, large enough to accommodate a stage and an auditorium for two hundred, was turned over to us. The upper floor would serve as storeroom for costumes and scenery. We could present one play a month.

This was really the start of a new life for me. Every day a screw took me to our future theater. I began to be at home in the hubbub of carpenters who were constructing the wings and the floor of the stage; it seemed to me that those hammer strokes were beating out the advent of freedom, bringing it a little nearer. Other guys put the seats in place, leveled the floor, arranged the benches.

I concentrated on getting together a repertory of plays. Lucien Rebatet agreed to write one for us, but since it would not be ready in time for the first presentation, we chose two proved successes, the first being *L'Anglais tel qu'on le parle* (*English As It Is Spoken*). We assigned the parts, giving the female ones to the less virile types, which was what they asked for. A wardrobe manager and stage director were appointed. I was the producer and also played the juvenile lead in a Tristan Bernard comedy, a short piece that opened the show.

Rehearsals started; we put a great deal of effort into them, prolonging our pleasure. Then one morning, the warden summoned me: "I've two pieces of news for you, one good and one bad. Let's start with the bad: your request for a parole has been turned down."

At that, my face fell. "There it is, I'll have to do my full five years." The police had given me a "favorable opinion" and I had been hopeful. It had been the district prefect in my home area who had, in the end, put obstacles in the way. I had wanted to return to Touraine, and, normally, I would have to give the name of my employer there. This was mandatory in the case of a parole. Alain, however, had written to me that it was an unimportant detail, and that the prefects were not taken in by false employment certificates. So we had simply put down: "Is going to live with his family." Unfortunately the local prefect thought I was making a fool of him and didn't give a damn for his authority and had sent in an unfavorable report, and the Ministry of Justice had refused the application.

"And now for the good news: the premiere of your play will take place on Easter Monday before some of our local bigwigs. I have invited the police prefect, the brigadier general, all the local authorities, in fact. There's to be a luncheon at my place and afterward your show will be staged before our guests and the prisoners. So you better get busy. . . ."

"But actually, Warden, that doesn't leave much time. It would be best to postpone the semipublic production until after the play has first been tried out for the prisoners only."

"No, no, there's no question of that. The premiere will take place Easter Monday, as I've just told you. That gives you a month still."

So we worked on double time and were ready for dress rehearsals pretty quickly. As the plays had contemporary themes, the office let us have back our civilian clothes. They awaited us at the property storeroom, where we left our prison uniforms and got into our suits and shoes. And then for a few minutes we allowed ourselves to dream, before going on stage.

A few days before Easter the warden summoned me once more, this time to his house. A widower, he lived alone in the large official building in the shadow of the outer wall of the prison. The rooms were furnished with fine pieces of furniture direct from the neighboring workshop: a very beautiful lectern in the hall, carved chests, various replicas of antiques with glowing patinas and made with an extraordinary skill that would even have provoked the admiration of an antiquarian.

"La Mazière, you'll have to give me a hand. As you know, I'm giving an important luncheon party and I want you to help me with the menu and seating arrangements."

He handed me a sheet of paper.

"Here is the list of guests who have accepted. I'm in a little difficulty about the seating arrangements: who should have priority, which women to have beside me. . . ."

He evidently planned a big do, a lengthy menu, special cooks, butler and uniformed waiters—something really smart. And with a new set of dining-room chairs and armchairs. While we discussed it all, he kept rubbing his hands. "If all this doesn't impress the general and the people from the prefecture . . ." he seemed to be thinking. He was not far from retirement and certainly had no further promotion to hope for. But, obviously, he was determined to make an impression.

Time passed. We worked away feverishly, the painters were finishing the scenery with broad strokes of the brush; by Easter Saturday the paint was just about dry. On Sunday morning at nine o'clock, when we were already rehearsing, a screw called to me, "You're to go to the warden at once."

I was expecting to be called to the visiting room to see Maud. Cursing and swearing, I marched off. "O.K., he's in a panic again; let him choke on his bloody menu!" I entered his office. He was at his desk. He seemed overwhelmed. He looked at me vacantly and pointed to a chair. "Sit down."

I sat. Normally he let me stand. I asked myself what disaster had overtaken him.

"Read this."

He gave me a yellow telegram, an official one. At once I thought of a death in my family, and kept it a few seconds in my hand before unfolding it. I was very frightened; but at last I opened it and read:

"Ministry of Justice: Release Christian de La Mazière at once. Full pardon. Signed: Vincent Auriol."

The words were blurred, the letters danced in front of my eyes.

"But what does it mean, it can't be true?"

"Yes, yes; read it, you've been pardoned."

"Then it's all over?"

"It's over, and I have to release you."

I had forgotten the petition for pardon. The High Council of the Bench of Judges had just begun its work in conjunction with the President of the Republic, and among the first three cases it presented to him, to exercise his right of clemency over, had been mine. I could not believe it was true, I felt so stunned.

The warden was looking at me with a long face. I could not understand why. Finally he said, "I'm bound to release you right away; and what about the play, and my luncheon party?"

Then, in the midst of my happiness, I felt like acting the generous fellow.

"But there's no question of my leaving today; I'll stay until tomorrow and leave after the performance."

In any case, now that I was free, what was twenty-four hours? But the warden shook his head.

"No, I'm not allowed to. If I kept you here one hour after the order of your release you would have grounds to attack the administration."

"Then what's to be done?"

"I don't know. Oh, how annoying!"

Furthermore, there was no understudy for my part. We had asked for them, with the idea of soft jobs for the boys, but had been refused, because the company would have gone from twenty to forty, twice the number permitted. And, at that point, the administration had thought best to be prudent, not wanting to find it was being superseded by the new reforms.

Both of us were considering the matter. Finally I said, "Anyhow, as far as I'm concerned, I'm willing to stay. If you like, I'll sign a paper to that effect."

"Fine. Sign a paper for me, asking to be allowed to stay, and set out the reasons for doing so. But I am releasing you immediately and it will be as a free man that you will come back to act in the play. Then you will leave again. . . ."

"Oh no, Warden, if I leave the prison, I don't come back. I'm going to stay, and tonight I'll sleep in my chicken coop."

Then I made my conditions, which were not many.

"It's understood that I remain a prisoner until tomorrow. As soon as the scene in which I appear is over, I'll clear out, I won't wait for the end of the performance. Before that, as you've asked, I'll take care of your luncheon, and I want to have my visiting hour tomorrow morning, just as if I was still a prisoner. After that, I want to take out some letters for my friends without them being scrutinized by the prison service. I know the men concerned and give you my word that their letters contain nothing critical of your administration. And, a last request—I ask that a guard carry my luggage as far as the third wall."

"Agreed, agreed. . . ."

He was ready to accept all of them, without asking the reason for my demands.

"Then no search at the gate, and my bags carried to the outer wall?"

"Yes, yes."

When I returned to the quad, it had become a forum. The screws had spread the news: "Do you know what, La Mazière is getting out, he's the first to be pardoned." It was like when I had returned from court to Fresnes, a sigh of hope went up. . . .

The prisoners had also heard that I was staying to take my

part in the play, and, all of a sudden, the prisoners were divided. My friends, Rebatet among them, approved of my decision. But others jeered, "What's come over the bastard, playing the noble fellow! He must be crazy. If it was me, I'd be off in a second. And all the better if some people were put out!" Small groups of ten or fifteen argued this way and that, some in my defense, others criticizing me. The screws listened, astonished. As for me, I said to myself, "I started the whole thing with pointless acts so I might as well let it end with one."

I went to my friends, trying to contain my happiness. One after another, they embraced me. I can still see that poor Guissen who was living through a life sentence. Some years were to pass before I would see those people again. . . . I told them about the arrangement I had made to take their uncensored letters. "So go and write them, and I'll take them with me."

Maud was waiting in the visiting room.

"Well, Christian, you know about it?"

"Yes, I know."

"Why haven't you left? I was expecting you."

I told her.

"You're right." Then she added, "This news, I couldn't believe it for forty-eight hours. Alain telephoned to tell me that the document with your pardon would be given the President of the Republic for signature. But I never imagined it would all go so quickly."

The great traditions persist, and Vincent Auriol, Socialist and atheist though he was, had signed the first pardons to celebrate the Easter holidays.

The longest day of my life had begun. I was in a feverish state, going from one place to another. I went to the office to get back my belongings and my money, which I turned over to my friends. I collected their letters. At chow that evening there were endless questions: "What's the first thing you'll do when you're free?" "Have a bang-up dinner, huh?"

Yes, no. I knew nothing anymore. I did not take in what was happening, my head was empty. All of a sudden I was afraid of this void. That night I could not sleep. I heard the hours strike, one after another, as I had the first night in the cellar. I turned and tossed on my cot, and by morning was worn out. I packed my things and rolled up my sleeping bag.

I went to "Ino 3," to say good-bye to the guys there, and when I returned, the screws came to shake my hand one after another. I looked in at the theater and paid a visit to the warden's house, checked the table setting and the seating arrangements. The luncheon began and from my corner I kept an eye on the room and the kitchens. My God, how long all this was taking!

At last, it was time to go to the theater. I ran my eye quickly over the script. The hall began to fill up. In an hour I would be a free man. . . . It was then that the warden came up to me in the wings.

"Monsieur de La Mazière . . ." It was years since anyone had addressed me thus. "Monsieur de La Mazière, these gentlemen would like to meet you."

I followed him into his reception room, still in my prison clothes. I had merely torn off my good-conduct stripes and cut away my number to keep as a souvenir. Now here was the police prefect: "My respects, Monsieur le Préfet." And his wife. "My compliments, madame."

The general: "My respects, Mon Général."

The Mayor, the parish priest . . . the faces seemed to mingle, I saw nothing clearly anymore and my legs were trembling.

I went backstage again, took off my prison uniform, for good, and got into my civilian clothes. It was funny that I should be dressed both for the city and for the stage. The three raps sounded and I stepped out into the lights and completely forgot my lines. I do not know how often *L'Anglais tel qu'on le parle* has been produced, but certainly never such a mess of it has been made as by me. It must have been hard to make head or tail of; I said whatever came into my head, the others talked similar nonsense. A wave of nervous laughter shook the scenery. All the same, I knew my final lines, and after that I wasted no time. I left my prison uniform in a corner, I embraced my comrades, ran to the office where I had left my luggage: a knapsack, a suitcase, a box of books. I had carefully packed away the letters I was taking in the suitcase. Nobody said a word about them.

I had said good-bye to everyone. Two guards picked up my things. Flanked by my porters, I crossed the various prison enclosures taking a last look at the post office and the church. Then I was outside the gate, all alone, my luggage at my feet. Suddenly I realized it was a very hot day. The sun dazzled me. What light; it was something I could not have imagined.

In front of me, men and women were going toward the prison for the next visiting hour, Admiral de Laborde's wife, the mother of Benoist-Méchin. . . . In their midst, Maud was standing motionless, smiling at me. Behind me were the walls, the two heavy swinging gates that had just closed on my past, on all my vain dreams.

I dared not go forward, I felt dizzy. . . .

"Now," I said to myself, "the real difficulties will begin."